1957

THE GENESIS OF DOCTRINE

Ike & Bunny Eichenberger
Doris Cheney
Cliff & Naomi Kraning
Marjorie C. Daeds
A. Dell Daeds
Hardy Kaiser

Budd Voigt
Mildred & Walter Davenport
Millie Mallett

Irene
Stella M. Hansin
Carmen M. Foogate
John H. Weare
F. Vaughn Tweedy
Audrey English
June English
Jon Marsh
Jean Marsh
Millie Mallett

A human being discovers his finitude in the fact that, first of all, he finds himself within a tradition or traditions.

Paul Ricoeur

C'est ça ma tradition, je n'en ai pas d'autre.
Ni la tradition orientale, ni la tradition juive.
Elles me manquent par mon historicité.

Jean-Paul Sartre

It is the tyranny of hidden prejudices that makes us deaf to the language that speaks to us in tradition.

Hans-Georg Gadamer

The Genesis of Doctrine

A Study in the Foundations of Doctrinal Criticism

ALISTER E. McGRATH

WILLIAM B. EERDMANS PUBLISHING COMPANY
GRAND RAPIDS, MICHIGAN / CAMBRIDGE, U.K.

REGENT COLLEGE PUBLISHING
VANCOUVER, BRITISH COLUMBIA

© 1990 Alister E. McGrath

First published 1990 by
Basil Blackwell Ltd, Oxford, U.K., and
Basil Blackwell Inc., Cambridge, Massachusetts

This edition published jointly 1997 by
Wm. B. Eerdmans Publishing Company
255 Jefferson Ave. S.E.,
Grand Rapids, Michigan 49503 /
P.O. Box 163, Cambridge CB3 9PU U.K.
and by
Regent College Publishing
an imprint of Regent College Bookstore
5800 University Boulevard, Vancouver, B.C. V6T 2E4 Canada

Printed in the United States of America

02 01 00 99 98 97   7 6 5 4 3 2 1

Library of Congress Cataloging-in-Publication Data

McGrath, Alister E., 1953–
The genesis of doctrine : a study in the foundations of
doctrinal criticism / by Alister E. McGrath.
p.   cm.
Originally published: Oxford, U.K. : Blackwell, 1990.
"1990 Bampton lectures" — P. ix.
Includes bibliographical references and index.
Eerdmans ISBN 0-8028-4316-6 (pbk. : alk. paper)
Regent College ISBN 1-57383-072-0
1. Dogma, Development of. 2. Dogma. 3. Authority — Religion.
I. Title.
[BT19.M37   1997]
230'.01 — dc21   96-37765
                                              CIP

Contents

Preface

The critical reappropriation of the doctrinal heritage of the Christian tradition is perhaps one of the most difficult tasks confronting contemporary theology. What criteria may be employed in the evaluation of the past, in order to select those aspects of the rich Christian doctrinal tradition which are of contemporary relevance and vitality? What is the authority of the past in the articulation of Christian theology in the present? There is a certain understandable tendency to adopt an uncritical approach to this question. The seductiveness of an uncritical *affirmation* of the Christian tradition is matched only in its appeal and absence of value by an uncritical *rejection* of the past. In practice, of course, all practitioners of Christian theology employ criteria in their evaluation of the present value of the past, whether or not these are consciously and explicitly articulated and defended. But what *are* these criteria? What have they been in the past? How are they selected and justified?

The discipline of *doctrinal criticism* seeks to evaluate the reliability and adequacy of the doctrinal formulations of the Christian tradition, by identifying what they purport to represent, clarifying the pressures and influences which lead to their genesis, and suggesting criteria – historical and theological – by which they may be evaluated and, if necessary, restated. My personal interest in the discipline arose first through a sustained engagement over a period of ten years with the history of the development of one specific doctrine (the doctrine of justification) within the western Christian tradition,[1] and secondly through a study of the intellectual origins of the Reformation,[2] as a new era in the history of doctrinal formulations dawned. Although my interests now extend considerably beyond this specific doctrine and period, these early studies served to convince me of the importance of a cluster of questions concerning Christian doctrine, which seem to be prior to engagement with doctrinal criticism itself. How is one to account for, and subsequently exercise control over, the development of doctrine? May purely historical criteria be used to evaluate the authenticity of doctrinal formulations? Is there such a thing as the 'essence of Christianity', and if so, by what means may it be identified in the first place, and incorporated into doctrinal reflection in the second? To what extent do doctrinal formulations reflect the socio-political situation of their generating community, and in what manner may such influence be assimilated *critically*? In wrestling with such questions, the possibility of writing a series of works – now in preparation – on their themes became increasingly appealing, if only as a means of assisting me to clear my own mind.

Prior to any such engagement, however, are three questions, which form the subject-matter of the present work. What pressures and factors cause the generation of doctrinal formulations? What *is* doctrine, anyway? And what authority is to be ascribed to the heritage of the past in Christian doctrinal reflection? These themes interrelate, making their treatment within a single work both realistic and potentially attractive. In effect, the present work may be regarded as a study in the foundations of doctrinal criticism, anticipating a more substantial subsequent engagement with the discipline. However tentative and provisional the probings of this work may prove to be, it is hoped that it will stimulate discussion of questions such as those noted above.

It is appropriate to acknowledge the impetus to such discussion already provided by the publication of George Lindbeck's *The Nature of Doctrine* (1984),[3] which has highlighted the challenges posed for contemporary theological reflection through the rise of what Lindbeck terms 'post-liberalism'. Without necessarily subscribing to Lindbeck's analysis of the current theological mood in North America, or to the particular proposal he advances in relation to our understanding of the nature of doctrine, I am sure that he is correct to suggest that the time is right – if not long overdue – for a careful re-examination of both the nature of doctrine and the role of the past in current theological reflection. Indeed, it would not seem unfair to suggest that serious engagement with precisely such questions is an essential prerequisite to an informed discussion of the nature, purpose and future of Christian doctrine.

The Genesis of Doctrine is partly an historical analysis, a study of how the phenomenon of doctrine arose, how it has been understood, and how the past has been restructured and reappropriated by Christian theologians, especially in the modern period. Historical analysis is not, it must be conceded, the most exciting of undertakings, tending to convey the impression that Christian theology is 'grey, meticulous and patiently documentary'.[4] Nevertheless, it is among the most important resources implicated in serious and critical contemporary theological reflection, in that it subverts the neat analyses of those who synthesize the past into an ordered and sacred tradition, imposing a preselected pattern upon its flux.[5] It champions the right of living history over and against artificial theoretical constructions, insisting on the priority of historical phenomena over abstract theoretical analysis. Doctrine, considered as an historical phenomenon, possesses a depth and richness which cannot adequately be captured by reductive theories of the nature of doctrine.

Nevertheless, this study is not purely historical in character, nor can the discipline of doctrinal criticism rest entirely upon historical analysis. Normative conceptual claims cannot be generated solely on the basis of historical detail. Implicit within this investigation is a creative dialectic between the historical and descriptive on the one hand, and the theological and prescriptive on the other. In exploring the delicate interplay between historical analysis and theological construction, the present work attempts to come to terms with the 'history of history' – in other words, with the uses which past generations of theologians of the modern period have found for the doctrinal heritage of the past in their own theological deliberations. While a full analysis of the dialectic between the historically descriptive and the theologically normative, between the historical and the conceptual, remains beyond the scope of this work, it is hoped that some preliminary clarification of its contours may nevertheless result.

In writing a work of this kind, an author incurs considerable debts to others, many of which are difficult to identify, let alone acknowledge. The stimulus to write this work arose from the invitation from Oxford University to deliver the 1990 Bampton Lectures. Those Lectures are here presented in a substantially modified and expanded form, appropriate to the complexity of their theme. The Bampton Lectureship has traditionally been held by senior theologians of considerable distinction; I am acutely aware that I can make no claim to any such seniority or distinction, and hope that the importance of the subject under consideration will go some way towards compensating for the obvious deficiencies of its exponent. My thanks are due to a number of European libraries and institutions which offered me hospitality and the use of their enviable facilities in the course of its preparation: the

Biblioteca Medicea-Laurenziana, the Biblioteca Nazionale, the Biblioteca Riccardiana, and the Biblioteca della Facoltà di Lettere e Filosofia (Florence); the Bibliothèque Publique et Universitaire and Institut d'Histoire de la Réformation (Geneva); the Institute of Historical Research (London); the Bodleian Library (Oxford); the Bibliothèque Nationale (Paris); the Stadtsbibliothek Vadiana (St Gallen); the Österreichische Nationalbibliothek and the Universitäts-bibliothek (Vienna); the Zentralbibliothek, the Institut für Hermeneutik and the Institut für schweizerische Reformationsgeschichte (Zurich). I owe sincere thanks to the British Academy for a research grant, to Oxford University for the award of the Denyer and Johnson Travelling Fellowship, and to Wycliffe Hall for a period of leave from academic responsibilities: without these, this work could not have been written. A number of individuals have read an earlier draft of this work, and I acknowledge their kindness in doing so and the value of their comments. Particular thanks are due to David F. Ford, John Macquarrie, Gordon J. Michalson Jr, Robert Morgan, and Rowan Williams. I am also grateful to Joanna McGrath, Gerhard Sauter, Stephen W. Sykes and Josef Wolmuth for helpful suggestions. In the end, however, what faults remain are entirely my own responsibility. Finally, I wish to thank Faber and Faber Publishers for permission to cite two lines from 'The Dry Salvages' from *Four Quartets* by T. S. Eliot. Scripture quotations in this publication are from the Holy Bible, New International Version, copyright 1973, 1978, 1984, International Bible Society, published by Hodder and Stoughton Ltd.

1

The Genesis of Doctrine

The precipitating cause of Christian faith and Christian doctrine was and is a man named Jesus, who appeared in Palestine in the time of the emperor Tiberius and was crucified under the Roman procurator Pontius Pilate. We know of him only through the traditions of his deeds and words preserved in the New Testament.[1] In a collective act of solidarity of recollection, the community of faith chose to align itself with *this* history as its fundamental legitimizing resource. The history of Jesus of Nazareth was and is the crucible of Christian doctrinal possibilities, the controlling paradigm of conceptual potentialities. Whatever the ultimate external referent of Christian doctrine might be, its proximate external referent is this history.

To attribute authority, however this may subsequently be articulated or defended,[2] to Jesus of Nazareth is to attribute authority to a past event not *because* it is past,[3] but because what thus happened in the past is perceived to be charged with significance for the transformation of the present and the construction of the future. In addition to memories of the life and death of Jesus, the New Testament transmits traditions of the impact made by him after he was raised from the dead,[4] and a range of attempts to explain his identity and significance in the light of this event. The New Testament is essentially the repository of the formative and identity-giving traditions of the Christian community, especially as they concern Jesus of Nazareth himself.[5] It does not encompass the totality of those traditions; rather, it contains those elements of early tradition which the first Christian communities perceived as decisive for their own identities and purposes, and thus preserved. Other traditions have unquestionably been silenced through the irreversibility of the historical process, and allowed to die.

Jesus is the primary *explicandum* of Christian theology. He is something and someone who requires to be explained.[6] The first community of faith recognized in him the one who brought divine judgement and, in its wake, the possibility of conversion and renewal. Christian doctrine is not primarily concerned with the insights of Jesus of Nazareth but with the insights of the community of faith concerning him. But how could this Jesus be placed upon the map of language about God and humanity? How could existing patterns of thought and styles of thinking – whether inherited from Judaism or Platonism – be employed to spell out the significance of Jesus as the bearer of divine judgement and renewal? In some way, the communities of faith had to preserve ways of thinking and speaking about Jesus which preserved his authority and comprehensiveness,[7] while at the same time setting to one side as inadequate those options which limited or compromised him in this respect. Within the New Testament, there is clear evidence that the early Christian communities were adopting fixed confessional formulae as a means of encapsulating and conveying the essential outlines of their understandings of the personal relevance of Jesus of Nazareth to their situation. The very term 'Christ', for example, so deeply embedded in the New Testament witness to Jesus of Nazareth, itself carries with it reference to a pervasive, if complex, strand of Jewish expectation.[8] Perhaps the clearest instance of the distillation of the gospel kerygma in a fixed confessional formula is found in 1 Corinthians 15.3–5, where Paul designates such a formula, taken from tradition, as 'gospel'.[9]

In the attempt to demarcate the significance of Jesus in such formulae lies the origins of Christian doctrine. For the loyal and uncritical repetition of formulae, however convenient it may have been for the liturgical affirmation of allegiance to the early Christian communities, was gradually found to be inadequate as a means of ensuring continuity, except at the purely formal level, with the apostolic church. The primitive instinct to preserve tradition by reiteration was obliged to give way to the perceived need to continue its history by restatement and interpretation. The dynamism of the New Testament traditions concerning Jesus was compromised through such a process of preservation, in that this process involved petrification, trapping something that was once living in a static form, as a fossil might be preserved in a rock or a fly captured in amber. These are symbols of the past, and of pastness itself – a past which once was living and vibrant but which is now dead, rigid and static. They appear as strange and unfamiliar exhibits in a museum of intellectual history, as anachronisms. The symbol which was intended to express today what was meant in the past degenerates into a symbol of pastness itself. The need for a 'rebirth of images' underlies the genesis of doctrine.[10] Thus doctrine must not be seen as an alienating move away from the gospel, being rather a development of a more advanced level of interpretative consciousness within the Christian community.

Furthermore, the New Testament traditions concerning Jesus themselves embody continuities of conflict concerning his identity and significance.[11] The romantic image of a nascent Christian church, unanimous in its affirmations concerning Jesus Christ,[12] has obscured the fact that internal conflict is inherent within the tradition concerning Jesus. The formative conflicts of the Christian community are transmitted and echoed in the pre-canonical traditions preserved in the New Testament. A remarkably short interval separates the death and resurrection of Jesus of Nazareth, and the development of a sustained intellectual struggle within the earliest Christian communities concerning the most appropriate means of articulating his identity and significance. Conflict is inherent within the tradition concerning Jesus: that tradition does not merely *generate* conflict but *transmits* it as an essential constituent element. As controversy flared further within the early church, it became clear that the deliberate critical reworking of the Christian tradition and its transmitted conflicts was both necessary and inevitable. The mere repetition of New Testament formulae had to give way to something more difficult, something more threatening and challenging – the formulation of doctrine, as a synthesis through which the formative and ineliminable conflicts of the Christian tradition could be resolved, or held in creative tension.

The genesis of conflict in doctrinal formulations is traditionally located in the characteristics of theological language.[13] If it is conceded that attempts to give full expression to the insights of Christianity can never be fully adequate, theologians of any given period will inevitably feel at liberty to draw upon the conceptual resources which their day and age recognizes as outstanding. Tensions thus arise on account of the differences in philosophical apparatus employed in giving substance to Christian affirmations. Furthermore, if it is true that the transcendent can never be wholly captured in finite language, so that we are obliged to rely upon images and models which elude precise definition, a certain degree of ambiguity and tension is inevitable on account of the provisionality of those models. The models and images may be well defined – but the manner in which they are to be used in building up our understanding of a transcendent reality (for example, by interacting with and qualifying each other) remains controverted. By suggesting that God is Christologically qualified, Christian theology has identified the tradition concerning Jesus Christ as the central controlling image and model of theological construct formation. The recognition that the tradition concerning Jesus itself mediates conflicts of interpretation thus adds significantly to the difficulties facing those concerned with doctrinal formulation.

A further point concerns the nature of the biblical material itself. While some writers of the Reformation period treated scripture as a doctrinal source-book – *doctrinae Christianae compendium* (Melanchthon) – there has been a recent, and entirely justified, tendency to stress the narrative character of the scriptural material. The New Testament presents us with the narrative concerning Jesus Christ.[14] At times, especially in the Pauline corpus, that narrative is overlaid with theological reflection: even at such points, however, a narrative substructure may be detected as underlying explicit theological formulations.[15] In asking the question concerning the significance of Jesus of Nazareth, we are posing the question of how the narrative concerning him may be interpreted and correlated with our situation, in order to illuminate and transform it.[16] Patterns of interpretation are already to be found in the New Testament, inviting further reflection upon the narrative concerning Jesus of Nazareth. Doctrine is thus concerned with the interpretation of this narrative, analysing and extending patterns of interpretation which already co-exist with that narrative.

The inevitability of doctrine arises partly on account of the transmission of conflict through the biblical source material upon which theological reflection is, however loosely, based,[17] partly through the narrative nature of the scriptural material itself, and partly on account of the need to interact with a language and a conceptual framework not designed with the specific needs of Christian theology in mind.[18] The expansion of Christianity into a Hellenistic milieu in the first centuries of its history illuminates this third point: rarely, if ever, did it prove possible simply to 'use' elements from a Hellenistic world-view, which carried with them an existing cluster of associations and values.[19] But which of these were to be denied, and which to be affirmed? The move from the repetition or reiteration of scripture to doctrinal exposition through an already existing language and conceptual framework, inevitably carried with it the demand for an engagement with the view, or range of views, of reality already associated with that language and conceptual framework.

There was thus a tendency to fuse the scriptural idiom concerning God with the classical philosophical theistic conventions.[20] The data of scripture and the Christian tradition were thus interpreted in the light of presuppositions, within a hermeneutical framework, alien to their sources. After all, Greek metaphysics had developed the idea of 'a god' before its encounter with Christianity,[21] with the result that the proclamation of the God of Jesus Christ in this milieu involved somewhat tortuous negotiations with this metaphysical god, leading to a complex and nuanced history of identifications and differentiations. Among these may be noted the distinct tendency to identify the figure of Christ with the mediating principle of Middle Platonism.[22] It is perhaps unfair to suggest that this represents the dominance of rationalism or philosophy over the data of Christian revelation. There is a temptation for every generation of theologians to bring a cluster of inherited metaphysical commitments as self-evident, requiring no further justification, to the task of theology. The engagement of the Christian tradition with an already existing view of reality thus required that certain elements of the philosophical concept of God be critically refined, remastered and reappropriated.

The nature of this engagement is perhaps more subtle than is usually thought. We fail to do justice to the pressures confronting early Christian thinkers if we represent them as simply incorporating pre-existing philosophical or civil views of the divine attributes (such as omnipotence) into their thinking,[23] or allowing that thinking to be shaped by such external influences. A potentially more subtle influence must be acknowledged – the prevailing conventions concerning the nature of informed discourse concerning so weighty a subject as the nature of divinity, and the manner in which such discourse is to be regulated and articulated. In other words, the manner in which discourse concerning God was conducted within pagan philosophy (such as discussion of formal attributes and properties) was, to a certain extent, treated as a model by Christian theologians. The engagement between Christian theology and pagan philosophy thus took place in the fields of grammar and logic as much as at the level of conceptualities.

The historical outcome of this engagement is a subject of considerable interest in its own right;[24] for our purposes, however, it is important to note that conflict over both the evaluation of existing conceptualities and modes of discourse appropriate to them, and the criteria to be employed in this evaluative process, contributed substantially to the great doctrinal controversies of the patristic era. Doctrinal formulation carried with it not merely an invitation, but a *demand*, for the revisioning of intellectual horizons, in order that the Christian tradition might enter into relation with – whether to transform or to affirm – the world-views of its environment. On the one hand, it was necessary to go beyond the insights of scripture in order to meet the new intellectual challenges faced by the Christian communities; on the other, it was necessary to ensure that these extensions of the scriptural vocabulary and conceptual framework were consonant with its central insights. The total rejection of innovation or development was an impossibility, if Christianity was to be seen as a genuine intellectual option in (for example) the fourth century; the question at issue concerned the nature and extent of these developments. The essential move towards doctrinal reflection inevitably entailed creative controversy concerning both the adequacy and the propriety of doctrinal formulations as vehicles for the transmission and affirmation of traditional ideas and images.

It is fatally easy to settle upon a single historical episode as representing a milestone or watershed in the development of the discussion of a given question. The risk is, nevertheless, worth taking. If any one such episode may be regarded as a turning point in this process of doctrinal development, it is the Arian controversy of the fourth century.[25] The debate between Arius and his opponents, considered at the purely biblical level, was essentially a stalemate. For example, both Arius and Athanasius alike were able to quarry the Fourth Gospel for ammunition in their Christological campaigns.[26] Both claimed to be accurately and adequately representing the Christological insights of the New Testament and Christian tradition, as expressed in the liturgy. Both regarded themselves as the defenders of certain centrally important formulae of the developing Christian tradition. Yet the Nicene crisis over the non-biblical term *homoousios* highlighted the inadequacies of a theology of repetition, of the strict adherence to archaic verbal formulae.[27] The meaning of the past was threatened with obliteration through the passage of time, as the church lost sight of the original meanings of past forms and, by failing to restate and interpret them, became prone to the temptation to invest them unconsciously with new and unintended meanings.

Scripture and tradition alike had to be re-read if a purely superficial engagement with their insights was to be avoided. A doctrinal hermeneutic was required, in which scripture and tradition were encountered creatively and profoundly, in order to recast their ideas and interpret their narratives in new images and terms. A theology of repetition – whether of biblical texts or liturgical formulae – left too many theological loose ends. The ideas behind the familiar formulae of the New Testament and the liturgy of the church had to be re-imagined and recreated through conceptual innovation, unless they were to become dead metaphors, petrified verbal moments from the past.[28] The Nicene crisis instantiates a general phenomenon, to which we shall return later in the present study: the perceived need to transfer theological reflection from commitment to the limits and defining conditions and vocabulary of the New Testament itself, in order to preserve its commitment to the New Testament proclamation. The genesis of doctrine lies in the exodus from uncritical repetition of the narrative heritage of the past.

It will therefore be clear that several major questions emerge from this preliminary discussion of the genesis of doctrine. In the first place, we are obliged to consider the manner in which the past may in any be sense authoritative for the present articulation of Christian doctrine. In what sense are our options limited, our horizons defined, our mental worlds already shaped, by what has happened in the past?[29] To what extent are we free to break away from the heritage of the past? In the second place, we are obliged to give an account of the genesis of doctrine. Why did doctrinal formulations evolve, and what is their significance? What significant pressures – whether religious or social – may be detected as having precipitated doctrinal affirmations? And in the third place, the theme of doctrinal criticism emerges as significant.[30] How does a doctrinal statement relate to its historical context? The suggestion, still occasionally encountered, that theological attitudes in general or doctrinal statements in particular may be totally abstracted from their historical situation is seriously deficient,[31] given the conceded insights of the sociology of knowledge.

Historical analysis of the evolution of doctrine permits us to begin the process of doctrinal criticism, the central questions of which integrate historical and theological matters: in what way may the truth and adequacy of a doctrinal statement be judged? On the basis of what criteria may doctrinal developments be evaluated?

Thus the mere antiquity of a tradition – to mention a purely *historical* criterion – is not necessarily a reliable guide to its validity. As Cyprian of Carthage pointed out, a 'tradition without truth' (to use Cyprian's pre-Wittgensteinian phrase without endorsing its ideational substance) is simply the improper perpetuation of an ancient mistake.[32] Doctrinal criticism obliges us to ask what specific theological insights lie behind a specific doctrinal formulation, and what specific historical contingencies influenced both those insights and the manner in which they were thus articulated, with a view to restating (if necessary) that formulation.

Doctrine and Dogma

Before turning to detailed engagement with the themes of this study, it is necessary to clarify the relation between 'doctrine' and 'dogma'.[33] The latter term is laden with unhelpful historical overtones, conveying ideas such as rigidity and authoritarianism, perhaps even irrationality and obscurantism, and evoking historical memories of the Inquisition and religious persecution and fears of the imposition of ecclesiastical authority within the sphere of academic freedom. It is the very idea of dogma, rather than any specific dogma, which is found distasteful in a period predisposed towards libertarian attitudes. Regrettably, theology cannot be conducted in a psychological or historical vacuum, which would allow these unhelpful overtones to be set aside in order to reclaim a legitimate theological concept. It is therefore important to make the historical observation that the modern Roman Catholic use of the term 'dogma' dates from the late eighteenth century, apparently being used in this sense for the first time in the polemical writing *Regula fidei catholicae* (1792) of the Franciscan controversialist P. N. Chrisman (1751–1810).[34] Chrisman used the term to designate formal ecclesiastical doctrine, as opposed to theological opinion.

The need for the distinction was evident, particularly on account of the detrimental effect of confusion between catholic doctrine and theological opinion in the later Middle Ages.[35] Many, on both sides of the Reformation debates of the first three decades of the sixteenth century, found themselves unable to ascertain what doctrines were officially acknowledged and recognized by the church, and which were merely the private, if publicly expressed, views of theologians. There is thus an intriguing possibility that Luther may have initiated his reforming programme at Wittenberg on the basis of the mistaken belief that the opinions of one theological school (the *via moderna*) were to be identified with the views of the catholic church itself. Luther's assertion that virtually the whole church of his day had lapsed into some form of Pelagianism may rest upon the improper extrapolation to the whole western church of what may conceivably have been a valid evaluation of the merits of the soteriology of the *via moderna*.[36]

By introducing the concept of 'dogma', Chrisman hoped to bring an element of clarity to interdenominational dialogues, by distinguishing ecclesiastical teaching from private theological opinion, and restricting denominational debates to the former. The term 'dogma' thus came to bear the meaning it possesses today within the Roman Catholic church: 'dogma' specifically designates that which is declared by the church to be revealed truth either as part of the universal teaching, or through a solemn doctrinal judgement.[37] Included in the concept of dogma are two quite distinct elements: the notion of divine revelation, or revealed truth; and the church's proposal or reception of such revelation or truth.[38] All dogma may be doctrine; not all doctrine, however, is dogma. The Jesuit scholar Deneffe gives the following succinct definition of dogma, explicitly including both these elements: *dogma est veritas a Deo formaliter revelata at ab ecclesia sive solemniter sive ordinarie definita*.[39] The term 'dogma' is not, of course, restricted to Roman Catholic usage, but also finds application in both Lutheran and Reformed writings, again tending to bear the general sense of 'an accepted teaching of the church'.[40] The term 'dogmatics', designating an organized body of Christian (or, more accurately, Protestant) theology, first came into use in the seventeenth century.[41]

A number of considerations underlie the reluctance to use the term 'dogma' in preference to 'doctrine' within the present study. First, the former term has now come to possess pejorative overtones which both overshadow and obscure an informed discussion of the nature and extent of the historically conditioned character of theological articulation within the Christian tradition, as expressed in doctrinal formulations. Second, the concept of 'dogma' may be thought to rest upon, or at least to reflect, an ecclesiastical positivism which may raise certain difficulties for the historian of the Christian tradition, who is reluctant to employ other than historical criteria in the course of such a study. Third, the concept suggests a preoccupation with, or particular emphasis upon, the formal authority, rather than the contents, of doctrinal formulations. Fourth, it limits the investigation to those doctrines which are accepted as 'dogma', such as the area of Christology, while excluding others of major historical interest, such as the doctrine of justification by faith. Fifth, the New Testament use of the term 'dogma' actually appears to carry with it no explicit reference to 'Christian doctrine'.[42]

It is therefore proposed to use the more general concept of 'doctrine' as a means of engaging with the history of the tradition of the theological affirmations of the Christian church. This is not in any sense to reject or criticize the modern concept of dogma as, for example, employed in contemporary Roman Catholic theology; it is merely to state that, on account of the both the assumptions underlying the concept and the pejorative associations the term now possesses, it is to be viewed as an inappropriate category for the more limited purposes of the present study. Equally, it is not to prejudge what terms such as 'doctrine' or 'doctrinal statement' themselves might signify: a wrestling with precisely such questions underlies this work.

Doctrine and Theology

'*Dogmengeschichte* has concentrated not on the history of what the Church believed, taught and confessed, but on the history of erudite theology.'[43] Since the establishment of the medieval universities in twelfth-century Europe,[44] theology has increasingly assumed the character of an academic subject, free from interference by secular or ecclesiastical authority. The disagreements between Peter Abailard and Bernard of Clairvaux in the twelfth century and between Fichte and Schleiermacher in the nineteenth point to a continued perceived tension between academic freedom and religious tradition.[45] Even if this tension may be regarded as fundamentally misconceived, resting upon a series of unhelpful misunderstandings or posturings, it does point to the need to make a distinction, however provisional, between corporate belief on the one hand and individual criticism or innovation on the other, and to note – with a view to criticizing – the tendency of works of historical theology to concentrate upon currents within academic theology, rather than within the life of the Christian churches.[46]

The use of the word 'doctrine' implies reference to a tradition and a community,[47] where 'theology' more properly designates the views of individuals, not necessarily within this community or tradition, who seek to explore ideas without any necessary commitment to them. Doctrine defines communities of discourse, possessing a representative character, attempting to describe or prescribe the beliefs of a community. As Clifford Geertz has emphasized, there are significant inter-relations between doctrine, schemes of symbolization and representation, and communities.[48] One could suggest that doctrine is essentially the prevailing expression of the faith of the Christian community with reference to the content of the Christian revelation.[49] Newman's essay *On Consulting the Faithful in Matters of Doctrine*, with its stress upon the communal matrix within which doctrine is formulated, received and developed, provided a much-needed corrective to the excessive emphasis upon the ideas of academic theologians, so irritating a feature of much German Protestant *Dogmengeschichte*. The community is not committed to the ideas of its theologians: such commitment would restrict their freedom to speculate, to explore, to criticize. The community is at liberty to appropriate or reject their speculation, in the manner, for example, that Vatican II's Constitution on Divine Revelation – perhaps the most significant achievement of this most impressive Council – was creatively influenced and enriched by the theological explorations of Yves Congar.[50] Nevertheless, the idea that doctrinal development is due entirely to the speculation of theologians is clearly incorrect: to note but three obvious examples, it was the sacramental life of the Christian community which evoked the doctrine of original sin; the religious life of monastic communities which gave rise to the Mariology encapsulated in the term *theotokos*;[51] and popular piety which gave rise (1950) to the dogma of the assumption of Mary.[52]

Doctrine entails a sense of commitment to a community, and a sense of obligation to speak on its behalf, where the corporate mind of the community exercises a restraint over the individual's perception of truth. Doctrine is an *activity*, a process of transmission of the collective wisdom of a community, rather than a passive set of deliverances. The views of theologians are doctrinally significant, in so far as they they have won acceptance within the community. The concept of 'reception'[53] is of central importance to the concept of doctrine, in that a community is involved in the assessment of whether a decision, judgement or theological opinion is consonant with their corporate understanding of the Christian faith, as perceived within that community.[54] Doctrine may thus be provisionally defined as communally authoritative teachings regarded as essential to the identity of the Christian community. Christian doctrine may be regarded as the present outcome of that long growth of tradition in which the Christian community has struggled to arrive at an interpretation of its foundational traditions, embodied in the New Testament, which both does justice to its own present place in tradition, and attempts to eliminate those doctrinal pre-judgements which are to be judged as inadequate. It is a historical phenomenon, grounded in history and conscious of its own historicity. To deal with the subject of doctrine is thus to deal with a matter which includes, but is neither restricted to nor totally dominated by, the academic study of theology.

Doctrine presupposes the existence of the church – not a *doctrine* of the church, but a community of faith which confesses Jesus Christ as Lord.[55] The common life and worship of this community sustains the sense of expectation and hope in the present of God, and provides the stimulus for doctrinal reflection. Doctrine arises within the community of faith, as it seeks to make sense and give order and structure to its experience of and encounter with God through the risen Christ. Doctrine is thus an 'insider' phenomenon, reflecting the specific perspectives of the community of faith. Outside this context, it seems barren and lifeless, in that its links with the worship and spirituality of the community, conscious of its calling and focusing on the death and resurrection of Jesus Christ, are not fully understood. To those outside the community of faith, what requires explanation and elaboration is not specific *doctrines*, but what doctrine attempts and purports to represent – the redemptive communal experience of the risen Christ as Lord. The source of pressure within the community to generate doctrinal formulations is its wish and perceived need to give substance and expression to its corporate experience of God in Christ. The impulse which animates the genesis of doctrine is thus prior to any specific doctrinal formulations as such – yet, paradoxically, requires precisely some such doctrinal formulation if it is to be transmitted from one generation to another.

In many ways, of course, the distinction between doctrine and theology is somewhat artificial at points, perhaps reflecting differences in emphasis rather than differences in substance. The themes to be analysed in this work are of relevance to both Christian doctrine and academic theology. Nevertheless, the distinction must be made, however unsatisfactory it may be considered. As recent ecumenical discussions have made abundantly clear, doctrinal affirmations are linked with a sense of community identity, and the very threat, whether real or imagined, posed to this identity by such discussions serves to remind us of the different levels at which doctrine and theology operate. It also provides a convenient point at which to begin an analysis of the nature of doctrine, to which the following two chapters are devoted.

On the basis of an historical analysis of the phenomenon of doctrine within the Christian tradition, four characteristic components of doctrinal formulations may be identified as the prolegomenon to a future theory of the nature of Christian doctrine. These four independently developed and justified theses, based on an engagement with the history of doctrine, are set out in detail in chapter 3. It is, however, proper to begin any discussion of the nature of doctrine with a preliminary evaluation of and response to the recent proposals of George Lindbeck. Although it is my conviction that Lindbeck's categorization of the history of doctrine is perhaps seductive and misleading, his criticism of certain experientially orientated theories of doctrine appears timely and persuasive. While I have no wish to perpetuate Lindbeck's taxonomy of doctrine, it would be improper to present a fresh analysis of the phenomenon without engaging, however briefly, with Lindbeck's proposals. The chapter which follows thus prefaces my analysis of the nature of Christian doctrine with an evaluation of and response to Lindbeck's *Nature of Christian Doctrine*.

2

The Nature of Doctrine: A Response to George Lindbeck

In his slender but greatly appreciated volume *The Nature of Doctrine*,[1] George Lindbeck provides a much needed stimulus to reflection on the nature of Christian doctrine. One of the many merits of this book is the debate which it has initiated over this unjustly neglected aspect of Christian theology, which has assumed new importance recently on account of the impact of the ecumenical movement.[2] It is therefore only proper that this attempt to explore the conceptualities associated with Christian doctrine should begin by outlining and – however provisionally – responding to Lindbeck's analysis.

Lindbeck suggests that existing theories of doctrine may be divided into three general types. The 'cognitive-propositionalist' theory[3] lays stress upon the cognitive aspects of religion, emphasizing the manner in which doctrines function as truth claims or informative propositions. The 'experiential-expressive' theory interprets doctrines as non-cognitive symbols of inner human feelings or attitudes. (A hybrid model, which Lindbeck suggests resorts to 'complicated intellectual gymnastics',[4] combines these two emphases.) A third model, which Lindbeck is particularly concerned to promote, is designated the 'cultural-linguistic' approach to religion. Lindbeck associates this model with a 'rule' or 'regulative' theory of doctrine.

I shall return to consider Lindbeck's 'cultural-linguistic' approach later. It is, however, important to observe that the motivation underlying the development of this theory appears to be Lindbeck's dissatisfaction with the existing models of religion and doctrine, particularly in relation to their failure to deal with ecumenical dialogue. How can doctrinal reconciliation – for example, between Lutherans and Roman Catholics (a dialogue in which Lindbeck was personally involved) – be achieved without doctrinal capitulation? In other words, how can doctrines which were once held to be divisive now be declared to be so no longer? The facility with which such declarations are made has frequently engendered the suspicion that those engaging in ecumenical theology employ language to conceal differences, rather than bring them into the open. Indeed, it is possible to suggest that the *explicandum* (if not necessarily the *explicatum*) of Lindbeck's book is the apparent anomaly which arises when doctrines remain unchanged, and yet cease to be regarded as conflicting.

Lindbeck suggests that the 'cognitive-propositionalist' and 'experiential-expressive' theories make it 'difficult to envision the possibility of doctrinal reconciliation without capitulation'.[5] By their very nature, he argues, they require us to reject either doctrinal reconciliation on the one hand, or doctrinal constancy on the other. Lindbeck suggests that the 'cultural-linguistic' approach relieves this perceived difficulty, where other approaches fail. This is not, of course, his only reason for adopting this approach; it is clear that Lindbeck believes that there is a general trend within many disciplines (such as history, anthropology, sociology and philosophy) towards a cultural-linguistic orientation: if theology is to avoid relegation to an 'intellectual ghetto', a similar development within this discipline would appear to be indicated.[6] Nevertheless, the ecumenical context is a particularly important element in Lindbeck's discussion, and requires attention in any critical and informed analysis of the nature of doctrine.

In what follows, I propose to repond critically to Lindbeck's three-fold taxonomy of doctrine, indicating what I perceive to be its strengths and weaknesses, before developing a more historically orientated approach to the subject.

The Cognitive-Propositional Theory

One view of doctrine, which Lindbeck designates 'propositionalist' or 'cognitive', treats doctrines as 'informative propositions or truth claims about objective realities'.[7] Lindbeck argues that this approach is to be rejected as voluntarist, intellectualist and literalist, even making the suggestion that those who 'perceive or experience religion in cognitivist fashion' are those who 'combine unusual insecurity with naiveté'.[8] A first hesitation about this criticism concerns its reliability: it appears to be based upon a questionable understanding of the 'cognitive-propositional' position, apparently grounded upon the belief that those inclined towards this position hold that it is possible to state the objective truth about God definitively, exhaustively and timelessly in propositional form.[9]

This cannot be considered to be an adequate representation of this position, in either its classical or post-critical forms. It fails to register the historical and linguistic sophistication of cognitive approaches to doctrine.[10] For example, Lindbeck's suggestion that the 'cognitive-propositional' approach to doctrine treats any given doctrine as 'eternally true'[11] fails to take account of the evident ability of proponents of this approach to reformulate, amplify or supplement a doctrine with changing historical circumstances.[12] Lindbeck attributes an unmerited inflexibility to cognitive approaches to doctrine through playing down the notion of 'relative adequacy' of doctrinal statements, where 'adequacy' can be assessed both in terms of the original historical context of a doctrinal formulation and whatever referent it is alleged to represent.

Most theologians of the medieval period understood dogma as a dynamic concept, a 'perception of divine truth, tending towards this truth (*perceptio divinae veritatis tendens in ipsam*)'.[13] It is true that certain medieval writings do indeed suggest that doctrine may be treated as Euclidean theorems: Alan of Lille's *Regulae theologiae* and Nicholas of Amien's *De arte catholicae fidei* are excellent examples of this genre dating from the twelfth century,[14] later found in such writings as Morzillus' *de naturae philosophiae* (1560) and Morinus' *Astrologia gallica* (1661). Nevertheless, a considerably more nuanced approach to the nature of theological statements is much more characteristic of the period.[15] Theology is recognized to be concerned with the clarification of the manner in which affirmations about God are, in the first place, derived, and in the second place, how they relate to analogous affirmations drawn from the more familiar world of the senses. It is an attempt to achieve conceptual clarity, to avoid confusion through subjecting statements concerning God to close scrutiny. What does the word 'God' stand for? How does the question, 'Does God exist?', relate to the apparently analogous question, 'Does Socrates exist?'? What reasons might be adduced for suggesting that 'God is righteous'? And how does this statement relate to the apparently analogous statement 'Socrates is righteous'? Thus Alan of Lille (to note one of the more propositionalist of medieval theologians) is concerned with identifying the ways in which we might be misled by theological affirmations – for example, by treating them as descriptions of physical objects, or assuming that terms and conceptualities relating to God possess the same meanings as in everyday discourse.[16] Underlying such attempts to achieve clarity of concepts and modes of discourse is the recognition that doctrinal affirmations are to be recognized as perceptions, not total descriptions, pointing beyond themselves towards the greater mystery of God himself.

For such theologians, doctrines are reliable, yet incomplete, descriptions of reality. Their power lies in what they represent, rather than what they are in themselves. The point at which interrogation is appropriate concerns whether such doctrines are adequate (to the strictly limited degree that this is possible) representations of the independent reality to which they allegedly relate. Given that they cannot hope to re-present it in its totality, and given the inevitable limitations attending any attempt to express in words something which ultimately lies beyond them, is the particular form of words employed the most reliable conceivable? The Nicene controversy is an obvious example of a struggle to articulate insights in this manner. If an experience is to be articulated in words, in order to communicate or to attempt a communal envisioning of this experience, some form of a 'cognitive-propositionalist' dimension is inevitable. Yet this is not to reduce the experience to words, but simply to attempt to convey it through words. (Interestingly, however, Lindbeck himself weakens his polemic against cognitivist propositionalism by his insistence that the proposition '*Christus est dominus*' may be 'not only intrasystemically but also ontologically true'.[17])

This point concerning the verbalizing of experience is valid, irrespective of whether the words used are thought to convey an ontological truth or not. For example, consider Longfellow's lines from the *Saga of King Olaf*: 'I heard a voice that cried, / Balder the beautiful / Is dead, is dead.' These words would not be thought of as ontologically true. To use Lindbeck's terms, they are intrasystemically true, in that they are consistent within the context of the Nordic Valhalla myth.[18] This statement implies nothing concerning ontological truth or falsity, unless the myth is improperly read as history. Yet C. S. Lewis wrote thus of his reaction to reading Longfellow's lines: 'I knew nothing about Balder; but instantly I was uplifted into huge regions of northern sky, I desired with almost sickening intensity something never to be described (except that it is cold, spacious, severe, pale and remote) and then . . . found myself at the very same moment already falling out of that desire and wishing I were back in it.'[19]

It would be absurd to suggest that words can adequately capture experience:[20] cognitive theories of doctrine, however, suggest that words are on the borderlands of such experience, intimating and signposting the reality which they cannot capture (see pp. 66–72). To apply pejorative epithets such as 'intellectualist' or 'literalist' to the 'cognitive-propositionalist' approach to doctrine is to fail to appreciate the power of words to evoke experience, to point beyond themselves to something inexpressible, to an experience which their author wishes to share with his or her readers. It is also, of course, to fail to do justice to the many levels at which cognitive or propositional statements operate.

Theological statements do not operate at the same level as mathematical equations. The charge of 'literalism' is vulnerable to the extent that it risks overlooking the richness of non-literal language, such as metaphor, as a means of articulation,[21] and the importance of analogy or 'models' as a heuristic stimulus to theological reflection.[22] It is simply a theological truism that no human language can be applied to God univocally;[23] indeed, it is from the recognition, rather than the denial, of this point that cognitive approaches to doctrine begin. It is this point which underlies Walter Kasper's qualified emphasis upon the provisionality of dogma.[24] At points, Lindbeck's unsympathetic and somewhat dismissive approach to cognitive theories of doctrine suggests he understands their proponents to adopt a crudely realist approach to theological statements, such as that criticized by John Robinson in *Honest to God* (1963) – for example, the idea that God really is an elderly man located at an unspecified point in the stratosphere. It must be stressed that such a crude correspondence theory of truth is neither a necessary consequence nor precondition of cognitive approaches to doctrine.

The imprecise charge of 'literalism' levelled against 'cognitive' theories of doctrine appears to lack the discriminatory apparatus necessary to distinguish, for example, the radically different interpretations of the statement 'This is my body' (Matthew 26.26) found with Luther (it is literally true), Zwingli (it is a form of metaphor) and Calvin (it is metonymical). Cognitive theories presuppose use of the non-literal 'four master tropes' of thought and discourse[25] (metaphor, metonymy, synecdoche and irony) in the process of conceptual thinking, rather than reducing them to a crudely literal conception of representation, as Lindbeck seems to suggest. Calvin and Zwingli are two sixteenth-century figures who make extensive use of rhetorical analysis and non-literal modes of discourse, both in their analysis of texts (such as scripture) and their positive theological affirmations.[26]

This rhetorical approach to reality may be illustrated from a seminal writer of the early modern period, Giambattista Vico.[27] Vico suggests that experience may indeed be captured in words, through proper use of the four master tropes of discourse. A initial metaphorical perspective on reality gained through an encounter with the domain of experience gives way to a reductive metonymic analysis of the situation. This process of deconstruction is followed by a process of synecdochic reconstitution of the relations between the superficial attributes of this encounter with reality and its presumed essence, finally yielding a reflective or dialectic or ironic comprehension of that experienced reality.[28] The precise ordering of these elements does not concern us at this point: I simply wish to draw attention to the sophistication of a rhetorical analysis of experience, by which a cognitive account may be given of experience without in any sense reducing experience to propositional form or degenerating into 'literalism' in the vague but pejorative sense of the term employed by Lindbeck. The impatience of many modern theological writers with 'cognitive' theories of doctrine seems at times to represent little more than impatience with the vexatious nature of human language, and a reluctance to engage with its ambivalence and polysemy.

It is also important to stress that the science of cognitive psychology has important insights to contribute to the 'cognitive' model of doctrine, in that it is able to address the cognitive processes by which experience is interpreted and expressed in words.[29] For example, there appear to be significant parallels between the cognitive processes implicated in aesthetic and religious reflection,[30] so that aesthetic cognition may be regarded as a relatively good analogue of religious cognition.[31] The attempt to symbolize personal experience (which also underlies important affinities between doctrinal formulations and psychotherapeutic insights)[32] suggests that both the difficulties and positive insights of defensible 'cognitive' approaches to Christian doctrine are paralleled at other points of major importance in the intellectual spectrum relating to human attempts to express experience in words. Although the study of these parallels is only now beginning, it is to be expected that cognitive models of doctrine may be better understood and appreciated in their light.

Lindbeck's criticism of 'cognitive' theories of doctrine has considerable force, when directed against neo-scholastic understandings of revelation.[33] For example, the view of the neo-scholastic writer Hermann Dieckmann, to the effect that supernatural revelation transmits conceptual knowledge by means of propositions,[34] is clearly open to serious criticism along the lines suggested by Lindbeck. In this respect, Lindbeck has provided a valuable corrective to deficient cognitive models of doctrine. Nevertheless, not all cognitive theories of doctrine are vulnerable in this respect. It is necessary to make a clear distinction between the view that an exhaustive and unambiguous account of God is transmitted conceptually by propositions on the one hand, and the view that there is a genuinely cognitive dimension, component or element to doctrinal statements on the other. Doctrinal statements need not be – and, as I shall argue in the following chapter, should not be – treated as *purely* cognitive statements.

The Experiential-Expressivist Theory

If I have felt obliged to register hesitations concerning Lindbeck's criticism of the 'cognitive-propositional' theory of doctrine, it is only proper to note that his account of those 'experiential-expressive' theories of doctrine which treat doctrine as referring to ubiquitous private prereflective experience underlying all religions appears to be fair and accurate, and that his criticism of this theory seems persuasive and effective, and may well be judged to be the most significant long-term contribution he has made to the contemporary discussion of the nature of doctrine. I here outline his criticism of this influential theory, while adding some additional material which seems to reinforce the general thrust of his remarks.

In the aftermath of the rise of experience-orientated religious theories, since the time of Schleiermacher, some have drawn the conclusion that an 'experiential-expressivist' approach, which 'interprets doctrines as noninformative and nondiscursive symbols of inner feelings, attitudes or existential orientations', is to be preferred to a 'cognitive-propositional' approach, which emphasizes 'the ways in which church doctrines function as informative propositions or truth claims about objective realities'.[35] Thus David Tracy argues for the need to bridge the gap between 'common human experience' and the 'central motifs of the Christian tradition',[36] so that religious language 're-presents' and reaffirms this common experience at the level of self-conscious belief. According to this approach, religions, including Christianity, are public, culturally conditioned manifestations and affirmations of pre-linguistic forms of consciousness, attitudes and feelings. As Lindbeck argues, the attraction of this approach to doctrine is grounded in a number of psychosocial features of the post-Cartesian, post-Kantian, privatistic context of late twentieth-century western thought.[37] For example, the contemporary preoccupation with inter-religious dialogue is considerably assisted by the suggestion that the various religions are diverse expressions of a common core experience, such as an isolable core of encounter or an unmediated awareness of the transcendent.[38]

The principal objection to this theory, thus stated, is its obvious gross phenomenological inaccuracy. As Lindbeck points out, the possibility of religious experience is shaped by religious expectation, so that 'religious experience' is conceptually derivative, if not vacuous. 'It is difficult or impossible to specify its distinctive features, and yet unless this is done, the assertion of commonality becomes logically and empirically vacuous.'[39] The assertion that 'the various religions are diverse symbolizations of one and the same core experience of the Ultimate'[40] is ultimately an axiom, an unverifiable hypothesis – perhaps even a dogma, in the pejorative sense of the term – not least on account of the difficulty of locating and describing the 'core experience' concerned. As Lindbeck rightly points out, this would appear to suggest that there is 'at least the logical possibility that a Buddhist and a Christian might have basically the same faith, although expressed very differently.'[41] The theory can only be credible if it is possible to isolate a common core experience from religious language and behaviour, and demonstrate that the latter two are articulations of or responses to the former.

Attempts to evaluate this theory are totally frustrated by its inherent resistance to verification or falsification. While conclusive empirical evidence is not available to allow us to evaluate the suggestion that religious language and rites are a response to prior religious experience, the possibility that religious language and rites *create* that experience (for example, through arousing expectation of such experience, and indicating in what manner it may arise, and what form it might assume) is at least as probable on both the empirical and logical levels. Equally, the suggestion that the experience of individuals is to be placed above, or before, the communal religion itself seems to invert observable priorities.[42] Thus Schleiermacher, who might be taken as the archetype of such an experientially grounded approach to theology, does not understand 'experience' to designate the undifferentiated and idiosyncratic emotions or existential apprehensions of each individual believer; rather, he understands 'experience' to be grounded in the memory, witness and celebration of the community of faith.[43] The theological significance of the Christian experience is articulated at the communal, not the individual, level.

The notion of a common core experience which remains constant throughout the diversity of human cultures and the flux of history, while being articulated and expressed in an astonishing variety of manners, remains profoundly unconvincing. The theme *semper eadem!*, once applied by an earlier precritical generation of alleged 'cognitive-propositionalists' (in Lindbeck's sense of the term) to the received deposit of catholic doctrine,[44] now seems to be applied to human religious experience by modern 'experiential-expressivists'. Empirically, this notion is highly questionable: thus Lonergan wisely concedes that religious experience varies from one culture, class and individual to another,[45] while apparently being reluctant to draw the conclusion his concessions suggest, however tentatively – that it varies from one *religion* to another. While the doctrinal tradition of the church is publicly available for analysis, however, allowing its allegedly 'unchangeable' character to be assessed critically, religious experience remains a subjective, vacuous and nebulous concept, the diachronic continuity and constancy of which necessarily lie beyond verification or – as seems the more probable outcome – falsification.[46]

The main lines of Lindbeck's critique of experiential theories of doctrine which treat doctrine as dealing with ubiquitous prereflective private experience common to all religions are timely and persuasive. I venture to add three further criticisms of such theories.

A second point of difficulty concerning this model concerns the emphatic insistence within at least one strand of the Christian tradition that experience and reality are, at least potentially, to be radically opposed. Doctrine does not necessarily express or articulate experience, but may contradict it. Perhaps the most celebrated instance of such an attitude may be found in Martin Luther's 'theology of the cross',[47] in which emphasis is laid simultaneously upon the importance of religious experience in the authentic Christian life, and its unreliability as a theological resource. There are important parallels between Luther's concept of faith and that found in the writings of St John of the Cross, especially as articulated in the concept of *noche oscuro*. The 'experience seeking expression' in the writings of a 'theologian of glory' and a 'theologian of the cross' (to use Luther's expressions) gives every appearance of being very different – yet both require to be subsumed under the same 'experiential-expressivist' model.[48]

A third difficulty which might be noted concerns the apparent assumption that the present experience of an individual, whatever that may be, constitutes the primary datum of religion. This emphasis appears to suggest that no fundamental distinction may be made between the experience of an individual who has deliberately and consciously determined to reject a religion, and one who has equally deliberately and consciously determined to embrace one. Consider, for example, an occurence which is increasingly common within the global religious situation, but with important roots in the formative stages of the Christian tradition – conversion.[49] Take the case of an individual, brought up within a purely secular environment and disposed towards a materialist atheism, who subsequently discovers Christianity and becomes a 'born-again Christian'. Is the experience of this individual in these two very different situations the same? It is, surely, inconceivable that they should be identical, or even similar, particularly if one of the more experientially orientated Christian traditions is implicated in the conversion experience. Further, empirical psychological studies have indicated that 'committed' religious individuals have markedly different psychological qualities and social attitudes from those who assume a merely 'consensual' position.[50] Such differences are expressed at both the experiential and cognitive level – for example, the manner in which prayer is experienced and interpreted.[51] Yet the experiential-expressivist approach to religion appears to lack the conceptual framework to distinguish these situations, on account of what Lindbeck terms the 'homogenizing tendencies associated with liberal experiential-expressivism'.[52] 'Experience' is treated as something which is homogeneous, common and unchanging, unaffected by alterations in religious affiliations.[53]

It may be objected that this is to confuse emotion and existential orientation. If there is any substance in this complaint, it is at least in part due to the failure, apparently reflecting an inability, on the part of experiential-expressivists to clarify the basis of such a distinction. It may nevertheless be pointed out that differences in existential orientation remain linked with the states of faith and unbelief. A series of existentialist theologies, drawing their inspiration partly from Heidegger's phenomenology of existence, categorize faith as instantiating authentic, and unbelief inauthentic, existence.[54] The transition from unbelief to faith would thus be held to involve a degree of existential reorientation, obliging an experiential-expressivist theory of religion to account for this change. In that conversion is a highly significant element in human religious experience, past and present, the need to differentiate between 'believing' and 'unbelieving' experience would seem to be a sufficiently important aspect of religion to require theories of religion and doctrine to be able to account for it.

A final difficulty might seem out of order, given the liberal presuppositions underlying this model of religion and doctrine. It is, nevertheless, a question which at least one important contemporary strand of Christian theology would demand receive attention. How can we know that – how, in fact, can we even begin to inquire whether, and in what manner – the experience we are attempting to capture in a verbal moment or symbol really is an experience *of God*?[55] What grounds do we have for suggesting that human experience is in some way related to a reality, traditionally designated 'God'? On what grounds are we entitled to identify a moment or moments as charged with the fragrance of divinity, and not simply an experience which is human and mundane? The great dilemma of the young Karl Barth, preparing his Sunday sermon at Safenwil, becomes our dilemma. For Barth, the crucial question concerned the words he would preach: how could he rest assured that these words in some way embodied or conveyed the word *of God*, rather than his own words? In what sense could he claim that he was proclaiming the word *of God*, and not merely lending a spurious legitimacy and unmerited authority to the words of Karl Barth? How can the 'experience seeking expression' be identified as an experience of God, and not as an experience of a secular and godless world, or an eccentric existential solipsism? And what of non-theistic religions? Doubtless an experiential-expressive account of Theravada Buddhism would insist that this tradition gives access to religious experience – but can it be regarded as an experience *of God*, when that tradition itself explicitly repudiates such a suggestion? Experience may indeed seek expression – but it also demands a criterion by which it may be judged.

This point could be developed further, particularly in the light of the trend towards secularism in western society. The 'experiential-expressive' approach to religion and doctrine asserts the primacy of present experience as the medium of God's revelation. The implicit presupposition of this approach is that there is some experience to express. For Tom Driver, the experience in question could be likened to stepping out of a bath tub and discovering that he was 'full of an energy that has no name.'[56] Other attempts to define this experience have been more restrained: for example, Schleiermacher's notion of piety as a sense of absolute dependence, Otto's category of the numinous, and Tillich's experience of the unconditioned.[57] But what if there is no experience to express? What happens if Driver ceases to have religious experiences on getting out of the bathtub? (Perhaps such theologians then write of the 'death of God' or the 'theology of the absence of God'?) If God is experienced as absent from his world – which Bonhoeffer suggests is the inevitable result in a 'world come of age'[58] – in what sense can we affirm that he is *present*? Luther, taking the event of the crucifixion as a paradigm, argues that experience is *corrected* by doctrine; that experience is properly interpreted, even to the point of being contradicted, by and within a theological framework. Experience, in other words, is the *explicandum*, rather than the *explicans*; it is what requires to be interpreted, rather than the interpreting agent itself. God is experienced as absent; doctrine affirms that God is present in a hidden manner.[59] Theology engages with existential realities, yet is able to avoid being trapped by them, and being reduced to their level.

Thus far, I have felt able to endorse Lindbeck's analysis. Nevertheless, I must also register disquiet over one of its components. Lindbeck's critique of 'experiential-expressive' theories of doctrine fails to discriminate between two quite different 'experiential' approaches to doctrine. Schleiermacher – who Lindbeck appears to treat as the intellectual forefather of the 'experiential-expressive' approach – is not an exponent of an 'experiential-expressive' theory of doctrine, in Lindbeck's sense of the term.[60] Christian doctrine, according to Schleiermacher, does not concern some 'prereflective experience' common to all religions but concerns the distinctively Christian experience of Jesus of Nazareth. Schleiermacher draws a clear distinction between human religious consciousness in general, and the specifically Christian consciousness.[61] It is this specifically

Christian 'feeling' or 'apprehension of an immediate existential relationship', deriving from Jesus of Nazareth, that Schleiermacher identifies as the referent of Christian doctrine. This crucial distinction is lacking in the 'experiential-expressive' approach, expounded and criticized by Lindbeck, suggesting that it may be impossible to draw such a distinction within their parameters and on the basis of their presuppositions.

Furthermore, Schleiermacher insists that the experience to which doctrine relates is not *private*, but *corporate*. 'Christian piety never arises independently and of itself in an individual, but only out of the communion and in the communion.'[62] The communal takes priority over the individual in Schleiermacher's account of the genesis and doctrinal articulation of religious experience. According to Schleiermacher, doctrines express an experience which has been constituted by the language of the Christian community (not some amorphous global prereflective experience) – a position which Lindbeck himself appears to endorse.[63]

The delicate interplay between language and experience suggested by Schleiermacher does not appear to be vulnerable to Lindbeck's critique, and does not even appear to fall within its scope. The example of Schleiermacher serves to remind us that not all experiential approaches to doctrine can be dismissed with quite the ease Lindbeck appears to suggest.

The Cultural-Linguistic Theory

Drawing on the writings of the cultural anthropologist Clifford Geertz,[64] although with obvious (and acknowledged) influences from Wittgenstein[65] and Polanyi, Lindbeck develops a theory of doctrine which he suggests may undergird a post-liberal age in theology. Religion, he suggests (and the parallel with Wittgenstein will be obvious), may be compared to languages, with religious doctrines functioning as grammatical rules.[66] Religions are cultural frameworks or mediums which engender a vocabulary and precede inner experience.

A religion can be viewed as a kind of cultural and/or linguistic framework or medium that shapes the entirety of life and thought....
It is not primarily an array of beliefs about the true and the good (although it may involve these), or a symbolism expressive of basic attitudes, feelings or sentiments (though these will be generated).

Rather, it is similar to an idiom that makes possible the description
of realities, the formulation of beliefs, and the experiencing of inner
attitudes, feelings and sentiments. Like a culture or language, it is a
communal phenomenon that shapes the subjectivities of individuals
rather than being primarily a manifestation of those subjectivities. It
comprises a vocabulary of discursive and nondiscursive symbols
together with a distinctive logic or grammar in terms of which this
vocabulary can be meaningfully deployed.[67]

Just as a language is correlated with a form of life (as Wittgenstein
pointed out in relation to 'language games'), so a religious tradition
is correlated with the form of life it engenders, articulates and
reflects. Lindbeck also suggests – tentatively, I think – that language
is capable of shaping areas of human existence and action that are
pre-experiential,[68] thus providing an important qualification to, and
extension of, the experiential-expressive theory.

A fundamental element in this understanding of doctrine, and its
attending theory of truth is the concept of *intrasystemic consistency*.
In part, this understanding concerns rational coherence of systems:
doctrines regulate religions, in much the way grammar regulates
language. The ideational content of a doctrinal statement is
effectively set to one side, in order that its formal function may be
emphasized. Lindbeck illustrates this point with reference to
Shakespeare's *Hamlet*: the statement 'Denmark is the land where
Hamlet lived' makes no claim to ontological truth or falsity, but
is simply a statement concerning the internal ordering of the
elements of Shakespeare's narrative.[69] Narrative in itself is neither
fact nor fiction: it is a vehicle for either or both.[70] Fact-like narratives
are not necessarily factual.[71] Only if the narrative is taken as *history*
are any claims being made concerning the ontological truth or
falsity of this statement. Thus the Bible may, Lindbeck suggests,
be read as a 'vast, loosely-structured non-fictional novel', the
canonical narrative of which offers an identity description of God.[72]
Developing this point, Lindbeck suggests – citing the Parable of
the Prodigal Son as an example – that the 'rendering of God's
character' is not necessarily dependent upon the facticity of the
scriptural story.[73]

Meaning is constituted by the uses of a specific language, rather than
being distinguishable from it. Thus the proper way to determine
what 'God' signifies, for example, is by examining how the word
operates within a religion and thereby shapes reality and experience

rather than by first establishing its propositional or experiential meaning and reinterpreting or reformulating its uses accordingly. It is in this sense that theological description in the cultural-linguistic sense is intrasemiotic or intratextual.[74]

The chief difficulty raised by this approach concerns the origin of the cultural-linguistic tradition regulated by doctrines. Lindbeck seems to assume it is simply 'given'. It is an axiomatic point of departure. The 'language' is just there. Lindbeck makes the point that languages originate from outside,[75] thus raising the obvious question concerning the origins of the Christian tradition of speaking about God, or articulating human aspirations, in its particular manner, or range of manners. How does the Christian idiom come into being? There are occasional hints that it may have something to do with scripture (note his discussion of Luther's *Turmerlebnis*).[76] Nevertheless, there is a studied evasion of the central question of revelation – in other words, whether the Christian idiom, articulated in scripture and hence in the Christian tradition, originates from accumulated human insight, or from the self-disclosure of God in the Christ-event. Lindbeck's insistence upon the primacy of 'the objectivities of religion, its language, doctrine, liturgies and modes of action'[77] raises the unanswered question of how these primary data may be accounted for.

It is, of course, possible that Lindbeck believes that this question may be dealt with at a purely phenomenological level, so that theology is concerned with the articulation and exploration of the intrasystemic aspects of Christian faith. If this is the case, then – in this respect at least – he follows Schleiermacher in adopting an essentially descriptive conception of doctrine. For Schleiermacher, dogmatic theology is 'the knowledge of doctrine now current in the church'.[78] In essence, theology is an inquiry concerning the adequacy of doctrines to articulate the faith which they express. The theologian is required to consider the 'ecclesiastical value' and the 'scientific value' of doctrines – in other words, their adequacy as expressions of religious feeling, and their consistency within the context of the theological vocabulary as a whole.[79] Doctrine is descriptive, concerned with intrasystemic cohesion and the ability to describe feeling.[80]

Doctrine, then, describes the regulatory language of the Christian idiom. But how did this language come into being, and to what, if anything, does it refer? Lindbeck appears to suggest that the cultural-linguistic approach to doctrine may dispense with the question of whether the Christian idiom has any external referent. Doctrine is concerned with the internal regulation of the Christian idiom, ensuring its consistency. The question of how that idiom relates to the external world is considered to be improper. For Lindbeck, doctrine is the language of the Christian community, a self-perpetuating ideolect. Indeed, at points he seems to suggest that conceiving theology as the grammar of the Christian language entails the abandonment of any talk about God as an independent reality and any suggestion that it is possible to make truth claims (in an ontological, rather than intrasystemic, sense) concerning him.[81] 'Truth' is firmly equated with – virtually to the point of being reduced to – internal consistency.

Thus while illustrating his understanding of the regulative function of doctrines within theology, Lindbeck suggests that the Nicene creed 'does not make first-order truth claims'.[82] In other words, the *homoousion* makes no ontological reference, but merely regulates language concerning both Christ and God.[83] This case study is important, in that it provides one of the few historical, worked examples of Lindbeck's thesis, thus allowing both his historical and theological competence to be judged, in however provisional a manner. Lindbeck asserts that Athanasius understands the term *homoousios* to mean 'whatever is said of the Father is said of the Son, except that the Son is not the Father', thus demonstrating that Athanasius 'thought of it, not as a first-order proposition with ontological reference, but as a second-order rule of speech'.[84] Only in the medieval period, Lindbeck suggests, were metaphysical concepts read into this essentially grammatical approach to the *homoousion*. In the patristic period, he argues, the term was understood as a rule of discourse, quite independent of any reference to extra-linguistic reality.[85] Yet Lindbeck appears to overlook the fact that Athanasius bases the regulative function of the *homoousion* on its substantive content. In other words, *given* the ontological relation of Father and Son, the grammatical regulation of language concerning them follows as a matter of course. For Athanasius, it would seem that 'the *homoousion*, regulatively construed, rules out ontological *innovation*, not ontological reference'.[86]

This is not, it must be stressed, to say that the patristic Christological debates failed to recognize the referential or regulative function of Christian doctrine. Nevertheless, it would seem that Lindbeck has perhaps attributed to the *homoousion* regulative functions which, strictly speaking, were associated with the *communicatio idiomatum*.[87] The grammatical or regulative functions of the *communicatio idiomatum* would seem to be grounded upon the ontological affirmations of the *homoousion*.

But how may we evaluate the Christian idiom, save by inquiring concerning what it purports to represent, interpret or convey? It may indeed be proper to ensure that the term 'Denmark' is consistently employed within the matrix of *Hamlet* – but how does this relate to a definite and identifiable geographical and political reality, located in the world of human experience? How can we ascertain whether *Hamlet* is fact or fiction? The significance of this question can hardly be denied. How does Shakespeare's Denmark relate to the Denmark of the real world? And how, we must ask as theologians, does the 'Jesus' of the Christian idiom relate to Jesus of Nazareth? Has it any identifiable connection with him? Does it *refer* to him, or to something else? Can it be shown to originate from him – or is it an independent construction of the human mind? Lindbeck appears to illustrate neatly what Rowan Williams identifies as one of the most serious weaknesses of modern theology – the perennial tendency 'to be seduced by the prospect of bypassing the question of how it *learns* its own language'.[88] The possibility – which Lindbeck seems unwilling and unable to consider – is that the discourse which he identifies Christian doctrine as regulating may be based upon an historical misunderstanding; that it may signify nothing other than the accidental forms of historical 'givenness', giving it a socio-historical rootedness which vitiates its wider validity; that it may represent a serious misrepresentation, or even a deliberate falsification, of historical events; that it may represent a completely spurious interpretation of the significance of Jesus of Nazareth. The Christian idiom cannot simply be taken as 'given': it must be interrogated concerning its historical and theological credentials.

Lindbeck's approach to the Christian idiom appears uncomfortably similar to Bultmann's approach to the *kerygma*: both are assumed just to be there, given, lying beyond challenge or justification. The interrogation to which the 'New Quest of the Historical Jesus' subjected Bultmann's kerygmatgic Christology[89] must be extended to Lindbeck's understanding of the nature of doctrine. Doctrine, like the *kerygma*, is not something that is just there, demanding that we take it or leave it: it is something which purports to represent adequately and accurately the significance of an historical event, and is open to challenge concerning its adequacy as an interpretation of that event. The Reformation and the Enlightenment are obvious historical instances of received doctrines being challenged concerning their historical credentials. Lindbeck, by accident or design, is perhaps somewhat equivocal over whether his cultural-linguistic approach to doctrine involves the affirmation or setting aside of epistemological realism and a correspondence theory of truth;[90] nevertheless, the overall impression gained is that he considers that consistency is more important than correspondence, raising precisely the questions I have just noted.

It is at this point that the question of the *genesis* of the Christian language becomes significant: what brought it into being? The Christian idiom is not a perennial feature of the intellectual landscape: it came into being, and developed within history. What pressures brought it into being? What factors governed its development? Lindbeck appears to treat the Christian language as something 'given', adopting an a-historical approach which parallels that of A. J. Ayer to language in general, so devastatingly criticized by Barfield: 'The linguistic analyst who attempts to tackle the problem of meaning without looking at its history, appears in much the same pitiful perspective as the earlier eighteenth-century biologists who attempted to tackle the variety of natural species as though there were no such thing as evolution.'[91] The history of the evolution of the Christian language is the essential prelude to the evaluation of that language and its grammatical regulators. For that language is not just 'given' in scripture or tradition: it was developed in a process of evolution which is partly susceptible to historical analysis and theological evaluation.

Throughout Lindbeck's discussion of cognitive approaches to doctrine, there may be detected a persistent Wittgensteinian reserve concerning the external referent of doctrinal statements, and a perceptible hesitation over the claims of epistemological realism.[92] There are important and illuminating connections here with recent debates within the philosophy of the natural sciences concerning the status of theoretical terms.[93] An instrumentalist interpretation of theoretical terms argues that theories relate to phenomena, to human preceptions, to *observabilia*, without making reference to what is 'really out there'.[94] A realist interpretation, however, carries with it a commitment to a belief in the reality of those things which constitute the denotation of the terms of the theoretical language of that theory. Thus on an instrumentalist view, no commitment is necessary to belief in the existence of positrons;[95] whereas a realist argues that there really are positrons 'out there'.

There are clear parallels between the instrumentalist approach and Lindbeck's 'cultural-linguistic' approach to doctrine. The chief difficulty associated with the instrumentalist approach to theoretical terms is that it 'leaves one in the uncomfortable position of holding that theoretical terms are necessary, but they do not mean anything or refer to anything. Rather than maintain such a position, most people who accept the legitimacy of theoretical terms in scientific theorizing also commit themselves to the position that they have real referents in the world.'[96] While the difficulties raised by the instrumentalist approach may be particularly acute within the scientific community, they are not without relevance to Lindbeck's analysis of the nature of doctrine.

A sense of unease, similar to that associated with the instrumentalist approach within the scientific community, attaches itself within the community of faith to the suggestion that doctrinal terms are purely intrasystemic, having no referent outside the theoretical system itself.[97] In the light of the considerations noted in this section, and without prejudice to the question of what the *ultimate* external referent of doctrinal formulations might be, I wish to suggest that its proximate external referent is the history of Jesus of Nazareth. This history, mediated by a tradition and a *Lebensform*,[98] generates and regulates doctrine in a manner which I shall explore in the following chapter.

A Preliminary Evaluation of Lindbeck's Analysis

In the above discussion, I suggested that Lindbeck's analysis of the nature of doctrine was open to criticism at points, particularly in his discussion of 'cognitive-propositionalist' and 'experiential-expressive' models. The attractiveness of Lindbeck's 'cultural-linguistic' theory, as his critics have suggested,[99] may rest partly on weak and unsympathetic expositions of alternative models; nevertheless, serious difficulties remain with this third model. A more general difficulty is Lindbeck's obvious reluctance to allow that the three models outlined above are in any sense complementary. Thus, for example, he criticizes those who suggest that there may be both cognitive and experiential dimensions to doctrine as resorting to 'complicated intellectual gymnastics'.[100] It is perhaps this reluctance to concede the polymorphic and polyvalent character of doctrine which occasions some hesitation on the part of the critical reader concerning Lindbeck's analysis of the nature of doctrine.

A more serious general criticism of Lindbeck's account of doctrine concerns his use of history. Lindbeck tends to use history but rarely, and then highly selectively, and for purely illustrative purposes. Selected incidents in the history of doctrine are used to illustrate Lindbeck's 'cultural-linguistic' approach to doctrine. Even here, however, Lindbeck's engagement with history is somewhat superficial, and gives every indication of being of questionable reliability. For example, he appeals to Athanasius and the Niceanum in support of his assertion that doctrines are rules, second-order propositions which regulate community discourse rather than first-order propositions which refer to extra-linguistic reality.[101] Both the text and the notes of Lindbeck's work, however, indicate that this conclusion is based upon secondary literature concerning Athanasius, rather than Athanasius' writings themselves.[102] Indeed, Lindbeck is here particularly dependent upon the writings of Bernard Lonergan, even if he makes a claim which represents a conclusion which Lonergan himself does not seem to have drawn.

But, it may reasonably be asked, can history be used in this manner? Lindbeck treats history as a source-book for illustrations for a theory of doctrine which is not itself necessitated, nor even plausibly suggested, by the historical evidence at Lindbeck's disposal. We are presented with controverted, highly selected, decontextualized episodes from the history of doctrine, without any serious attempt to engage with the total historical phenomenon of doctrine. Perhaps this is inevitable, given the brevity of Lindbeck's work: it is possible that this manner of handling doctrinal history is adequate and proper for his specific purposes. Nevertheless, it is fair to register the suspicion that history is being exploited to support, rather than employed to establish, a theory of doctrine. A necessary prelude to any theory of doctrine is a precise understanding of the genesis of doctrine, of the factors which stimulate and govern doctrinal formulation, in all their historical and systematic complexity. Lindbeck's theory of doctrine ultimately rests upon his perception that 'cultural-linguistic' insights already finding application within the social sciences ought to find their way into theological reflection: the phenomenon of doctrine is then effectively *reduced* to this model, with history being treated in an atomistic manner as a convenient quarry for illustrative material for the model.

This grand retreat from history reduces doctrine to little more than a grammar of an ahistorical language, a language which – like Melchizedek – has no origins. It is just there. It just happens to be located in history. It is given. The historian, however, will wish to inquire concerning its origins and its historical points of reference. Like a biologist who sees behind the present complexity of species to discern a common process of evolution, the historian will suggest that the Christian language came into existence under certain quite definite historical conditions, and that its subsequent development may be accounted for by historical factors. Its present form is to be explained (and subjected to criticism) on historical grounds.[103] On the basis of this premise, the historian will suggest that a study of the development of doctrine as a historical phenomenon must underlie any theory of the nature of doctrine.

A related criticism concerns the referent of the term 'doctrine'. How does what has been described as 'doctrine' within the history of the Christian church relate to what Lindbeck defines as 'doctrine' on the basis of his cultural-linguistic model? Do they designate the same entity? I would suggest that there is at best a partial overlap between what Lindbeck describes as 'doctrine', and the historical phenomenon of doctrine which I shall explore in more detail in the following chapter. What Lindbeck chooses to designate 'doctrine' does not coincide (although there are obvious points of contact) with the complex agglomerate of social, cognitive and existential parameters implicated in a fully nuanced account of doctrine as an historical phenomenon. To put it more briefly, Lindbeck's concept of doctrine is strongly reductionist, facilitating theoretical analysis at the cost of failing to interact fully with the phenomenon in question.

I therefore venture to develop a somewhat more nuanced account of the nature of doctrine, which allows the complexity of doctrine as an historical phenomenon to be more fully appreciated. Although appreciative echoes of Lindbeck's analysis may be detected during its course, it will be clear that my basic conviction, very reluctantly drawn, is that Lindbeck's proposals require revision. Cognitive and experiential approaches to doctrine have perhaps more to commend them than Lindbeck suggests – partly because they are not quite what he suggests them to be.

3

The Nature of Doctrine:
Four Theses

The history of Jesus of Nazareth may be regarded as the precipitating or generative event of Christian doctrine. A community and an associated foundational narrative arose in direct response to that history, which sought to identify and legitimate both the existence of that community as a social entity and its distinctive understanding of God and human nature and destiny with reference to the perceived significance of Jesus of Nazareth. At a purely historical level, Jesus of Nazareth may be regarded as the historical source of both the community of faith and its foundational narrative, in a manner perhaps similar to that suggested by Liberal Protestantism.[1] Nevertheless, the doctrinal system generated by that community on the basis of its foundational narrative makes claims which transcend a purely historical account of its origins, and extend to both the existential and ontological domains.

In turning to deal with the nature of doctrine, it is necessary to note the endemic tendency within much recent theology towards what, for want of a better word, might be termed reductionism. Phenomena must be capable of being reduced to their bare essentials, with all hints of complexity and ambiguity eliminated. They must be amenable to being dismantled to yield a simple univocal conceptual structure. It is this precommitment to reductionism which has so seriously inhibited responsible analysis of the concept of doctrine in recent years. It is not just that certain theological criticisms, such as those noted in the previous chapter, may be brought against them: it is that they are often inattentive to the history of Christian thought, perhaps occasionally even to the point of near-total disengagement, failing to render a sufficiently nuanced account of the historical development of doctrine as an historical phenomenon, and the specific roles allocated to doctrinal formulations in the history of the Christian church. An historical analysis of the phenomenon of doctrine itself (rather than any specific doctrines) suggests that Christian doctrine is fundamentally an integrative concept, which brings together a number of elements into a greater whole. Reductionist approaches to the subject must thus, in retrospect, be judged to have surrended much that is essential to Christian self-understanding in an attempt to render doctrine – or, more accurately, a truncated and idealized reconstruction of the concept – intelligible to outsiders.

The history of Christian theology is an adequate, if not particularly eloquent, witness to the consequences of a failure to maintain the integrative nature of doctrine. For example, the debate between Lutheran Orthodoxy and Pietism in the seventeenth and eighteenth centuries illustrates the consequences of isolating the cognitive and the experiential elements of doctrine: Pietism was prepared to concede that Orthodoxy was probably true, but insisted that it appeared to lack any relevance to ordinary life.[2] It was not lodged in the realities of the experiential world of individuals, who thus perceived it as something of an irrelevance. A more modern failure to correlate doctrine and worship threatens to isolate doctrine from the public world of the community to which it relates.[3] More recently still, as noted in the previous chapter, the treatment of doctrine simply as the regulator of theological discourse, while setting to one side its external referents, gives rise to visible hesitations on the part of those who believe that Christianity is concerned with catching and preserving a glimpse (in however fragmented and limited a manner) of some reality, rather than merely with attaining (possibly arbitrary) internal systemic consistency.

An analysis of the development of Christian doctrine and the manner in which doctrinal formulations have functioned in the history of the Christian church discloses the nuanced character of doctrine. Such historical study disrupts simplistic theories of doctrine, which fail to account for the multifaceted character of doctrine as an historical phenomenon. Such simplistic theories display a tendency towards idealism, towards a disengagement with history, failing to interact with the extraordinarily historical and systematic complexity of the functions assigned to and associated with doctrinal formulations in the course of the history of the Christian church. There is generally at best a fractional degree of phenomenological isomorphism between 'doctrine', as it is encountered as an historical phenomenon on the one hand, and as it is defined by such historically- and socially-abstracted theories (such as that of Lindbeck) on the other. It is my contention that such reductive theories demonstrate an inherent tendency to deal with an idealized and historically abstracted conception, rather than an historical and social phenomenon.

Without in any way prejudging the question of what doctrine *ought* to be, I wish to suggest that, as a matter of historical fact, doctrine *has* been understood to possess four major dimensions, as follows:

1 Doctrine functions as a social demarcator.
2 Doctrine is generated by, and subsequently interprets the Christian narrative.
3 Doctrine interprets experience.
4 Doctrine makes truth claims.

In what follows, these four theses and the complex manner in which they interplay will be explored. They cannot be isolated as non-interactive and independent entities, but are rather to be viewed as mutually interacting constituents of a greater whole. I must stress that I am not concerned with presenting a *theory* of doctrine, but rather a descriptive account of the essential elements of doctrine as an historical phenomenon, which any theory of doctrine must be capable of accommodating. (An abstract account of doctrine as a purely ideal concept is vulnerable to the charge of theoretical idealism, a particular difficulty in the case of formulations which may be argued to rest ultimately upon an historical event – the history of Jesus of Nazareth.) Any theory of doctrine must be capable of accounting for the historical phenomena associated with doctrinal formulations. Historical analysis allows the four theses which follow to be identified both as the historical starting point of any future theory of doctrine, and as an implicit criticism of past theories.

Doctrine as Social Demarcation

There is an obvious need for a religious group to define itself in relation to other religious groups, and to the world in general. The general phenomenon of 'doctrine' – although not specific *doctrines* – is linked with the perceived need for social definition, especially when other factors do not adequately define a group. An ideology which legitimates its existence is required. Thus Niklas Luhmann,

perhaps the most significant recent writer to address the question
of the social function of Christian doctrine, stresses that doctrine
arises in response to threats to religious identity, which may be
occasioned socially (through encounters with other religious systems)
and temporally (through increasing chronological distance from its
historical origins and sources of revelation).[4] Doctrine is, according
to Luhmann, the self- reflection of a religious community, by which
this religious sub-system maintains its identity and regulates its
relations with other such religious sub-systems and the whole social
system in general.[5] The social function of doctrine is particularly
evident in cases in which a religious group originates through
rupture with an older grouping (for example, in the case of
Christianity's appearance from within the matrix of Judaism,[6] or
the emergence of the churches of the Reformation from the medieval
catholic church). There is a perceived need for a theological
justification of the separation of the Christian church from its Jewish
matrix, and subsequently in justifying its distinction from the
Hellenism of the patristic period. Doctrine is thus linked with the
affirmation of the need for certain identity-giving parameters for
the community, providing ideological justification for its continued
existence.

Doctrine thus defines communities of discourse. It does not
merely structure the conceptual frameworks and specific modes of
discourse of those communities; it identifies them as social entities,
marking them off from other social groupings. It serves as a means
of creating a sense of social identity, shaping the outlook of a
community and justifying its original and continued existence in
the face of rival communities with comparable claims. It assists in
defining both the limits of, and the conditions for entering, such a
community. Effective social cohesion requires the fixing of boundaries, and the sense of community identity.[7] Doctrine is one such
social demarcator, serving to enhance the sense of identity of a
community, and facilitating its distinction from other communities.
Other means of social demarcation associated with the Christian
communities (such as the sacraments)[8] have a clear doctrinal
component.

The early Christian communities do not appear to have regarded
precise and elaborate doctrinal formulations as essential to their self-
definition. 'Their doctrinal distinctiveness, however defined, was
reinforced, sustained, perhaps even eclipsed, by their sociological
distinctness as groups set, literally, apart from the world.'[9] Thus

the Johannine community regarded its circumstances as a group set apart from the world as being explained and legitimated by the accounts of Jesus transmitted within the Fourth Gospel.[10] The very early Christian communities, although clearly bearing a Wittgensteinian 'family resemblance' on account of their beliefs concerning Jesus of Nazareth, did not require doctrinal formulations to distinguish themselves from the world: that distinction was already forced upon them by the world, which isolated them as visible and readily identifiable social groups.[11] To become a Christian was (at least potentially) to be liable to a change in social location.

Gradually, however, this situation altered, as Christianity became increasingly widespread. Unlike the Essenes, the early Christians saw no need to withdraw into the wilderness: they remained within the world of the *polis* and *agora*, apparently mixing with the remainder of the population. 'We Christians', Tertullian wrote to his pagan audience, 'live with you, enjoy the same food, have the same manner of life and dress, and the same requirements for life as you.'[12] Christians declined to adopt the cultic rituals of Judaism (such as food laws, sabbath observance and circumcision) which served to identify Jews within a Gentile community; on the other hand, Marcion's proposal that Christianity should be declared utterly distinct from Judaism failed to gain support. There was an obvious polarity within the relationship of Christianity and Judaism. As a result, Christian self-definition was initially directed towards clarification of the relationship of Christianity and Judaism, centering upon the identity of Jesus, and subsequently upon the role of the Old Testament Law.[13] (Incidentally, the importance of the person of Jesus of Nazareth in precipitating bifurcation between Christianity and Judaism serves to highlight his function as the fundamental legitimizing resource of Christianity). It is thus perfectly acceptable to suggest that the Pauline doctrine of justification by faith represents a theoretical justification for the separation of Gentile Christian communities from Judaism, thus identifying the obvious social function of the doctrine[14] – providing, of course, that the naive conclusion is not drawn from this, that the Pauline doctrine of justification is *solely* a social epiphenomenon. The question of its ideational content remains to be discussed, and is only to be dismissed by those precommitted to an unacceptably reductive approach to doctrine.

Initially, then, the early Christian communities felt obliged to define themselves in relation to Judaism. As Christianity became

increasingly influential, however, the need for self-definition over
and against society as a whole became evident. The expansion of
Christianity rapidly led to it becoming a predominantly non-Jewish
community, and demanded that it define itself in the world of late
Hellenic culture within the frontiers of the Roman Empire.[15] The
question of its relation to Judaism became perceived increasingly as
something of an irrelevance. Two movements were of particular
importance in occasioning this self-definition: Gnosticism and
Platonism.

The encounter between Christianity and 'gnostic' movements
precipitated a crisis of identity during the second century, necessitating the formulating of criteria by which the claims of groups to be
'Christian churches' could be evaluated and authenticated. Gnosticism posed a powerful challenge to the Christian church, in
effect forcing the latter to clarify its boundaries.[16] Although the
contribution of Irenaeus to this process was pivotal, the importance
of Tertullian in urging self-definition and the maintenance of self-
identity within the Christian communities must not be overlooked.[17]
Yardsticks – such as the canon of the New Testament, or adherence
to the apostolic rule of faith – were agreed by which the claims of
religious communities to be Christian churches could be tested.

In this trend towards shaping Christian self-identification in the
face of a rival religious movement, it will be clear that doctrinal
formulations began to become particularly significant towards the
end of the second century. Nevertheless, the historical observation
must be made, that this does not appear to have been understood
as an attempt primarily to define what individual Christians believed;
rather, it seems to have been intended as a means by which the
credentials of a community claiming to be a Christian church might
be validated. There is no sense of 'orthodoxy' in the Eusebian sense
of a universal and uniform teaching of the Christian church: rather,
we find 'doctrine' being understood to refer to a range of options,
corresponding to the received range of traditions, subject to the
restraints imposed by a common central doxological core.[18] As I
emphasized in chapter 1, the New Testament itself generates and
transmits a definite, if limited, range of intellectual options: the
movement towards explicit doctrinal formulation in the second
century does not appear to have been conceived as eliminating that
diversity, but merely with ordering it within the limits of an agreed
central core – a core which is primarily doxological (rather than
purely ideational), a cluster of attitudes, practices, beliefs and

expectations, shaped by patterns of worship, adoration and prayer.[19] It was this central core which was held to be normative for communities wishing to regard themselves as 'Christian'.

The second century also witnessed the beginning of the clarification of the relationship of Christianity to the Platonic tradition. 'The most important part of the task of intellectual self-definition in relation to Hellenic culture undertaken by educated Christians from the second century onwards was the determination of what they could accept and what they must reject in contemporary Platonic–Pythagorean tradition.'[20] As Meijering as shown, even Christian thinkers who are generally regarded as not owing much to Hellenic philosophy (such as Athanasius) actually incorporate a remarkable number of late Platonic ideas into their thinking.[21] As noted earlier, it is at this point that doctrinal formulation became of particular significance: if Christian writers were to distinguish themselves from the Academy, they were obliged to demonstrate their distinctive ideas. For example, the Christian use of the term *logos* had to be distinguished from its Platonic equivalent. The dialogue between Christianity and late Platonism did much to encourage self-definition within both groupings.

With the conversion of Constantine, Christianity assumed a new status within the Roman Empire, and doctrinal formulations became of increasing political importance. Where the Donatist schism (313–16) had merely obliged Constantine to determine which of two rival *social groupings* could legitimately claim to be the true church, the Arian controversy obliged him to determine which of two rival *doctrines* was the teaching of the catholic church.[22] With the imperial resolution of the Arian crisis, 'doctrine' rapidly assumed the character of legally sanctioned ideology – a concept perhaps accurately designated 'dogma'. The relative pluralism of an earlier understanding of doctrine (that is, of a central core of ideas, and agreement concerning the texts to be used in teaching, preaching and theological exploration) reflected the unintegrated social structure of the Christian church of the period; with the advent of centralization during the Constantinian period came the idea of the church as a single institutional unit, requiring doctrinal uniformity in order to preserve its new-found social function and status.

With the development of the post-Constantinian concept of 'Christendom', doctrine lost its function as a social demarcator. The distinction between church and society in the Middle Ages was difficult to draw, and it is arguable that some would not even have considered this distinction possible. The high medieval ideology which insisted upon the identity of 'church' and 'society' fostered the suggestion that concern for matters of doctrine was potentially divisive, characteristic of heretics or monks, both of whom had effectively withdrawn from the world. Medieval heretical movements – such as the Hussites, Waldensians and Cathars – are now increasingly recognized to be political as much as religious movements, often with well-defined political goals, social institutions and power structures, incapable of being reduced to their religious ideas alone.[23] Thus, for example, Hussitism cannot be considered in isolation from Bohemian nationalism and the distinctive socio-political situation in that region which contributed in no small manner to its local attractiveness and the threat it was perceived to pose to political stability. For the medieval heretical movements, doctrinal issues were essential to self-definition, even if they were linked to, perhaps even dominated by, other concerns.

Although it is possible to suggest that social, economic and political factors may account for the genesis as much as for the ultimate success or failure of the medieval heresies, the fact remains that these movements chose to adopt doctrinal criteria in their self-definition, thus occasioning a doctrinal response from the church. Thus Hussitism was censured for its doctrinal ideas, giving the impression that these ideas existed in a socio-political vacuum and were in themselves capable of giving an exhaustive account of the movements. Similar observations may be made concerning the papal condemnation of Luther in 1520. The expediencies of medieval ecclesiastical power politics must not, however, be allowed to obscure the fact that the medieval heresies were social and political movements, posing a challenge to medieval society which far transcended the sphere of ideas. Doctrine served as a convenient way of identifying medieval heresies as social units, prior to their neutralization as a social, economic and political threat to the social stability of the age (which both church and society had a vested interest in maintaining).

This is not to say, of course, that the medieval church had no interest in doctrine whatsoever, or that the period was totally devoid of doctrinal development. It is, however, to draw attention to the fact that doctrine was not perceived to function as a criterion of social demarcation in the period, save in the specific area of combatting heresy. The threat posed by heresy was, of course, social and political, as much as religious. The penalty of excommunication served to emphasize this social function of doctrine: inability to subscribe to the chief doctrines of the medieval church would result in expulsion from the church, and hence effectively from the social order which it embodied. 'Christendom' was sufficiently stable and well-defined an entity to allow the need for doctrinal self-definition to become of perceived irrelevance. It is, of course, precisely this lack of interest in doctrine which is widely held to underlie the origins of the Reformation:[24] as doctrinal confusion and vagueness became increasingly widespread, uncertainty concerning what the church taught on certain issues in the first two decades of the sixteenth century led to some difficulty in recognizing that the ideas of individuals such as Luther or Zwingli were innovatory, let alone heretical, and subsequently blunted the force of the catholic response to these thinkers.

With the advent of the Reformation, however, the situation changed significantly. The emerging evangelical faction at Wittenberg, associated with Martin Luther, chose to define itself in relation to an explicitly doctrinal criterion: the doctrine of justification by faith alone.[25] It was on the basis of this doctrine that the Lutheran faction, soon to become the Lutheran church, would take its stand against the papacy.[26] The affirmation that the doctrine of justification is the *articulus stantis et cadentis ecclesiae*[27] confirms the importance of this doctrine to the self-definition of the Lutheran church, as is evident from Luther's ecclesiological criterion concerning the identity of the true church.

Once the Lutheran church became established as a serious and potentially credible alternative to the medieval church, self-definition through doctrinal formulations once more became of crucial importance to the catholic church. The significance of the Council of Trent lies in its perception of the need for the catholic church to define *itself* – rather than define *heretics* – at the doctrinal level. Earlier medieval councils had tended simply to condemn heretical opinions, thus defining views which placed those who entertained (or were prepared to admit to entertaining) them as heretical, and thus as lying outside the bounds of the church. In other words, they defined who was *outside* the bounds of the church, on the assumption that all others, whose views did not require definition, were *within* its bounds. The Council of Trent, in discussing the doctrine of justification, felt obliged to do more than simply censure Lutheran ideas: it defined catholic ideas with unprecedented clarity.[28] In an extensive series of anathemas, Trent defined who was outside the bounds of the church; it also, however, provided a remarkably comprehensive statement of catholic doctrine,[29] thus providing an explicit definition of the intellectual (and hence the social) bounds of the church.

This development reflected the growing need to demarcate catholics from evangelicals in sixteenth-century Europe, especially in disputed regions such as Germany. The catholic church was obliged to offer a criterion of self- identity, in order that its bounds might be defined in the face of the threat from Protestantism. The Reformation may therefore be regarded as precipitating the reclamation of doctrine as a criterion of social demarcation, a function which had not been of decisive importance during the medieval period.

Elsewhere in the sixteenth century, however, the need for doctrinal self-definition was not perceived as of crucial importance. An excellent case in point is the English Reformation, in which the reformed English church was under no pressure to define itself in relation to any other ecclesial body in the land. Powicke's generalisation, despite its obvious historical vulnerability, contains an important insight: 'The one thing that can be said about the Reformation in England is that it was an act of State . . . the Reformation in England was a parliamentary transaction.'[30] The manner in which the English Reformation initially proceeded demanded no doctrinal self-definition, in that the church in England was defined socially by precisely the same parameters before the Reformation as after, whatever political alterations may have been introduced. This is not to say that no theological debates took place in England at the time of the Reformation;[31] it is to note that they were not perceived as possessing decisive significance in relation to the self-definition of the Henrician English church. They were not regarded as identity-giving. The Lutheran church in Germany was obliged to define and defend its social existence and boundaries through explicitly doctrinal criteria precisely because it had broken away from the medieval catholic church; the Henrician church in England, however, was both contiguous and continuous with the medieval church at the institutional and social level, ensuring its adequate self-definition without the need to resort to explicitly doctrinal criteria. The English church was sufficiently well defined as a social unit to require no further definition at the doctrinal level.[32]

The re-emergence of doctrine as a criterion of social demarcation

in certain geo-political regions of Europe during the sixteenth
century is also evident from events in Germany during the period
of the so-called 'Second Reformation',[33] as Lutheran and Reformed
communities found themselves entering a period of increased tension
in the 1560s and 1570s due to the expansion of the Reformed church
in what had hitherto been regarded as exclusively Lutheran territory.
The principle *cuius regio eius religio*, established by the Religious
Peace of Augsburg (1555), appeared to allow political geography
to function as a criterion of religious demarcation: this possibility
was eliminated through the rise of Reformed influence (not envisaged
by the Peace), again forcing demarcation to be grounded on
doctrinal criteria. The late sixteenth-century phenomenon of 'Con-
fessionalization'[34], by which both Lutheran and Reformed communities defined themselves by explicit and extensive doctrinal formulations, represents the inevitable outcome of a quest for self-
definition on the part of two ecclesial bodies within the same
geographical region, both claiming to be legitimate outcomes of
the Reformation. At the social and political level, the communities
were difficult to distinguish; doctrine therefore provided the most
reliable means by which they might define themselves over and
against one another. The contrast with the earlier Henrician church
will be obvious: there was no rival ecclesial body then in existence
in England, which might have obliged that church to envisage the
necessity of self-definition along doctrinal lines. As Robert Morgan
remarks, 'in a fairly monolithic Christian culture, cut off by sea
from neighbouring states, when Roman Catholics and other
nonconformists could be penalized and marginalized, it was possible
to maintain a church's boundaries largely by a common liturgy and
polity'.[35]

This point may be given added weight through a consideration
of the legal significance of doctrine in the very differing circumstances
of the German and English Reformations. The phrase 'Church of
England', as defined as a legal term in Halsbury's *Laws of England*,
makes no reference to explicitly doctrinal formulations: the 'Church
of England' is regarded as continuous with the church established
in England during the period 597–686.[36] By law, according to
Halsbury, the 'Church of England' is defined as a matter of political
geography, rather than of doctrine. During the period of the
'Second Reformation' in Germany, however, the need to define
Reformed and Lutheran churches as *legal* entities led to doctrinal
formulations (such as the Augsburg Confession of 1530) assuming

legal, as well as theological, significance. *Sensu theologico*, the Augsburg Confession might be regarded as doctrine binding on the faithful; *sensu politico*, however, the document served as a convenient way of defining the Lutheran church for secular legal purposes,[37] distinguishing it from other ecclesial communities present within the same geo-political area in the increasingly complex German religious situation of the 1570s. Doctrinal formulations thus served as criteria by which churches might be identified as legal entities in the German situation.

This analysis of the social function of doctrine could be extended considerably, for example by dealing with the North American religious situation in the seventeenth century. Considerations of space, unfortunately, preclude such further analysis, and require some general observations to be made.

In the first place, it will be clear that the distinction between 'doctrine' and 'theology' serves to emphasize the social function associated with the former, yet denied to the latter. Doctrine identifies social communities. Ecclesial bodies may indeed 'receive' – in the technical sense of the term – theologies, thus altering their status to that of doctrine: this process of reception, however, as noted earlier (pp. 11–12) takes place at the communal, not the individual, level. Theology may be received as doctrine; without reception, it remains theology.

In the second place, the importance of the social function of doctrine for modern ecumenical discussions will be obvious.[38] How, it may be asked, may agreement be reached between Lutherans and Roman Catholics on justification, when this doctrine has traditionally divided their churches? Have they not altered their beliefs, which is unthinkable? While fully recognizing the importance of scholarship in clarifying the precise points at issue in the sixteenth-century debates (and hence eliminating misunderstandings), one crucial point has not received the attention it merits. The doctrine of justification by faith alone was of essential importance as a criterion of social cohesiveness to sixteenth-century Lutheranism in its formative phase: it has that function no longer. Agreement may be reached, precisely because doctrines which were once regarded as essential to the self-definition, and hence to the social cohesion, of the Lutheran church no longer possess that function. Ecumenical agreement on the doctrine of justification involves the recognition that doctrinal matters which were, as a matter of historical contingency, essential to the self-definition of either Lutheranism or Roman Catholicism at the time of the Reformation need no longer be regarded as having this function. The self-identity of Lutheranism is no longer perceived to be shaped by this doctrine.

The recognition of the social function of doctrines in no way weakens their truth-claims. Certain specific contingent historical circumstances lead to the perception that a given doctrine is of normative importance for the self-definition of a community in that situation. The identification of a given doctrine, with its particular emphases, as a criterion of ecclesial demarcation is *standortsgebunden*, linked with a specific set of historical circumstances. With the passing of those circumstances, the community may wish to define itself with reference to different parameters. The doctrine does not cease to be 'true'; it merely assumes a different social function. Thus, to give one particularly luminous example, the early Lutheran community in Germany perceived the doctrine of justification by faith to be of central importance to its self-definition. This perception derives from a number of historical contingencies: for example, Luther's formative engagement – central to his personal development – with a cluster of questions concerning this doctrine,[39] the popular preoccupation with purgatorial concerns (evident in the indulgence traffic), the ecclesial and political situation in Germany in the 1520s, and Luther's personal influence over the development of the Lutheran church.[40] Since then, however, the situation of the Lutheran churches has altered. Their centre of gravity is no longer Germany. They need no longer look over their shoulders at the pressing social concerns of the sixteenth century, in Germany or anywhere else. They no longer regard Luther as of decisive importance to the shaping of their identity.[41]

With the emergence of the very different ecclesial circumstances of the twentieth century, it is the occasion for no surprise that the doctrine of justification by faith should no longer be perceived as functioning as a social demarcator for Lutheranism – but this is not to deny that the doctrine is *true*, even if its central insights may be accommodated within a different framework acceptable both to Roman Catholics and Lutherans.[42] Central to modern ecumenical discussions is the fact that doctrines which functioned as social demarcators in the Reformation period have lost that function, partly by a process of historical erosion and partly on account of a recent willingness to set that function aside in the interests of the unity of Christendom. No ecclesial body which defines itself totally or largely in relation to a specific set of historical circumstances can avoid shifts in paradigms of self-identity with the progress of time.

In the third place, recognition of the social role of doctrine allows a theologically significant prediction to be made. The need for ostensive social demarcation arises primarily through two circumstances: on account of the existence of a rival religious ideology in a given geo-political arena (for example, in the case of Lutheranism in sixteenth-century Germany, a serious threat to its legitimation was initially posed by Roman Catholicism, and subsequently by Reformed theology); or on account of the need to distinguish the body of believers from society as a whole (particularly important in the early patristic period, but also significant in relation to the Radical Reformation in Europe and the growth of new religious movements in the United States during the twentieth century). Where no rival religious ideology exists which may be regarded as posing a serious threat to an ecclesial body, or where that body either feels no need to distinguish itself from society or positively wishes to identify itself with a given society, then it may be predicted that doctrine will not be perceived as significant by that ecclesial body.

Those who hold that 'religion' – which may, but need not, specifically refer to Christianity – is a phenomenon which embraces society as a whole will thus regard doctrine as potentially insignificant, or perhaps even as a phenomenon of purely negative significance. Doctrine serves to differentiate one community from other communities: those who regard religion as one aspect of social existence will therefore tend to resist the phenomenon of doctrine, in that it threatens to introduce inappropriate and unnecessary social division.[43] Doctrine divides that which ought, according to this view of religion, to be a unity. (It would, however, be more accurate to suggest that doctrine does not necessarily divide in itself; it may merely give expression to differences which already exist, in order that these may be confronted, assessed and possibly resolved.)

This phenomenon may be observed historically in those sections of the church which, following an ideology characteristic of the Middle Ages, regard 'church' and 'society' as essentially contiguous and continuous. This distinctive ideology held that 'church' and 'society' represent essentially the same entities, viewed from different aspects. Faithful to, although critical of, the medieval view of church and society, Erasmus of Rotterdam was hostile to explicit doctrinal formulations in the 1510s and 1520s, on account of their potential divisiveness.[44] Doctrine was, in Erasmus' view, associated with the formation of factions. With characteristic perception, Erasmus had observed the social function of doctrine, and noted its implications for the fate of the church in the sixteenth century, as the medieval social ideology which assumed the virtual identity of 'church' and 'society' began to lose its credibility.

The view that 'church' and 'society' designate precisely the same entities is one of the more significant characteristic features of the late medieval urban ideology. The great free imperial cities regarded themselves as a single community at both the political and religious levels, and regarded anything which posed a threat to this unity as unacceptable. In a seminal essay on the Reformation in the imperial cities of Germany, Berndt Moeller pointed out that the social contexts addressed by Luther in the northeast and by Bucer in the southwest were fundamentally different. Luther's religious thinking, according to Moeller, was the inevitable product of the less culturally developed part of Germany, which lacked the sophistication of the more developed regions, such as Strasbourg. Coming from a small town (Wittenberg corresponds well to the popular American notion of a 'hick' town) which lacked the corporate structures of guilds and the communal impulses of the great free imperial cities, Luther could hardly avoid producing a theology which was inward looking and doctrinally orientated, failing to engage with communal discipline and corporate urban structures.[45] Luther's ecclesiology is thus founded on a doctrine orientated towards the individual, rather than the community, and on explicitly doctrinal criteria: the church is the arena of authentic doctrine.

The great urban reformers, such as Bucer and Zwingli, however, based their programmes of reform and their ecclesiologies on the concrete realities of urban existence. In line with the prevailing urban ideology, 'church' and 'city' were treated as identical. The Reformation was not primarily concerned with doctrine, but with the reformation of the structures and existence of a community. Doctrine was regarded as potentially divisive, and initially marginalized for this reason. The failure of the Reformation in Erfurt, for example, reflects internal urban division arising from matters of doctrine.[46] The central premise of the urban Reformation was the maintenance of civic unity, for both ideological and political reasons. Doctrine threated to divide what both the late medieval urban ideology and political realism dictated should be a unity.

Zwingli's Reformation in Zurich thus proceeded on the characteristic assumption that 'church' and 'society' were essentially the same.[47] Fidelity to the church and to the city were regarded as equivalent, with the sacraments serving the dual function of demonstrating publicly both ecclesial and civic loyalty. The doctrinal content of Zwingli's reformation, as has often been noted, was initially negligible;[48] with the rise of a threat from a rival religious ideology (that of the *Wiedertaufern* in the 1520s), however, Zwingli was obliged to move towards making (and enforcing) explicit doctrinal formulations. Luther was obliged from the beginning to defend the evangelical faction at Wittenberg against catholic opponents – thus immediately necessitating doctrinal formulations (in hymns, liturgies, sermons and Confessions) as a means of demarcating that faction from its catholic opponents. The Zurich Reformation, in contrast, initially faced no internal opposition of any substance from catholicism, and thus demonstrated a marked disinterest in matters of doctrine at this stage. It is a change in historical circumstances, rather than any major theological shift on Zwingli's part, which led to the Zurich Reformation developing an explicit doctrinal component.

At the time of the Reformation, the tensions between Lutheran, Reformed, Radical and Roman Catholic ecclesial bodies on mainland Europe were so pervasive that doctrinal formulations were perceived to possess major importance. In England, however, a distinctively insular form of Reformation led to the Church of England developing without any major rival religious ideology arising internally, and being perceived as a serious threat to that Church. Furthermore, the English church was conceived by Henry VIII as a national church, no distinction between 'church' and 'society' being envisaged. The historical devaluation of doctrine, so central a feature of the life of the Church of England,[49] partly reflects the fact that the Church of England – maintaining the medieval social ideology – did not feel under any obligation to distinguish itself from the English social structure as a whole, and initially faced no serious internal threat from a rival religious ideology. The traditional Anglican devaluation of doctrine may thus ultimately rest, at least in part, upon a matter of political geography, rather than theology. (It will be recalled that Jules Michelet used to begin his lectures on British history with the words, 'Messieurs, l'Angleterre est une île', drawing attention to the importance of the geographically and politically insular character of England as the key to its historical development.) England was 'insulated', to exploit a pun, from the factors which made doctrine so significant a matter on the mainland of Europe in the Reformation and post-Reformation periods.

Fourthly, the recognition of the social role of doctrine suggests that doctrine is likely to become of increased, rather than diminished, theological importance in the final decade of the twentieth century and the opening of the new millenium. The reasons for this may be illustrated by considering the situation of the Church of England. The characteristic English devaluation of doctrine, far from reflecting insights or methods peculiar to 'the English mind',[50] arises partly from a specific set of historical circumstances which pertained in the sixteenth century, as I have argued. Those circumstances have been eroded by a process of historical decay: the Church of England is no longer the only significant ecclesial body in England, on account of the growth of non-conformism, the house church movement, and the new confidence evident within English Roman Catholicism; the notion of 'establishment' has become little more than a legal fiction; society as a whole is now not merely non-Christian (due to patterns of immigration from the Indian subcontinent, amongst other factors), but at points aggressively secularist. There is thus a growing need for self-definition on the part of the Church of England, if it is to survive as a distinctive ecclesial entity – and an inevitable part of that process of self-identification is ostensive doctrinal formulation, transcending the minimalist position associated with the Elizabethan Settlement. We argued above that the traditional marginalization of doctrine within the Church of England partly reflects the specific social, religious and political situation of sixteenth-century England, now radically altered through a process of historical erosion. A new social situation demands a new – and more positive – attitude to doctrine, unencumbered by the illusion that it is possible to maintain, or return to, the defining conditions of the sixteenth century. The new interest in doctrine evident among younger English Anglicans reflects this perception,[51] and echoes a wider recognition of the importance of doctrine within many other churches.

Finally, recognition of the social function of doctrine allows insight to be gained into the phenomenon, particularly associated with (although by no means restricted to) the Roman Catholic and Orthodox churches, in which institutional affiliation precedes the acceptance of doctrinal formulations. An individual may make a conscious decision to be associated with an ecclesial body, and, as a consequence, come to adopt its doctrinal formulations as a way of envisioning reality. Acceptance of the community, of the group, here precedes acceptance of its social demarcators. Acceptance of the doctrines of such a community may be less than total, and may take place over an extended period of time, even though the decision to align oneself with this ecclesiastical grouping may be total and instantaneous. These comments are not intended to suggest that this attitude towards doctrine is normative, or even particularly common: it is, however, to state that it is an observable phenomenon, illustrating the interaction of cognitive and social elements which is so characteristic a feature of Christian doctrine, requiring explanation by any comprehensive theory of doctrine.

Doctrine as Interpretation of Narrative

In his superb recent essay 'Per la storia del mito di Firenze', Christian Bec shows how the development of a communal narrative (Bec deliberately uses the term 'myth', to indicate that this story is an interpretation, rather than a mere reiteration, of history) was perceived to be central to Florentine self- identity throughout the period 1300–1527.[52] This communal narrative, bearing vital suggestive parallels with that of ancient Rome, was seen as a means of preserving the city's identity, self-consciousness and values. The narrative made certain significant statements concerning Florence's origins, its present situation and its hopes for the future, as well as stating (in narrative form) its cultural values, particularly at times where these were seen to be under threat. Bec points out that 'Florence' thus assumes a symbolical literary role in Dante, as it does pictorially in Giotto, by recalling this narrative and the values it entails.[53]

In doing this, however, the Florentines were not in any way suggesting that their situation was identical with that of classical Rome or Athens. Rather, they were convinced that these classic models illustrated patterns of behaviour which could be conceived as genuine contemporary possibilities. Heidegger draws a significant distinction between an era characterized by an authentic historical consciousness, in which history is grasped as an recurrence of the possible, of a genuine possibility of existence, and a historiographically orientated era (such as the nineteenth century) preoccupied with expressions and the theory or methodology of expression of the past.[54] Unencumbered by imperialist theories of history which prohibited the perception of present-day relevance in past history, the Florentines saw the story of Rome as *their* story, with (for example) the Medicis as the kings, and themselves as the republicans. The Florentine 'retelling' of the story of the ancient world allowed them to make sense of what was happening to them, lending historical dignity and ideological legitimacy to their situation and strategy.

A similar situation existed within the Helvetic (Swiss) Confederation in the early sixteenth century, especially in the aftermath of the disastrous defeat of the Confederates at Marignano (1515). The Confederation – a fragile political and cultural entity, even at the best of times – felt its existence was threated by outside elements, and supplemented its military defences by the vigorous development of a cultural programme. The Swiss humanists (in marked contrast to Erasmus of Rotterdam, who regarded national identities and languages as outmoded) were committed to a nationalist vision, by which Swiss national identity was affirmed and sustained by the republic of letters.[55] One of the more important ways of affirming this sense of national identity was through narratives of the formative period of the Confederation. As Stephan Schmidlin has shown in his seminal study of the culture of the period, by far the most celebrated of these narratives is the legend of William Tell, which assumed its definitive form in 1512, and rapidly assumed the status of a national myth.[56] The story of the background to the formation of the Confederacy identified the communal values it affirmed, enhanced its sense of communal identity, and explained why it was worth defending in the face of an external threat. The narrative of the past was thus seen as illuminating the present situation, disclosing both insights and possibilities.

The insights to be gained from treating such communal foundational narratives as a model for the reappropriation of the past assume particular importance if read in conjunction with Alasdair MacIntyre's *After Virtue*.[57] MacIntyre stresses the importance of narratives in shaping the outlook of a community, in that it is able to ground the particularity of that community in history. Narrative functions as the bearer of a tradition, which illuminates the present and opens up options for the future. 'Living traditions, just because they continue a not-yet completed narrative, confront a future whose determinate and determinable character, so far as it possesses any, derives from its past'.[58]

Bec's analysis of Florence's image-making illustrates MacIntyre's point that 'the history of each of our own lives is generally and characteristically embedded in and made intelligible in terms of the larger and longer histories of a number of traditions'.[59] The history of Florence was an extension of the narrative of ancient Rome, so that the character of the Florentine community derived from that narrative. A fundamental resonance was detected between the 'here and now' of that community and the 'there and then' of classical Rome. In much the same way, the character of the Christian community arises from its historical derivation from the precipitating event of Jesus of Nazareth, and a willingness to let his story govern that community's understanding of its historical situation and future: its attitudes to power, to pride, to loss, to death, to grief, to despair – all are governed by the narrative of Jesus of Nazareth. 'Jesus' assumes a role within the community of faith equivalent to that assumed by 'Florence' for Dante or Giotto – it evokes a deep sense of 'happening', the memory of a foundational narrative and its present significance for the community whose identity is inextricably bound up with it. It provides a focus of identity for the community.[60] The New Testament affirmation of the conformity of the believer to Christ – that, through faith, those who believe in Christ are somehow caught up in him, so that *his* history becomes *their* history[61] – provides a significant theological foundation for this correlation of narratives. His death is their death, his life is their life – and the narrative of Jesus gives some specification to Christian existence by aligning that existence with a lived life, with a specific historical person.

This process of establishing the conformity of the structure of existence of both the community of faith and the individual believer to that of Jesus is already clearly evident in the New Testament itself.[62] Particularly in the Pauline writings, participation in Christ points to a conformity of one's existence to his. Through faith, the believer is caught up in a new outlook on life, a new structure of existence, embodied paradigmatically in Jesus Christ – and both in their proclamation and person, the community of faith and its members reveal this story of Jesus Christ. The narrative of Jesus is thus interpreted as a story which grounds Christian existence, which gives some shape and specification to what human outlooks on life, what form of actions, what moral motivations, are appropriate expressions of our own sharing in the life of Christ. Narratives are grounded in history, in actions, enabling us to avoid thinking of Christianity in terms of universal abstractions, and instead to ground it in the contingencies of our historical existence. Our vision is shaped and informed by the story of Jesus of Nazareth, recalled in the eucharistic celebration of his death and resurrection and the benefits which these are understood to bring us, which we recognize as embodying the shape or pattern of our lives and communities as Christians.

The correlation of the narratives of ancient Rome and Renaissance Florence casts light upon the manner in which the narrative of Jesus of Nazareth bears upon the existence and outlook of the modern community of faith, and the way in which the past may have a bearing upon the present. In a period in which the consciousness of historical location dawned, the past was still found to be charged with present relevance, on account of the conscious decision to allow the reclamation of a broken tradition of narrative. Florence had to remember its connections with the past; it had to reassert – perhaps even to the point of inventing – its continuity with the classical period; it had to decide to allow itself to be governed by the narrative of Rome. The community of faith, however, stands in an unbroken tradition with another narrative, which it recalls *as given* in its worship (as *anamnesis*) and proclamation. The community of faith stands in anamnetic solidarity with its apostolic forebear; it has no need to invent this continuity, which is historically and theologically *given*. The narrative of Jesus Christ, mediated through scripture and eucharistic celebration, is presented, proclaimed *and accepted* as the foundational and controlling narrative of the community of faith.

This narrative is transmitted through scripture, or channels which may be shown to be directly derived from this source. The primary source of Christian doctrine is thus scripture, in that it is scripture which mediates Jesus of Nazareth to us. Scripture is the manger in which Christ is laid (Luther). While the theologian may feel at liberty to explore other sources of potential interest, doctrine is historically linked with scripture on account of the historicity of its formulating communities. Christian communities of faith orientate and identify themselves with reference to authoritative sources which are either identical with, or derived from, scripture. A church which accepts the authority of the creeds does so on account of a belief that they correctly express what is contained in scripture.[63] Scripture, whether approached directly or through a filter of creeds and traditions, is regarded as constituting the foundational documents of the Christian church.

Scripture does not primarily take the form of credal and doctrinal statements, although these are unquestionably interwoven within its structure. Its primary – although by no means its *exclusive* – concern is with narrating what happened at moments held to be of particular importance to the self-definition of the community of faith – moments such as the exodus from Egypt or the resurrection of Jesus of Nazareth. Scripture presents us with a narrative,[64] which purports to tell of God's dealings with humanity, culminating in – bot not ending with – the history of Jesus of Nazareth.[65] Where doctrine is concerned with what should be (or is) believed, scripture appears preoccupied primarily with narrating what happened.[66] (While the New Testament includes much material that is not narrational in character, this can be argued to represent the outcome of engagement with the narrative of Jesus of Nazareth). In that Christianity is centered on the figure of Jesus of Nazareth, a mode of discourse capable of structurally expressing that history is required. Scripture does not articulate a set of abstract principles, but points to a lived life, a specific historical existence, as in some sense embodying and giving substance to some such set of principles.

This point could be illustrated with reference to a number of literary examples. Perhaps one of the most interesting such illustrations is provided by Alessandro Manzoni's *I Promessi Sposi*, which may be regarded as an exposition, in narrative form, of a set of aesthetical principles. *I Promessi Sposi* is basically the narrative transformation of a framework of values,[67] in which values are given historical substance. In evaluating the methodology of Manzoni, the contemporary literary critic Francesco de Sanctis argued that the statement of abstract ideas or values was of little practical relevance, being destined to remain little more than theory: it is necessary to incarnate these ideas in 'una società reale', and in 'un tempo particolare della storia'.[68] The narrative form (of which *I Promessi Sposi* is a classic expression) provides the link between ideas or values and their actualization in history and historical forms: the impact of *I Promessi Sposi* (Manzoni's only novel, incidentally) upon the *Risorgimento* testifies to the effectiveness of narrative in addressing and engaging with history. A narrative does not merely recount what has happened or is now happening: it discloses possibilities.[69] To relate abstract values to our own specific location in history is greatly facilitated by a concrete example, a narration of how these values are fleshed out and given historical substance. Any correlation between theory and practice requires the establishment of a link between the realms of ideas and of history, and thus indicates the narrative form as the primary means of analysing the dialectic between them.

Scripture, then, provides a narrative of a real historical existence, affirmed to be of foundational significance to the community of faith, incarnating both values and ideas.[70] But how is the transition from narrative to doctrine to be effected? The importance of this question in relation to the genesis of doctrine may be illustrated with reference to two historical examples, which illuminate the difficulties encountered in making the transition from narrative to doctrine.

I begin by considering the so-called *Christus Victor* theory of the Atonement. This theory, prominent in the patristic period,[71] is essentially narrative – even dramatic.[72] The soteriological markers and metaphors of the New Testament are expanded and reconstructed, to yield a narrative account of the drama of the redemption of humanity. This narrative has certain presuppositions – for example, that humanity is in bondage to tyrants or hostile powers. Nevertheless, these presuppositions are identified by the narrative itself, in the course of recounting the manner in which the death and resurrection of Jesus of Nazareth represents the divine conflict with and victory over the evil powers of bondage.

Our concern is with the structure, rather than the content, of what Gustaf Aulén infelicitously designates the 'classical theory of the Atonement'. The narrative proved to raise more questions than it answered. Why was humanity held bondage to demonic forces? In what way does the cross and resurrection represent a *divine* conflict and victory? Why couldn't God just have taken out the devil? And, faced with these difficulties, the proponents of the theory were obliged to provide a conceptual substructure in the light of which the narrative might be interpreted. The concept of the *ius diaboli* was thus developed as an attempt to make sense of the narrative at its more perplexing points.[73] A substructure of doctrinal formulations thus began to emerge, as a means of interpreting the drama narrated by the *Christus Victor* theory. With the theological renaissance of the late eleventh and early twelfth centuries, this substructure came under intense critical scrutiny from theologians such as Anselm and Abailard,[74] eventually to be rejected as unsatisfactory and replaced with a doctrine – rather than a *narrative* – of redemption. Our point, however, concerns the structure of the *Christus Victor* theory, which may be seen as an intermediate stage between the scriptural narrative and doctrinal formulations. The narrative required the presupposition of a set of axioms if it was to be meaningful: those axioms were identified and elaborated, in the process of the genesis of doctrine. What narrative lacked, or could plausibly be argued to presuppose, was provided by a doctrinal substructure.

Our second example is the Origenist Christological tradition,[75] in which a 'mythology' and a 'metaphysic' – that is, a narrative and various frameworks of conceptualities, ultimately of Platonic provenance – demanded correlation. How could the scriptural narrative be related to such an interpretative framework? And which of the various frameworks available (or conceivable) was most appropriate? The Arian controversy illuminates this tension between differing interpretative frameworks as they bear upon a common narrative tradition: both Arius and Athanasius claim to be interpreters of the same narratives. Although Arius was no philosopher, it is clear that his reading of the scriptural narrative required both a monist and absolutist metaphysic;[76] the scriptural narrative centred upon a creature, not the creator. For Athanasius, the same narrative centred upon the incarnation of the Son of God, implying a correspondingly different metaphysic.

This controversy illustrates a crucial phase in the genesis of doctrine: the need to test the adequacy of doctrinal formulations as interpretative frameworks for the scriptural narrative. The frameworks proposed by both Arius and Athanasius were sufficiently internally consistent to necessitate their evaluation on other grounds (an important point, incidentally, in relation to Lindbeck's 'cultural-linguistic' approach to doctrine, which would appear obliged to treat each option as possessing equal merit, on the basis of the criteria at its disposal): those grounds included the degree of correlation with both the scriptural narrative itself, and the evaluation of that narrative within the community of faith as expressed in its prayer, worship and adoration.[77] Athanasius' insistence upon the significance of the maxim *lex orandi lex interpretandi* sets him apart from Arius at this point:[78] for Athanasius, worship is the crucible within which theological statements are refined; for Arius, theology provides a framework for the criticism of worship.

How, then, are narrative and doctrine related? Prior to more detailed exposition, the relation of doctrine to the scriptural narrative may be summarized provisionally as follows. Doctrine provides the conceptual framework by which the scriptural narrative is interpreted. It is not an arbitrary framework, however, but one which is suggested by that narrative, and intimated (however provisionally) by scripture itself. It is to be discerned within, rather than imposed upon, that narrative. The narrative is primary, and the interpretative framework secondary. The New Testament includes both the narrative of Jesus of Nazareth and interpretation of the relevance of that narrative for the existence of the primitive Christian communities; doctrine represents the extension of the quasi-doctrinal hints, markers and signposts to be found within the New Testament.

Narratives demand interpretation. Most narratives – for example, William Golding's novel *Lord of the Flies* – admit to interpretation at more than one level. The scriptural narrative is no exception. The Old Testament may be read as a story of the quest for identity among a nomadic people of the Ancient Near East, just as the synoptic gospels may be read as the story of a misguided Galilean revolutionary or a frustrated Jewish rabbi. Doctrine articulates the particular interpretation, or range of interpretations, of the scriptural narrative appropriate to the self-understanding of the Christian community, calling others into question. Thus the assertion 'Jesus is the Christ' is a doctrinal affirmation which allows the narrative of Jesus of Nazareth to be viewed in a particular light. This assertion is not, however, arbitrary: it is held to be legitimate in the light of that narrative itself. Romans 1.3–4 legitimizes Paul's claim that Jesus is the Christ with reference to the narrative of Jesus of Nazareth, just as a narrative substructure may be detected in the case of other Pauline theological or ethical affirmations.[79]

The doctrine of the 'two natures' affirms two vital insights: 'Jesus is God' and 'Jesus is man'. Whatever metaphysical or ontological implications may be suggested by these claims, it is important to appreciate that *initially* they refer to the interpretation of the narrative of Jesus of Nazareth. Within the context of this narrative, Jesus may be discerned as playing two roles – the human and the divine. Two roles which had hitherto been regarded as mutually exclusive, demanding different actors, are held by the narrative to be intimately related and focused on the single person of Jesus. Within the context of the narrative, Jesus acts as God (for example, by forgiving sin: Mark 2:5–7), as well as assuming the more conventional role of a human actor. The doctrine of the two natures thus provides a means of interpreting the scriptural narrative, and ensuring its internal consistency.

Similarly, the doctrine of the Trinity may be regarded as an interpretation of the Christian narrative. 'Father, Son and Holy Spirit' is an identifying description of God, as he is perceived to act in the New Testament.[80] 'Father', 'Son' and 'Spirit' are identified as related roles within the New Testament narrative. The doctrine of the Trinity provides a hermeneutical key to the correct interpretation of the Old and New Testament narratives, which might otherwise be understood to concern three different deities. Trinitarian discourse is an attempt to identify the God at the centre of the scriptural narrative. In common with doctrine as a whole, it neither explicitly makes, nor does it explicitly preclude, metaphysical statements. It is initially concerned with interpretating a narrative.

It is at this point that Lindbeck's analysis of doctrine as regulative discourse has a fruitful role to play, ensuring that a consistent interpretation of the scriptural narrative results. To use Lindbeck's own example: if 'Denmark' is identified by the narrative of *Hamlet* as being 'the land where Hamlet lived', intrasystemic consistency demands that 'Denmark' shall not suddenly assume some other meaning.[81] (In a similar manner, I might define 'Narnia' as 'the land where Aslan lives' to emphasize the point that we are dealing with *consistency* at this stage, rather than questions concerning whether 'Narnia' has any external referent. 'Narnia' is identified and given its meaning by a narrative.) Analysis of a narrative engenders a network of relations, demanding intrasystemic consistency. If Jesus of Nazareth is defined as 'God', then consistency demands that traditional monotheism either recognizes that there are at least two gods, or begin rethinking the question of just who the 'God' implicated within this narrative might actually be.

There is thus a dynamic relationship between doctrine and the scriptural narrative. That narrative possesses an interpretative substructure, hinting at doctrinal affirmations. It is evident that there are conceptual frameworks, linked to narrative structures, within scripture: these function as starting points for the process of generation of more sophisticated conceptual frameworks in the process of doctrinal formulation. On the basis of these scriptural hints, markers and signposts, doctrinal affirmations may be made, which are then employed as a conceptual framework for the interpretation of the narrative. The narrative is then re-read and re-visioned in the light of this conceptual framework, in the course of which modifications to the framework are suggested. There is thus a process of dynamic interaction, of *feedback*, between doctrine and scripture, between the interpretative framework and the narrative itself, paralleling the related process of mathematical iteration. There is an instructive parallel here with Hegel's understanding of the relation of *Vorstellung* and *Begriff*: the philosophical mediation of truth is characterized by the constant dynamic oscillation between representation and concept, as one is compared with the other and refined and modified accordingly.[82] Alternatively, one might describe this dialectical relationship in Piagetian terms, as one of assimilation and accommodation: the narrative is assimilated to concepts, and the concepts are accommodated to the narrative. In the course of the 'hermeneutical spiral'[83], new levels of interpretation are achieved through a progressive interactive oscillation between the generative narrative of scripture and the interpretative framework of doctrine.

With these points in mind, we may consider a statement such as that of Wiles: 'Incarnation, in its full and proper sense, is not something directly presented in scripture.'[84] Quite so. Neither, it may be added, is an oak tree directly presented in an acorn.[85] The essential question concerns whether the doctrine of incarnation, in 'its full and proper sense', is a legitimate interpretation of the scriptural narrative. Given that metaphysics and narrative are different, yet not mutually exclusive, modes of discourse, it would not be expected that such advanced metaphysical assertions as those associated with incarnation 'in its full and proper sense' would be found within the scriptural narrative. The genuine point at issue is whether such a metaphysical statement is consistent with, and legitimately generated by, this narrative. Is it continuous and contiguous with the narrative which it purports to interpret, and within which its seeds are to be discerned? Is the transition between this narrative and that framework of conceptualities justified? The process of interactive oscillation between narrative and interpretative framework which I have identified allows an elementary, but nevertheless decisive, distinction between conceptualities already present, in however nuanced a manner, in scripture, and those which may be inferred from the interpretative process. For many scholars, the idea of incarnation is already present in scripture;[86] for others, it is a reasonable, perhaps even necessary, inference. The essential biological continuity between acorn and oak is ensured by its genetic code;[87] can we discern a corresponding framework of identity between the narrative of Jesus and the doctrinal framework of the incarnation? If a radical discontinuity or discontiguity may be demonstrated, the doctrine of the incarnation may be set to one side as improper.

The question does not concern whether the doctrine of the incarnation is a proper deduction from the premises of scripture, as has often been suggested. This is to misunderstand the literary genre and manner of discourse associated with scripture. The primary literary form encountered within scripture is that of narrative, rather than propositional formulation, suggesting that the appropriate mode of analysis is inference rather than deduction. In that scripture recounts a narrative, a set of particularities, a process of inferential, rather than deductive, analysis is clearly indicated. The question concerns what framework of conceptualities may be inferred from this narrative. In making this statement, I am attempting to draw attention to some points frequently overlooked or misunderstood within the debate concerning the incarnation. Scripture is not primarily a set of premises, from which deductions may be made. It is a specific mode of discourse and pattern of thinking, which requires transposition into an interpretative framework. This involves a shift in modes of discourse and patterns of thinking, in that two quite different genres – narrative and metaphysics – require correlation.

The decisive transition in ancient Greek thought, giving rise to metaphysics, is often portrayed as a transition from myth to *logos* – in other words, from narrative to conceptual frameworks.[88] The shift away from the narrative mode of discourse associated with *mythos* to an argumentative and conceptual mode of discourse and thought may be traced through the Pre-Socratics, Plato and Aristotle.[89] (A significant debate, worthy of note at this point, concerns whether the narrative structure of human existence is ontologically given, or is historically and contingently acquired;[90] the outcome of this debate is not of direct relevance to my analysis, which rests upon the observation that narrative structures – whether given or acquired – constitute the medium, structurally capable of expressing time and space, through which the history of Jesus of Nazareth is transmitted to us.) The recognition that doctrine involves the interpretation of narrative, and hence a shift from one literary genre and mode of thinking to another, forewarns us of the potential futility of certain criticisms of doctrine on the grounds of its alleged 'Hellenism'. The doctrine of the incarnation is perhaps the classic example of the outcome of a prolonged interaction between narrative and metaphysical modes of discourse, an interaction which is of central importance to the genesis of doctrine. There will always be those who will be content simply to retell the Christian story, without critical reflection or any attempt to correlate it with other patterns of thought or modes of discourse. Doctrinal formulations are the result of the early church's correct perception that the mere reiteration of the scriptural narrative was not enough; it was necessary to interact with other modes of discourse, such as those associated with Platonism, correlating narrative and conceptual frameworks.

As I suggested earlier, Christian doctrine may be regarded as the present outcome of that long growth of tradition in which the Christian community has struggled to arrive at an interpretation of its foundational traditions, embodied in the New Testament, which both does justice to its own present place in tradition, and attempts to eliminate those doctrinal pre-judgements which are to be judged as inadequate. This interpretation involves a continuous interaction between scriptural narrative and doctrinal formulations, in an attempt to find an interpretative framework, or range of such frameworks, already hinted at within the New Testament, on the basis of which the narrative of Jesus of Nazareth might be viewed at enhanced levels of meaning. The doctrinal framework which embraces the concept of incarnation was arrived at with some hesitation, on account of its evident implications for Jewish monotheism, and has been subjected to the most sustained criticism in the Enlightenment and post-Enlightenment period. Nevertheless, radical discontinuity between the narrative of Jesus of Nazareth and the primitive interpretative frameworks contained within the New Testament on the one hand, and the doctrine of the incarnation on the other, remains to be shown.

In chapter 1, I located the genesis of doctrine as lying within the need to transfer theological reflection from the limits and defining conditions and vocabulary of the New Testament, in order to remain faithful to the New Testament proclamation. The deficiencies of a theology of repetition being painfully obvious, the need for critical theological reflection was soon conceded (pp. 2–5). But what form might this reflective development take? The supplementation or abbreviation of the scriptural narrative was self-evidently deficient, given the potential distorting influences attending any such amend-ation. The only serious possibility lay in transposing the scriptural narrative conceptually, generating new images and idioms by an attempt to recast this narrative in a different (yet not totally unrelated) mode of discourse. This is a secondary move in the articulation of the significance of Jesus of Nazareth, and a precarious one at that – yet it is unavoidable, unless the gospel proclamation was to be petrified in its first-century Palestinian matrix. The transition from *mythos* to *logos* thus implicated parallels that historically associated with the genesis of philosophical modes of discourse in ancient Greece; to dismiss it as the baleful influence of 'Hellenism' is to demonstrate a regrettable impatience with the different ways of thinking available in specific historical situations, thus effectively prohibiting the proclamation of the gospel in different historical situations. The metaphysical and ontological implications of the scriptural narrative concerning Jesus of Nazareth will not go away, and cannot be ignored or dismissed out of hand, just because some individuals find them difficult or indigestible.

The transition from a narrative to a conceptual framework of thinking would have potentially destructive effects for Christian theology if the narrative concerning Jesus of Nazareth, having being allowed to generate a specific framework of conceptualities, were forgotten. Had a conceptual approach to Christianity (such as that associated with the concept of incarnation) been regarded as self-sufficient and autonomous, the narrative which originally precipitated it might have disappeared into the mists of history. Had this occured, serious anxiety would necessarily have resulted concerning the propriety and adequacy of this framework. It would have been left suspended without visible support. No criteria, save those imposed from outside by rival ideologies, could be adduced by which it could be evaluated. However, the foundational narrative has been preserved by the community of faith, and accorded primary status in doctrinal reflection (particularly within the churches of the Reformation). The *sola scriptura* principle is ultimately an assertion of the primacy of the foundational scriptural narrative over any framework of conceptualities which it may generate.[91] We do not have access to the history of Jesus in its entirety. We do not possess the totality of traditions concerning Jesus. Nevertheless, we do have access to the part of that history and those traditions which the first Christian communities regarded as foundational and identity-giving, along with hints of possible interpretative frameworks, allowing us to evaluate any resulting conceptual representations of the gospel – past, present and future. We retain possession of the criteria by which any proposed framework of conceptualities may be generated or evaluated. In the end, Christian doctrine stands or falls in relation to scripture, not any particular set of concepts.

The relation of narrative and metaphysics may be further explored by considering Luther's 'theology of the cross', perhaps one of the most theologically acute accounts of this theme.[92] Luther's theology is often incorrectly described as 'anti-metaphysical', which has led to a cluster of unhistorical judgements concerning his theology. Luther's fundamental point, however, is that the narrative of the crucified Christ must be interpreted on the basis of a framework established by that narrative itself, rather than upon the basis of an imposed alien framework. Luther's hostility towards Aristotelian metaphysics is based on his conviction that it imposes upon the scriptural narrative an interpretative framework which leads to serious distortion of the narrative.

Luther's particular concern centres upon a cluster of divine attributes, such as the 'glory of God', the 'power of God', and the 'righteousness of God'. If these attributes are defined on the basis of prior metaphysical presuppositions (including an uncritical use of the principle of analogy), the gospel is distorted. How can the revelation of the 'righteousness of God (*iustitia Dei*)' (Romans 1.16–17) be good news for sinful humanity, when (on the basis of an Aristotelian analysis of *iustitia*) this revelation can only imply condemnation?[93] Luther's theological breakthrough (to be dated at some point in 1515) centred upon his realization that it is the narrative of Jesus of Nazareth, centring upon the crucified Christ (who assumes the function and identity of *Deus crucifixus et absconditus* within the parameters of the narrative), which defines the meaning of such terms as the 'righteousness of God'.[94] The 'theologian of the cross' is one who generates a conceptual framework on the basis of the scriptural narrative; a 'theologian of glory' is one who interprets the scriptural narrative on the basis of a predetermined conceptual framework.

Luther thus has no objection to metaphysics, as even a cursory reading of his writings in the period 1515–21 demonstrates; his concern is to allow the scriptural narrative of Jesus of Nazareth, as it is focused upon the crucified Christ, to generate its own framework of conceptualities. Luther's assertion of the autonomy of the scriptural narrative does not involve the rejection of metaphysics; it merely denies to any preconceived metaphysics the right to impose its interpretative framework upon scripture. For Luther, conceptualities such as 'the righteousness of God' are defined by the scriptural narrative. Even 'God' is defined in this manner, as may be seen from Luther's celebrated reference to the 'crucified and hidden God (*Deus crucifixus et absconditus*)'.[95] Aristotle's definition of 'God'[96] has, according to Luther, no direct bearing upon the interpretation of scripture, which identified a somewhat different God as its chief agent. It is possible to regard Luther's axiom *crux sola nostra theologia*[97] as a sophisticated statement of the *sola scriptura* principle, which asserts the priority of a historically based narrative – rather than abstract concepts of divinity – in theological reflection.

Doctrine as Interpretation of Experience

Christianity is concerned with human experience.[98] This is not, however, to say that it is concerned with a universal private experience, common to all religions;[99] rather, it is concerned with a communal experience within the Christian community. It addresses the human experience of alienation, of feeling cut off from a homeland, as points of contact. It addresses such experiences in order to transform them, and to indicate what the shape of the experience of redemption through Jesus Christ might be like.[100] But how can an experience be expressed in words, in the broken and fragmentary units of human language? If words are but the counters of human logic, how can something incapable of expression in the form of syllogisms be articulated? As Wittgenstein wryly pointed out, human words could not even describe the aroma of coffee.[101] Their failure to describe this experience (presumably a quintessential memory of his native Vienna) points to the need of an unattainably better vocabulary, if human experiences are to be echoed in words.

The fundamental insight here, noted in the previous chapter, is that human words cannot adequately define experience, but may nevertheless point towards it, as signposts. Although emphasis upon the experiential aspects of doctrine are especially associated with the later Renaissance and the rise of experientially orientated theologies in the Romantic period, hints of such insights are evident in the writings of Augustine of Hippo and his medieval interpreters. Christian doctrine attempts to give shape to the Christian life by laying the foundations for the generation of, and subsequently interpreting, Christian experience. In this sense, Schleiermacher is right to insist that Christian doctrines are individually accounts of

Christian religious feeling, set forth in speech.[102]

Schleiermacher's emphasis upon the communicability of the self-consciousness of Jesus rests upon a cluster of significant premises: that the self-consciousness of Jesus may be distinguished from natural (or, we might say, unredeemed) self-consciousness; that, although ultimately indefinable, it may be described in such a manner as to permit its communication to others at different points in history, in such a way that it may be recognized on its development; that an account may be given of the conditions under which this self-consciousness may arise in an individual; that in the specific historic existence of Jesus of Nazareth may be seen the definitive instantiation of this self-consciousness, so that Jesus may be treated as defining the shape of the redeemed life.[103]

The concept of 'the self-consciousness of Jesus' appears outmoded today, possessing associations deriving from the 'life of Jesus' movement which modern historical research finds questionable; the category of 'religious experience' is undoubtedly more appropriate as a means of articulating Schleiermacher's insights concerning the nature of doctrine in the modern period. Nevertheless, the relevance of Schleiermacher's experiential account of doctrine to the contemporary debate will be evident. The continuity of Christianity is to be established at the experiential level of the Christian community (not that of the pious sentient individual),[104] and articulated in a purely descriptive manner at the level of doctrine.

Underlying the profundity of human experience and encounter lies an unresolved tension – the tension between the wish to express an experience in words, and the inability of words to capture that experience in its fullness. Everything in human experience which is precious and significant is threatened with extinction, in that it is in some sense beyond words, and yet requires to be stated in words for it to become human knowledge.[105] It is threatened with the spectre of solipsism, in that unless an experience can be communicated to another, it remains trapped within the private experiential world of an individual. Words can point to an experience, they can begin to sketch its outlines – but the total description of that experience remains beyond words. The words of John Woolman's associate express this point: 'I may tell you of it, but you cannot feel it as I do.'[106] Words point beyond themselves, to something greater which eludes their grasp. Human words, and the categories which they express, are stretched to their limits as they attempt to encapsulate, to communicate, something which tantalizingly refuses to be reduced to words. It is the sheer elusiveness of human experience, its obstinate refusal to be imprisoned within a verbal matrix, which underlies the need for poetry, symbolism and doctrine alike. An impatience with precisely this elusiveness appears to underlie the rejection of any cognitive component to doctrinal statements.

The intimation of something further, lying beyond and signposted by experience, is characteristic of human experience. We live on the borderlands of something more – something intimated, something ultimately lying beyond the horizons of our comprehension, yet on occasion intruding into our consciousness. Experience and language point beyond themselves, testifying that something lies beyond their borderlands, yet into which we tantalizingly cannot enter. Everyday language founders as it attempts to grasp beyond the threshold of the empirical and observable, to capture what it knows lies beyond. As Wordsworth suggests, human beings are 'borderers', firmly based in the real world of human experience, yet reaching out in aspiration beyond its limits.[107]

This sense of reaching after something unattainable, intimated yet not delivered by experience, has strongly religious overtones and important religious consequences. It is, however, not in any way confined to what we might reasonably designate 'religious' experience or 'religious' situations. The observation is often made that humans entertain lofty ideals, which they repeatedly – and often tragically – fail to meet. There is a tension at the moral level between the faulty and finite creatures which we are, and the high destiny to which we feel ourselves called. A similar tension, captured by C. S. Lewis, exists at the aesthetic level, in the quest for beauty.

> The books or the music in which we thought the beauty was located will betray us if we trust to them; it was not *in* them, it only came *through* them, and what came through them was longing. These things – the beauty, the memory of our own past – are good images of what we really desire; but if they are mistaken for the thing itself they turn into dumb idols, breaking the hearts of their worshippers. For they are not the thing itself; they are only the scent of a flower we have not found, the echo of a tune we have not heard, news from a country we have never yet visited.[108]

The same sense of bittersweet longing, of *Sehnsucht*, of the inability both of experience to deliver what it promises, and of human words to capture that experience and the aspirations it engenders, permeates the writings of Evelyn Waugh, perhaps most powerfully in the exquisite poignancy of *Brideshead Revisited*, as memories of the past invade, illuminate and transform the present.

> Perhaps all our loves are merely hints and symbols; vagabond-language scrawled on gate-posts and paving stones along the weary road that others have tramped before us; perhaps you and I are types and this sadness which sometimes falls between us springs from disappointment in our search, each straining through and beyond the other, snatching a glimpse now and then of the shadow which turns the corner always a pace or two ahead of us.[109]

Christian doctrine exists under constraints similar to those affecting poetry: it is obliged to express in historical forms, in words, those things which by their very nature defy reduction to these forms; nevertheless, there is a fundamental resonance between words and experience. Keats' experience on reading Chapman's Homer; Wordsworth's experience on seeing a vast expanse of Cumbrian daffodils; both demanded expression and communication through words, a medium perhaps fundamentally unsuited for their purpose, but which remained the only vehicle at their disposal. Schleiermacher suggests that the function of Christian doctrine is to effect a decisive transition within the language of the Christian community from the poetic and rhetorical to the 'descriptive-didactic':[110] poetic and doctrinal language are thus distinct, but related, levels of discourse available to the community of faith. Precisely because the primary language of the Christian community is poetic and rhetorical, doctrine is essential for the sake of responsible preaching to the community in its primary language.[111]

This insight can be developed, to take account of the apologetic and evangelistic aspects of doctrine. Preaching may be directed towards those outside the community of faith, not merely those within, with a view towards evoking understanding and a response on their part. This point is made in what is perhaps one of the most brilliant discussions of the relationship of poetic language to the language of religion, found in C. S. Lewis, who writes thus:

> This is the most remarkable of the powers of Poetic language: to convey to us the quality of experiences which we have not had, or perhaps can never have, to use factors within our experience so that they become pointers to something outside our experience – as two or more roads on a map show us where a town that is off the map

must lie. Many of us have never had an experience like that which Wordsworth records near the end of *Prelude* XIII; but when he speaks of 'the visionary dreariness', I think we get an inkling of it.[112]

In addition to noting the power of poetic language to communicate emotion, Lewis points to its ability to arouse that emotion in others. The reader of Wordsworth is not merely enabled to understand the poet's feelings – those feelings are evoked, aroused within him, as he reads.[113] Here we find the principle of the communicability of emotion and feelings *through* words, despite their innate irreducibility *to* words. The communal Christian experience may be communicated verbally to those who have yet to discover it, in such a manner that an individual may, in the first place, experience it, and in the second, subsequently recognize this experience for what it is.

To caricature Christian doctrine, then, as mere word-play or as an attempt to reduce the mystery of God to propositions is to fail to appreciate the manner in which words serve us. In order for my experience to be expressed, communicated to or aroused in another, it demands statement in cognitive forms. That these cognitive forms fail to capture such an experience in its totality is self-evident, and hardly a matter for rhetorical exaggeration: it is one of the inevitable consequences of living in history and being obliged to communicate in historical forms. Schleiermacher recognized that doctrine expressed an experience constituted by the language of the Christian community, thus pointing to the delicate interplay of cognitive and experiential elements in doctrinal formulations. T. S. Eliot's lines from *The Dry Salvages* express the situation with insight and economy:

> We had the experience but missed the meaning,
> And approach to the meaning restores the experience.

'Experience' and 'meaning' are two sides of the same coin, forbidding us to reduce Christianity to bare propositions on the one hand, or to inchoate experience on the other. Every experience includes, and is modified by, interpretative elements.[114] As modern theories of scientific observation stress, experience is not pre-theoretical data, but is actually theory-laden:[115] it is accompanied by interpretative elements. The 'brute empiricism[116] which treats experience purely as raw data which requires interpretation is inadequate: experience is actually 'given' within an interpretative framework, however provisional. Theory plays a much more constitutive role in our approach to experience than pure empiricism suggests: theory itself determines, at least to some extent, the experience which that theory is suuposed to explain or interpret. As Husserl's phenomenology stresses (see p. 182–3), prior knowledge and beliefs play a constitutive role in determining what we observe and experience. It is for this reason that Lindbeck's treatment of 'cognitive' and 'experiential' models of doctrine as antithetical is so profoundly unsatisfactory. The cognitive dimension of Christian doctrine is the framework upon which Christian experience is supported, the channel through which it is conveyed. It is a skeleton which gives strength and shape to the flesh of experience.

Doctrine also provides a conceptual apparatus by which the provisional intimations of reality provided by experience may be interpreted and criticized. The preliminary judgements (to use Gadamer's nuanced understanding of *Vorurteil*) of experience themselves are interpreted within a conceptual framework, ultimately based upon the scriptural narrative and its doctrinal intimations, expressed by doctrine, in order that it may be viewed in a new light. This point has been stressed by Ebeling, who notes the need to be able to approach experience itself in such a way that it may be experienced in a new manner.[117] By being viewed in a particular light, experience is correlated with the scriptural narrative and the conceptual framework it engenders, and allowed to assume a new significance. Doctrine thus opens the way to a new 'experience with experience' (Jüngel).[118]

The tragic human feeling of alienation from the grounds of our being is thus interpreted as alienation from God, carrying with it preliminary intimations of the possibility of redemption. The great medieval spiritual writers interpreted this sense of human alienation as a sense of a lost homeland, a desire to return to Eden, thus correlating experience with an interpretative framework (the doctrine of the Fall). The feeling of absolute dependence, to use Schleiermacher's characteristic starting point, is interpreted as an intimation of our dependence upon God. In such manners, doctrine is able to address, interpret and transform human experience, correlating it with the parameters of the Christian proclamation. The Christian proclamation is thus enabled to establish points of contact with human experience, in order to allow that experience to be take on new and hitherto unexpected depths of meaning. A fundamental resonance between Christian doctrine and the experience of the community of faith is thus presupposed.

The preliminary intimations of experience may, however, occasionally be contradicted by doctrine. Perhaps the most significant discussion of this point is provided by Martin Luther, especially in his 'theology of the cross'.[119] For Luther, the normative paradigm for Christian theology is provided by the scene of dereliction at the crucifixion. Luther modifies the traditional dictum *experientia docet* with an appeal to the narrative of the crucified Christ as a corrective to the raw data of experience. *Crux probat omnia!*[120] The preliminary judgement of experience on the scene of helplessness and hopelessness presented to it in the crucified Christ is that God is absent. This preliminary verdict of experience, however, is contradicted by doctrine, which affirms that God is present in a hidden manner.[121] Experience is exposed as an inadequate foundation for theological affirmation; nevertheless, on being interpreted, experience affords central insights into the existential dimension of the Christian faith. The new relevance of the 'theology of the cross', as expounded by Moltmann and Jüngel in the modern situation, points to the need for doctrine to interpret experience, without being reduced to its categories or bound by its preliminary intimations.

Doctrine as Truth Claim

For Plato, a philosopher is a lover of truth. Most would wish to regard themselves as philosophers, given this inoffensive definition. The concept of 'truth' itself, however, remains controverted, to the point at which many philosophers have abandoned as fundamentally misguided the quest for a single universal concept of truth. 'There is no single criterion of truth. Different disciplines have different criteria, often unspecified, sometimes, where specified, liable to conflict.'[122] Nevertheless, the concept of 'truth' has moral, perhaps even revelatory, overtones which render its quest or possession a significant human achievement. Thus both Marx and Engels understand 'truth' to mean 'correspondence with reality',[123] thereby lending moral, as well as intellectual, authority to their claims to present a true (i.e., corresponding to the way things actually are) account of social existence. The Marxian community of discourse would lay claim to the possession of certain significant insights concerning social, political and economic situation, which merit the epithet 'true'.[124] Christian doctrine similarly represents a communal claim to possession of significant true insights concerning God and humanity.[125] It is the intellectual self-expression of a living and thinking community. That there are difficulties associated with this claim is self-evident: that the claim *has* been made consistently and persistently throughout the entire period of Christian history is equally evident as a matter of historical fact, necessitating its inclusion in any phenomenological account of Christian doctrine.

A preliminary clarification of three classical concepts of truth[126] is appropriate in beginning to consider the Wittgensteinian 'family resemblances' which underlie the characteristic human instinct to regard truth as significant, and to view diverse disciplines as making *related*, if distinct, claims to the same 'truth'.

The Greek term *aletheia* was understood by the Greeks, and is traditionally interpreted, as a term derived from the verb *lanthanein*, with the prefix α-*privativum*. This lends itself to the interpretation of truth as 'the state of discoveredness or unhiddenness', 'that which is uncovered or unveiled'.[127] Its primary point of reference would naturally be taken to be the thing in itself, and only secondarily as a statement concerning that thing. This statement, however, in so far as it makes evident or declares how the thing is, could therefore be regarded as 'truth'. *Aletheia* thus concerns the way things *are* in the present, in the manner suggested by Parmenides' insistence that the first attribute of being is its character of 'being present' in both the sense of being contemporaneous and immediately present to the mind.

The Latin term *veritas*, however, has the sense of exactness or precision of utterance. What is *verum* is what is faithful and exact, complete and without significant omission. The primary reference is to the past – a past narrative, a recollection of past events. *Veritas* refers to the past, the mode of truth particularly associated with history as *vera narratio*,[128] or with the legal requirement that a witness shall give a truthful account of what was observed to happen. An account is true if it is veridical, 'speaking the truth'. History tells stories[129] – and the appropriate point at which it may be interrogated concerns the present accuracy of a narrative concerning the past, especially in a legal context. Does it correspond with what actually happened? Is this witness telling the truth, by accurately recounting events? Cicero is perhaps the most noted exponent of this historically orientated concept of truth. 'Who does not know the first law of history to be that an author must not dare to recount anything except the truth? And its second that he must endeavour to recount the whole truth?'[130]

The Hebrew term *emunah* contains a personal reference: truth in the sense of trust. The true God is not simply a God who exists, but a God who is trustworthy, who is faithful to his promises. Thus a false friend is not a non-existent person, but a person who cannot be trusted. As such, *emunah* has an implicit future reference, to trust in fulfilment, grounded in the present and pointing towards the future. There is an obvious semantic connection between 'truth (*emunah*)' and 'faithfulness (*emeth*)'.[131] It is, of course, important to note how *emunah* and *emeth* are related in biblical narrative: although the context is unquestionably the past (and here the parallel with *veritas* is clear), its objective is not primarily to recall the past but to shape the present through paradigms of predictive hope. In other words, past narrative shapes present hopes by providing a paradigm for understanding the way in which history is moving.[132]

These three approaches to the question of the nature of truth alert us to the various nuances the term has been understood to possess, and which have contributed to the shaping of the family resemblance underlying contemporary concepts of truth.[133] It is thus appropriate to indicate how the truth-claims of Christian doctrine relate to each of these understandings of truth.

In the first place, doctrine concerns an historical event. Perhaps the term 'Christ-event' is unhelpful in respects:[134] nevertheless, it serves to emphasize that the primary referent of Christian doctrine is an historical event, rather than any static or timeless concepts. To make use of Emil Brunner's characteristic emphasis,[135] truth is something which *happens*. It concerns something which is presented to and present to human inspection, to note a characteristic insight of the Johannine circle. Jesus *is* the truth (John 14.6).[136] God, to note another insight of the Johannine circle, is not defined with reference to static timeless realities, but with reference to Jesus of Nazareth: 'anyone who has seen me, has seen the Father' (John 14.9). Jesus is treated as a lens, a window, through which reality may be illuminated and viewed. Jesus of Nazareth is the primary *explicandum* of Christian theology. Truth is grounded in history, and subsequent reflection upon an historical event. The Enlightenment depreciation of history, evident, for example, in the writings of Spinoza and Lessing,[137] exists in tension with the biblical tendency to value history as the arena within which God acts, and through which he may be known. Christian doctrine is thus concerned with the unfolding and uncovering of the significance of the history of

Jesus of Nazareth, in the belief that this gives insights into the nature of reality.

In a perceptive and provocative study,[138] George Vass suggests that in any issue of interpretation (and Christian doctrine is unquestionably a case in point) it is of central importance to consider the question asked, as much as the answer given. In attempting to evaluate the 'truth' of Christian doctrine, it is not simply the cognitive content of those doctrines which demands examination; it is the question to which they are a response that must be identified. Does the Christ-event precipitate the questions to which doctrines are answers?[139] It is Jesus of Nazareth who precipitates the questions, the process of reflection and construction, which eventually leads to doctrinal formulations. We might perhaps take this argument further, and suggest that the essential continuity underlying Christian doctrinal affirmations throughout history is the fact that they are responses to the Christ-event. The question to which doctrines are an affirmative response is constant, whatever variations may be detected in the answers given.

I therefore feel it is proper to suggest that there is an ineradicable cognitive element to Christian doctrine,[140] considered as an historical phenomenon. It purports to be a representation, however inadequate or provisional, of the way things really are, in response to the questions arising from the history of Jesus of Nazareth. As Luther emphasized, of course, it is impossible to represent God exhaustively at the cognitive level, yet possible to represent him adequately for the purposes of Christian proclamation and existence. Christian doctrine claims to possess significant insights concerning, for example, the character of God and human nature and destiny. Implicit within these truth–claims, however, is a subordinate claim: that they are mediated through, perhaps even instantiated in, the person of Jesus Christ. There is, in other words, an implicit Christological reference within the truth-claims of Christian doctrine. In declaring that 'God is love', for example, I am not merely declaring my allegiance to a community that affirms that 'God is love', irrespective of what God may actually be like. Nor am I merely affirming a broad positive personal attitude to God, irrespective of what he may actually be like. I am affirming that I understand that 'God is love' to be an authentic and valid insight into the character of God, and that this belief is grounded, and the hitherto undefined concept of 'love' implicated therein is instantiated, in the history of Jesus of Nazareth.

This emphasis upon the event-character of 'truth' is of importance, in that it represents a strategic move away from any understanding of revelation as the disclosure of general principles. The concept of 'love', so central to the Christian self-understanding, is not left undefined and suspended in mid-air, as it were, but is fleshed out and given substance in the history of Jesus of Nazareth. It is exemplified. 'Examples are the final food of thought. Principles and laws may serve us well. They can help us bring to bear on what is now in question. They can help us to connect one thing with another and another. But at the bar of reason, always the final appeal is to cases.'[141] Christian theology could thus be said to be casuist, in the sense that it does not proceed from general timeless principles relating to God, but from a generative event which precipitates the hermeneutical spiral – the case of Jesus of Nazareth. The history of Jesus of Nazareth, as transmitted to us in the memory of the church, is the case-study which stimulates, controls and corrects our theological reflection.

In the second place, this history is transmitted in a narrative form, in a literary form which can structurally express time and history. Doctrine does not assume a narrative form, yet is based upon a narrative which it purports to interpret. In that direct access to Jesus of Nazareth is now denied to us on account of our historicity, we are obliged to approach him indirectly through the formative transmitted narratives of the Christian tradition. The question of the veridical character of these narratives is thus of central importance. It must, incidentally, be stressed that it is not necessarily a challenge to this veridical character – as some of the writers of *The Myth of God Incarnate* seem to think – to suggest that the narrative is partly 'mythical'. In that this narrative employs human language in its transmission, the use of mythology in some form – whether disarmed or not – is virtually inevitable. In Schelling's famous words, 'language itself is only faded mythology'.[142] Myth, like metaphor, is simply a non-literal level of representation, which the interpreter of the narrative learns to handle accordingly, refusing to prejudge the veridical character of a narrative on account of the literary and linguistic devices it may employ in the process of narrating. In suggesting that Christian doctrine makes truth-affirmations, we are therefore implicitly asserting that it is based upon narratives of past events which are of primary importance in shaping our understanding of reality, and the reliability of which thus demands consideration. I have considered the narrative-based character of doctrine in more detail above (pp. 52–66).

In the third place, doctrine is concerned with the internal consistency of Christian truth-affirmations. At this point, the insights articulated by George Lindbeck (pp. 26–32) are to be welcomed: doctrine is indeed concerned with the internal regulation of the language of the Christian faith, as one of its several functions. The importance of this point may perhaps be appreciated best by considering Schleiermacher's understanding of the nature of heresy, probably one of his most creative contributions to Christian theology.[143]

For Schleiermacher, the distinctive essence of Christianity consists in the redemption of humanity through Jesus of Nazareth.[144] The denial of this assertion involves a break with the Christian tradition, yielding a non-Christian or anti-Christian ideology. If the assertion of the redemption of humanity through Jesus of Nazareth is accepted, however, there is a danger that internal inconsistency will arise, on account of an inadequate understanding of the constituent elements presupposed by this assertion. '*Either* human nature will be so defined that a redemption in the strict sense cannot be accomplished, *or* the Redeemer will be defined in such a way that he cannot accomplish redemption.'[145] The principle of the redemption of humanity through Jesus of Nazareth is thus upheld, yet the constituent elements of this principle are understood in such a manner that internal inconsistency results: either human nature or the person of Jesus is understood in such a manner as to render redemption an impossibility. For example, if Jesus of Nazareth is simply a human being like the rest of us (Ebionitism, according to Schleiermacher), he shares our need for redemption, and hence cannot redeem us. He is perceived to be part of the problem, rather than a potential solution. Schleiermacher thus suggests that the Pelagian and Manicheaen heresies concern inadequate conceptions of human nature; that the Docetic and Ebionite heresies concern inadequate views of the identity of Jesus; and that these four heresies taken together are the 'natural heresies' of Christianity.[146]

The importance of Schleiermacher's contribution is clear. First, it allows us to draw a distinction between *unbelief* (refusal to accept the principle of the redemption of humanity through Jesus of Nazareth) and *heresy* (internal inconsistency within the principle, as its constituents are understood). While Schleiermacher makes clear that his account of the four natural heresies do not coincide with their precise historical forms (and, as I have already indicated, neglects the social dimension of heresy), his intention is to demonstrate that these historical forms embody and instantiate the threat posed to the proclamation of Jesus of Nazareth through internal inconsistency. Secondly, it clarifies the role of doctrinal formulations. Doctrine is concerned with the generation of a consistent framework of conceptualities, in which each constituent interacts with others and impinges upon them – rather than with individual isolated *doctrines*. Christology, soteriology and anthropology, for example, clearly interact with each other, and cannot be discussed in isolation.

Finally, doctrine is orientated towards faith, representing a demand for personal involvement, rather than passive assent. An emphasis upon the subjective or existential dimension of truth is, of course, particularly associated with Kierkegaard: nevertheless, it is important to observe that it is already implicit in the biblical material. 'Truth' is something which must be personally appropriated. Whatever social or communal function Christian doctrine may possess, it includes an appeal to the individual. It is an affirmation of trustworthiness, inviting a response of faith. To use Kierkegaard's famous phrase, truth demands 'an appropriation process of the most passionate inwardness'.[147] Doctrines define the object of faith – God – not in order that God may be comprehended but in order that the believer may relate to God in faith. There is an existential, as well as a cognitive, dimension or component to the truth-claims of Christian doctrine:[148] it claims to represent (adequately, but not exhaustively) the situation, and demands an inwardly- appropriated and assimilated response to it.[149] 'Christianity is not a doctrine, but an existential communication concerning an existential paradox . . . Christianity has to do with existence, with the act of existing.'[150] The proper context of doctrine – for example, the doctrine of the incarnation – is not a speculative philosophy of divine-human unity (as with Hegel), but the existential challenge to the unredeemed human situation. Truth is not simply something one knows about, but something which one possesses and is possessed by. Thus Kellenberger points out that religious insights are not arrived at in a detached manner (as in the natural sciences), and possess an emotional impact and life-changing power rarely, if ever, associated with scientific discovery.[151]

To speak of doctrine as 'truth' is rightly to draw attention to the fundamental Christian conviction that doctrine has to do with veridicality, rationality and comprehensive elucidation; nevertheless, it is also concerned with maintaining the possibility of *encountering* the truth, which the Christian tradition firmly locates in Jesus Christ as the source of her identity. At the outbreak of the Second World War, William Temple identified the tension between these concepts of truth in his remark, 'our task with this world is not to explain it, but to convert it.'[152] Although the phrase is clearly derivative (borrowing from Marx), the point scored by Temple is important. Doctrine does not merely describe reality, but articulates the manner by which it may be renewed and refashioned; by which the creation may be recreated. It is not a static representation, but an invitation to the dynamic transformation, of the human situation. It is this recognition of the power of doctrine to effect what it signifies – to convert *homo peccator* to *homo iustus* – that underlies its significance.

Kierkegaard readily concedes the descriptive importance of doctrine in defining Christianity: it is, he argues, important that the intellectual content of Christianity should be capable of being described publicly, however provisionally and partially. 'The possibility of knowing what Christianity is without being a Christian must therefore be affirmed.'[153] In other words, the need for a capacity to give a publicly accessible description of Christianity must not be permitted to obscure the fact that it is possible to *know about* Christianity without being a Christian. For Kierkegaard, doctrine is to be viewed, not merely as a description of Christianity, but as an existential imperative, a challenge to *become* a Christian. Doctrines are descriptions which propose to be actualized in human existence; there is a demand for the interiorization of doctrine. Doctrines do not contain the meaning of the truth as such, but define how an individual is – or comes to be – 'in the truth', by orientating his or her existence towards God and Jesus Christ. Implicit within doctrinal formulations is an invitation to adopt a 'discovery perspective' on God.[154]

To speak of doctrine as making truth-claims is thus to note the significant affinities, points of contact and parallels between 'doctrine' and 'truth', as the latter term is employed in human discourse and reflection. It is most emphatically not to commit oneself exclusively to a 'correspondence theory of truth', or any other theory of truth; rather, it is to observe the significant degree of isomorphism that exists between the inherently polyvalent concepts of doctrine and truth, and to register an historically-informed unwillingness to reduce either concept to univocity. The concepts of doctrine and truth each cover a broad spectrum of meaning; our concern is to suggest that there exists such a degree of overlap between those spectra that it is meaningful and legitimate to continue to speak of doctrine making 'truth-claims'.

Finally, to recognize that doctrine makes truth-claims allows a further important insight into the social function of doctrine (pp. 37–52). Doctrines are not invented to serve social functions, as we shall indicate in the following chapter; rather, their claims to truth are foundational for their social function. Doctrine generates a community of faith – and having brought such a community into existence, it safeguards the identity of that community, and differentiates it from its social and intellectual alternatives. Doctrine may thus be said to generate, sustain and demarcate the community of faith.

These preliminary clarifications of the nature of doctrine completed, we may begin to engage with some of the more important questions underlying the discipline of doctrinal criticism. In what way may doctrines formulated at one moment in history be transferred to a different period? How can the ideas of the past be appropriated by the present? To what extent are doctrinal formulations conditioned by the historical conditions under which they were generated? The first matter to be considered concerns the consequences for this discipline of being located within the flux of history. Doctrinal critics stand within history, not above it. What are the implications of this historical locatedness on the part of both doctrine and doctrinal critic?

4

On Being Condemned to History

We are all condemned to live and speak in history and historical forms. Like an intellectual prison, our very historicity limits our intellectual options. The very fact of human language itself reminds us that our modes of discourse and imagination are limited by an inherited framework of communication.[1] Language, like tradition, affirms the afterlife of the past. The theologian, in common with every other inhabitant of the flux of history, finds himself or herself within a tradition – an inherited complex of symbols, values and pre-understandings which fixes a world-view and functions as a framework for communication, in which the past obstinately impresses itself upon the present. In this present chapter, I propose to begin exploring the consequences of being condemned to history for Christian theology.

The Strangeness of the Past

The confident and restless culture of the Enlightenment experienced the past as a burden, an intellectual manacle which inhibited freedom and stifled creativity. To ascribe authority to the past, or even to particular features of the past, was seen as becoming incarcerated – needlessly – in a prison of one's own making. It was viewed as a mark of intellectual servility and spiritual immaturity. Among the intellectual superstitions from which we are alleged by its proponents to have been liberated by the advent of the Enlightenment is the view that the past discussion of a question can in any manner possess binding significance. As Kant defined 'Enlightenment', it is 'man's emergence from self-incurred immaturity. Immaturity is the inability to use one's own understanding without the guidance of another. This immaturity is self-incurred if its cause is not lack of understanding, but lack of resolution and courage to use it without the guidance of another. The motto of Enlightenment is therefore: *Sapere aude!* Have courage to use your own understanding!'[2] The past is dead and unusable,[3] threatening to haunt us in a manner which is as irrational as it is menacing. Just as the New World had thrown aside the political hegemony of the Old in the final quarter of the eighteenth century, so it also sought to destroy the last vestiges of intellectual colonialism. Ralph Waldo Emerson's Phi Beta Kappa address of 1837 was received as an intellectual declaration of independence – independence from the bondage of the past, and freedom to embrace the future.[4] At the heart of the Enlightenment's anti-traditionalist rhetoric lay a belief in radically autonomous human reason. The chords of this theme have resonated throughout modernity. Iris Murdoch writes thus of its heritage.

> How recognizable, how familiar to us, is the man so beautifully portrayed in the *Grundlegung*, who confronted even with Christ turns away to consider the judgement of his own conscience and to hear the voice of his own reason. Stripped of the exiguous metaphysical background which Kant was prepared to allow him, this man is still with us, free, independent, lonely, powerful, rational, responsible, brave, the hero of so many novels and books of moral philosophy.[5]

The past, however, remains an obstinate aspect of the present. We do not live within a vacuum, but within a context, the intellectual, cultural and social contours of which have been shaped by the past. The present has a history, whereby the past extends its influence into the present. The influence of the past, paradoxically, is at its greatest precisely when it is undetected or unacknowledged – when certain present-day axioms and presuppositions, allegedly self-evident, in fact turn out to represent the crystallized prejudices of an earlier generation. For example, Michel Foucault has unravelled the arbitrariness of what has come to be regarded as self-evident in the field of 'social management' – such as pervasive attitudes to the criminal, to the insane, and to codes of personal sexual morality.[6] Far from being (or reflecting) universal patterns of rationality, these have been exposed as social constructs, serving the needs and prejudices of the specific social situations which engendered them. To the social anthropologist, the very idea of 'common sense' appears as a socially constructed agglomerate, varying significantly from one contemporary culture to another;[7] to the historian of ideas it often appears as little more than an amalgam of past confusions and clarities, tending to do little more than preserve what past generations, through intuition as much as through critical insight, regarded as self-evident.[8] Much of what, for example, was self-evident to writers of the patristic or medieval periods would find little support in the modern period,[9] reminding us that 'self-evident truths' are often only 'self-evident' within a specific and restricted socio-historic situation. Whether approached at the synchronic or diachronic level, whether sociologically or historically, the assumption that there is some universal framework of rationality (which might be designated 'common sense') is quite untenable. Yet the assumption of English Deism (and, it may be added, much English theological speculation since then) is that 'reason' provides a *fundamentum inconcussum* for theological reflection, as if 'reason' was something timeless and global, independent of the historical location of the thinker. The demonstration of the social rootedness of 'rationality' is one of the most significant achievements of the sociology of knowledge, even if the full implications of this for 'rationalist' theology have yet to be recognized and explored.

The bold assertion that we can break free from the past – for example, by shutting ourselves in a stove, isolated from all resources of knowledge apart from our own thoughts or 'rationality' – may well, in fact, turn out to be sheer intellectual bravado, which, by asserting the illusory nature of the influence of the past, contributes to our deeper bondage to it. Thus Kant's 'knowing subject' gives every indication of being an ideal mental construction, rather than an empirical reality, in that his or her mind has acquired its shape through the process of social living,[10] shaped by a corporate tradition and socially transmitted patterns of rationality. The 'man . . . who confronted even with Christ turns away to consider the judgement of his own conscience and to hear the voice of his own reason' cannot be allowed to escape close interrogation concerning the social factors (ignored by Kant, who was historically located in an age largely innocent of any awareness of relativism) which have shaped his conscience and influenced the patterns of rationality which he presupposes. There is a significant ideologically conditioned component to patterns of rationality which cannot be overlooked. 'Reason' and 'conscience' are, if not necessarily totally socially constructed, at least significantly influenced by communal traditions which are in turn affected by its memory of the past. To understand the present and to shape the future, it is thus necessary to investigate the past.

In part, the investigation of the past serves to remind us of our own historical location. An encounter with the past calls into question the historically generated assumptions of our own situation, permitting a radical questioning which cannot take place within the confines of present experience. Precisely because it cannot and does not totally reflect our present experience and assumptions, the very *strangeness* of the past[11] relativizes that experience and assumption. The strangeness of the past discloses the historically located character of the present, which will one day itself seem strange to future observers. The fact that the past seems strange questions the beliefs of the present (which make it seem strange), as much as those of the past itself. The plausibility of the belief that the present possesses privileged observer status is diminished through an historical awareness that every period has entertained such beliefs, whether they are explicitly and consciously brought to expression. The study of the past allows a critical element to enter our evaluation of the present, subverting unconscious attitudes towards the essential 'rightness' of its precommitments, the 'self-evident' character of its assumptions, and the 'rationality' of its frameworks of thought. It invites us to see our own situation from the perspective of the future, and anticipate the relativizing verdict of 'strangeness' which future observers will pass upon our situation.

Underlying the total rejection of the past and the demand for radical innovation, at least in their more sophisticated forms, is the idea of total incommensurability between diachronic frameworks. In other words, certain frameworks may have such different notions of truth, method and rationality that they cannot communicate with each other.[12] Truth is thus perceived to be a relative matter: '*p* is true' may be valid in situation A but not in situation B.[13] Pascal's *bon mot* is worth recalling in this context: 'truth on this side of the Pyrenees is error on the other'.[14] Thus for Ernst Troeltsch, what is doctrinally true in one specific historical context is not so in another.[15] In that the past constitutes a different framework, the present is unable to understand, let alone make use of, its ideas and methods. To add more substance to this point, the ill-defined concept of 'cultural relativism' is often introduced: each doctrinal statement is specifically conditioned by its historical and cultural context, rendering its alleged truthfulness in another context questionable.[16] The radical historicization of reality, it is suggested, demands the recognition that what is 'true' for one generation may reflect a specific cultural framework, and be invalid outside that context.

In turning to evaluate this consideration, a preliminary difficulty must be noted. The concept of 'historicism'[17] and the sociologies of knowledge deriving from it both engender and shelter a variety of metaphysical claims, which must themselves be made explicit as a prelude to their critical evaluation. Consider the statement, 'all truth-claims are historically conditioned'. There is a perplexing intrinsic self-reference within this statement, similar to the paradoxes beloved of the philosophers: the Cretan who states that all Cretans are liars, or the blackboard with only one statement inscribed, to the effect that all statements on the blackboard are untrue. The fallacy in these paradoxes, as exposed by Bertrand Russell, is that the definer or definition of a class of statements or objects must stand outside that class. The definer cannot be included in the class of objects which it defines.[18] The above statement, however, clearly includes a self-reference: all truth-claims are historically conditioned – including this one.

The suggestion that all truth-claims are historically conditioned must itself be treated as a historically conditioned insight, reflecting a specific cultural framework, outside of which it may not be valid. Radical historicization, like the anti-historical philosophy of Diderot and Voltaire,[19] is itself a historical phenomenon. It is conscious of its own historical location, and lack of privileged status. This point was noted by Troeltsch. 'Historicism knows the ideas of all ages, and even its own ideas, as historically conditioned. For this reason it knows of no belief which could be normative for it.'[20] Cultural relativism – indeed, any form of relativism – is thus logically, if not epistemologically, self-destructing: if all truth is totally culture-specific, so is the truth of the cultural relative analysis – hence it cannot really be said to be 'true'.[21] It is certainly not to criticize or undervalue the insights of this approach to point out that this very attitude to history is, by its own criteria, itself a product of its times, thereby demonstrating the inescapability of its own historical relativity.[22] It is, however, to raise a significant hesitation concerning both the universality and the long-term relevance of the approach. The very preoccupation with history itself cannot necessarily be regarded as a permanent feature of the western intellectual landscape.[23] The significance of historicism may ultimately relate chiefly to the formulation of pivotal philosophical problems through a creative exploitation of the tension between structures of knowledge grounded in universal theories of human nature and those grounded on concrete historical experience.[24]

The Concept of Cultural Relativism

In more recent times, the theological implications of historicism
have been pursued in terms of 'cultural relativism'. The general
tenor of this approach may be illustrated from a recent work of
British radical theology, *The Myth of God Incarnate*.[25] Underlying
many of the contributions to this collection of essays is the proposal
that no Christian doctrines or documents may be regarded as of
permanent intelligibility or validity, or as possessing permanent
'truth' on account of 'the problem of cultural relativism'.[26]
Incarnational Christologies, it is argued, are 'culturally conditioned',
inextricably enmeshed in an obsolete patristic *Weltanschauung*. The
modern-day theologian is locked into a very different cultural milieu
– that of the Enlightenment – and cannot find any meaningful link
with the past. 'We must accept our lot, bequeathed to us by the
Enlightenment, and make the most of it' (Leslie Houlden.)[27]

At this point, a very obvious difficulty must be noted concerning
this ideological fatalism. The primacy of any given ideology is a
matter of historical and cultural contingency, and its dominance is
subject to a process of historical evolution and erosion. There is an
unresolved paradox in the suggestion that we are locked into our
cultural situation. If we cannot escape from our cultural milieu,
how does cultural change occur? Houlden's statement paradoxically
(given the intentions of its author) actually appears to suggest that,
since some unspecified point around the year 1750, cultural
development does *not* occur (so that we are trapped within the
Enlightenment mindset), or that it has not *yet* occured (so that
while the Enlightenment mindset will one day be outmoded, that
day has yet to arrive). Any understanding of cultural relativity
which is unable to account for cultural *development* may legitimately
be criticized for gross phenomenological inaccuracy. The fact that
such development *does* occur cannot be ignored – and its very
occurrence suggests that it is possible for individuals to escape, at
least in part, from their present cultural situation. A cumulation of
partial breaks eventually leads to a total break, and the dawn of a
new cultural situation.[28] There is a paradigm-shift, a revolution in
our way of thinking and dealing with questions (Kuhn). If, however,
our thinking at any one time is *totally* conditioned by the prevailing
historical and cultural situation, an epistemological scepticism would
appear to be implied, taking away all possibilities of rational

discrimination and of new departures of thought – yet the very recognition that there *is* an ideological component to our thinking provides a means by which the total dominance of hidden ideological factors to our ways of thinking may be reduced. It is precisely when the ideological component to frameworks of rationality is ignored or denied that its influence is at its greatest.

Furthermore, implicit in some writing on 'cultural relativism' is the notion of a 'cultural totality', implying an essential quantal approach to history.[29] History may, on this approach, be divided into discrete cultural totalities, each of which is incommensurate with its diachronic and synchronic neighbours. This assumption irritatingly ignores the fluidity of cultural development, an essential part of the intellectual equipment of any social historian. For example, to speak of 'Victorianism' or 'the Victorian world-view' may be helpful in differentiating some aspects of nineteenth-century thought-patterns from those of the eighteenth or twentieth centuries. It is also, however, to de-emphasize the wide diversities and conflicts within 'Victorian culture', and the extent to which there is continuity with both the preceding and succeeding cultural epochs. To speak of the 'Enlightenment world-view' is, if we may borrow a term from the field of quantum theory, to *quantize* (that is, to divide what was once thought to be continuous into discrete, distinct and non-interacting units) intellectual history in a crude and arbitrary manner, implying a geographical, cultural and historical uniformity which is obviously lacking in the modern period.

To assert the totality of difference between present and past cultures is dogmatic, rather than empirical. As I shall stress, many writers of the Renaissance, for example, felt perfectly at home in the long-dead classical world, adopting and shaping its ideas and methods, however selectively, in their vision of a new classical age (see pp. 104–17).[30] The 'strangeness' of the ancient world is significantly reduced through the fact that both Christianity itself and classical culture in general have influenced our modern culture to the point at which we do *not* feel totally alien in the world of ancient Rome or the New Testament. Aspects of one culture are carried over into, even deliberately appropriated by, another. The selective appropriation of the past decreases its strangeness, in that we feel familiar with at least some aspects of its outlook. It is for this reason that there is often more continuity between diachronic than synchronic cultures, in that two cultures, differing in time (shall we say, those of Ciceronian Rome and fifteenth-century

Florence) may share a substantial common ideological heritage denied to two synchronic cultures (for example, those of 'New Deal' America and the Azande tribe in the 1930s).[31] For all its chronological and cultural distance, the modern Christian church continues to find vital continuities with the world of the New Testament and early Christianity.

It is perfectly proper to suggest that there are certain genuine difficulties in understanding and interpreting a past text, event or idea. This point is familiar to historians, who do not feel unduly intimidated about studying the past, nor totally alienated from it, as a result.[32] It is only through confusion concerning what 'historicism' designates that the importance of historical research and the possibility of attaining of historical knowledge and understanding are minimized.[33] Through an effort of informed empathetic imagination, the historian attempts to understand past texts or ideas, whether he or she is able to agree with them or not. To suggest that there is no continuity between past and present is to rule out the possibility of an intelligent understanding of the past, denying us any insights into the intellectual worlds of Ancient Greece or the Middle Ages. This dismissive approach to the past effectively likens it to 'a cypher text of which it was laid down in advance that the solution must elude us.'[34] Furthermore, it is important to note that the historian who investigates other periods or cultures does so as an investigator, not a participant who merely exchanges one world (his or her own period and culture) for another, with no resultant gain in investigative understanding.[35] The critical appraisal of another period or another culture demands a certain degree of distance between the investigator and the situation.

Underlying the analysis to be found within *The Myth of God Incarnate*, however, is the more radical suggestion that modern thinkers cannot, on account of their different cultural frameworks, share the meaning attached to the person of Jesus Christ by patristic writers. There is no state of affairs that would count as being 'right' or 'true' in terms which are sufficiently absolute or culture-free to justify a comparison between the past and present. If the Christian proclamation could be expressed in terms of mathematical, logical or chemical equations, this difficulty would presumably be alleviated – but in that words and concepts are employed in its articulation, it is suggested that it is impossible to make use of the theological resources of the past in the present. The identification of the meaning of the past is thus overshadowed, and to a certain extent rendered pointless, or of purely academic interest, by the *a priori* unacceptability of that past meaning. The perceived meaning of Jesus Christ to the writers of the patristic period is determined by their cultural context; we, who inhabit a different culture, cannot share it. The past is a cypher, whose solution, if it can be uncovered at all, is of essentially antiquarian interest.

There are, of course, some modern writers who appear to suppose that they are somehow exempt from the flux of cultural relativism. The past may be conditioned or determined by cultural considerations; the present, however, is not. Thus some critics of the idea of incarnation appear to suggest, or allow it to be understood, that while the doctrine of the incarnation is 'culturally conditioned' and simply 'an interpretation of Jesus appropriate to the age in which it arose',[36] their modern criticisms of and alternatives to this doctrine are of permanent validity. This position, however, is indefensible,[37] and is not to be found within more responsible discussions of the subject.

Consistent cultural relativism involves the explicit recognition that *all* truth-claims, whether ancient or modern, whether metaphysical, moral or theological, are shaped by their total cultural context – in short, by an ideology. The term 'ideology' was introduced by Destutt de Tracy in eighteenth-century France to designate a secular (as opposed to religious) approach to society,[38] and was initially devoid of the Marxian overtones of 'false consciousness'[39] – overtones which, for the purposes of the present study (and, it may be added, for virtually all other purposes as well) have strictly limited interpretative potential. Thus Ernst Topitsch suggested that various philosophical positions rested upon and reflected certain ideologies,[40] despite the truth-claims naively being advocated on their behalf by their proponents. Similarly, the idea that biblical exegesis is a neutral or value- free enterprise is to be rejected: its methods and presuppositions are *seins-* and *ortsgebunden*. The exegete brings to the text questions which he or she has been conditioned to ask through his or her experience, social position, political conviction, gender and so forth. The recognition that human thought – whether sociology, theology, ethics or metaphysics – arises in a specific social context is of fundamental importance to the sociology of knowledge. All social movements, whether religious or secular, including the literature which they produce, involve implicit or explicit ideological perspectives and strategies by which personal experience and social reality may be interpreted and collective needs and interests may be defined and legitimated.[41] This suggestion clearly demands that we consider the religious implications of the sociology of knowledge, to which we may now turn.

Theology and the Sociology of Knowledge

The recognition that frameworks of rationality are not universal, but are socially and historically located, is of considerable importance to Christian theology, particularly in assessing the significance of Enlightenment rationalism. For example, consider the Enlightenment criticism of the traditional Christian notion of the revelation of God in Jesus Christ. For Reimarus and Lessing, this notion was unacceptable, in that it denied access to such 'revelation' to those whose historical location was, for example, chronologically prior to the birth of Jesus of Nazareth.[42] The force of this objection, one assumes, is primarily moral, in that the *accessibility* of historical or empirical truth has no direct bearing upon its veridicality. For Lessing, this point served to highlight the moral superiority of rational religion, which was able to make an appeal to the universal truths of reason.

With the advent of the insights of the sociology of knowledge, the advantages of Lessing's position are seriously eroded, probably to the point of rendering them specious. 'Universal truths of reason' may indeed be found within the somewhat restricted confines of logic and mathematics; patterns of rationality in general, however, are socially and historically located and conditioned.[43] 'Reason' must be taken to refer to those frameworks of rationality and preconceived notions of self-evident truths appropriate to specific social groupings at specific moments in history, rather than some universal and perennial feature of human ratiocination. Precisely the same criticism directed by Reimarus against Christianity may be laid against Lessing's appeal to the fictitious notion of universal reason: the social location of an individual determines the intellectual options open to him or her. 'Reason' and 'revelation' are both subject to the limitations of historicity.

This insight is of considerable importance, and naturally leads to further consideration of the relation of patterns of rationality and their social context. Certain older sociologies of knowledge have laid particular interpretative weight upon the concepts of 'superstructure (*Überbau*)' and 'substructure (*Unterbau*)', reflecting the origins of many sociological concerns in the writings of Karl Marx.[44] According to Marx, thought and knowledge are essentially a superstructure erected upon, or thrown up by, an underlying social reality. They are protective ideational cocoons spun around themselves by vulnerable social groupings. When ideas are shorn of their ideological trimmings, no solid independent core necessarily remains.[45] For many Marxist writers, ideas are essentially an intellectual superstructure erected upon an economic substructure.[46] Thus the religious ideas of the Reformation may be interpreted as arising through socio-economic changes in the late Middle Ages, culminating in the early bourgeois revolution.[47] For the Durkheim-ian, religious ideas are erroneous cognitive responses to social structures.[48] The historicist emphasis upon the *Standortsgebundenheit* and *Sitz im Leben* of knowledge – leading to a stress upon the relativity of all perspectives upon human life, and the recognition that no historical situation could be understood except in its own specific terms – laid the foundations of the sociological insistence that no human thought is exempt from the pervasive influence of ideology.[49] It is thus important to note, for example, that – as a matter of historical fact – philosophy is not some perennial feature or universal mode of expression of human rationality, but a 'style of thinking' which arose in a specific social stratum in a definite historical situation.[50] It is, of course, equally important to observe that sociology itself developed historically from the philosophical, moral and political concerns, presuppositions and methods of early nineteenth-century western Europe.[51] Like every other area of human knowledge, it is characterized by *Standortsgebundenheit*, and the suspicion that it may represent nothing more than a conceptual epiphenomenon of underlying economic, political and social realities. The tensions which this may occasion even within philosophies orientated towards social theory will be evident: it is thus particularly interesting to note the endemic dualism within much recent Marxist epistemology (for example, in the writings of Louis Althusser, Lucio Colletti and Jürgen Habermas) between thought as 'truth' on the one hand, and as historically situated on the other, apparently reflecting a reluctance to allow that frameworks of rationality – such as those drawn upon by Marxist theorists – are simply the consequence of a given historical situation, and a stubborn belief that they possess wider validity, despite the theoretical contradictions this might seem to imply.[52]

This radical historicization of human knowledge has, however, been subjected to considerable modification, in the light of certain significant internal contradictions and failures to interlock adequately with the history of ideas.[53] In its defensible forms, historicism does not reduce all ideational structures to epiphenomena erected upon social, economic or cultural foundations; nor does it imply nor presuppose conceptual relativism. Rather, it lays stress upon three essentially modest considerations which it suggests are essential to human understanding.

1   All thought is historically located.
2   Historical insight is essential to self-understanding.
3   A flight from history is improper and impossible.

It will therefore be evident that one primary target of historicism is the grand retreat from history characteristic of the tradition of Descartes and Kant, in which an attempt is made to transcend the limitations of historical location by purifying thought of its historical contingencies. Ideas and theories – including Christian doctrines – must be situated historically, prior to their analysis and evaluation. The historical context of the ideas of an individual or community is not merely dispensable background material to understanding those ideas: the evaluation of those ideas cannot proceed on the basis of the questionable assumption that thought is a socially disembodied process dealing with essentially timeless issues. In that human thought is both tradition-constituted and tradition-constitutive, such thought cannot be divorced from types of community and forms of practice in which they are, to whatever extent, embodied.[54]

The insights of historicism thus render questionable the notion of a doctrine which lays claim to be 'eternally true'.[55] This position, maintained by linguistic absolutists designated as 'cognitivists' by George Lindbeck (see pp. 15–20), fails to engage with the historical phenomenon of the genesis of doctrine – that is to say, the observation that doctrines come into being under certain historical circumstances, in response to a historic event (the history of Jesus of Nazareth, as transmitted within the Christian tradition). The Cartesian-inspired enterprise of eliminating historical contingencies from Christian doctrine founders on account of its historically contingent (if, it might be argued, theologically necessary)[56] primary referent. The very fact that Christian doctrine comes into being in history renders it susceptible to historical investigation. An account may be given of the factors and pressures underlying the genesis of doctrine. Nevertheless, in its defensible forms, historicism neither presupposes nor implies that recognition of the historical location of a specific Christian doctrine, nor the phenomenon of doctrine in general, constitutes adequate grounds to relativize its ideational content, or to cease deploying the adjective 'true' when describing that content.

What, then, is the importance of the sociology of knowledge, including the central thesis of relativism, to questions such as the genesis of doctrine and the authority of the past in Christian theology? In its early period, sociology tended to treat Christian doctrine, where it chose to address it at all, as nothing more than an epiphenomenal superstructure, which obscures the underlying economic, political and cultural realities of religious behaviour. A more mature approach to such questions, fortunately, has now developed within the discipline. In turning to discuss this development, an initial difficulty should be noted: generalizations concerning contemporary sociology of knowledge are problematic, on account of the remarkable pluralism evident within the discipline.[57] There are fundamental differences evident, for example, between Marxist and non-Marxist, between phenomenologists and empiricists, and between French, German and American approaches to the discipline.[58] Even to speak of 'the sociology of knowledge' is to invite the pivotal, and properly inevitable, question: 'which one?'? Contemporary sociology of knowledge exhibits a degree of diversity and pluriformity which renders generalizations concerning the subject hazardous, inviting comparison with modern theological pluralism. It is somewhat pointless to speak of 'the insights of the sociology of knowledge', as if the discipline possessed anything even approaching the uniformity this phrase implies. Nevertheless, it seems proper and important to draw attention to some recent developments within contemporary sociology of knowledge which have obvious theological significance, without necessarily suggesting that these developments command universal assent within the discipline.

Peter Berger identifies the central question with which the theologian is obliged to wrestle as follows: 'When everything has been subsumed under the relativising categories in question (those of history, of the sociology of knowledge, or what- have-you), the question of truth reasserts itself in almost pristine simplicity. Once we know that all human affirmations are subject to scientifically graspable socio-historical processes, *which affirmations are true and which are false?*'[59] This point is of crucial importance in relation to the advocation of truth claims, and it is an unquestionable sign of the growing maturity of the sociology of knowledge as an intellectual discipline that its importance is now being recognized. To say that all beliefs are equally true faces an obvious, and virtually insuperable, difficulty: how can beliefs which contradict one another be handled? Can one really say that the views of Galileo and Bellarmine were equally justifiable?[60] How can one account for Herschel's changed views on the nature of radiant heat?[61] Is the scientific theory that the universe evolved on the basis of the laws of physics to be accorded the same status as the belief of a west African tribe, to the effect that the world was created from a pile of ant excrement?[62] If one belief denies what the other asserts, how can both be true?[63] This totally agnostic epistemology, usually taken as a corollary of relativism, appears to vitiate its potential function as a tool for the evaluation of truth claims. Equally, to suggest that all beliefs are equally false raises serious difficulties for the relativist, who is obliged to number his or her own relativist beliefs among those recognized to be erroneous. It is this agnosticism which has increasingly been viewed as unsatisfactory by more recent contributors to this debate; I shall review their solution to this impasse presently.

It is also appropriate at this point to highlight a point of genuine difficulty for contemporary sociology of knowledge: the assumption of privileged status on the part of the sociologist as an observer.[64] Marx's *Theses on Feuerbach* develop the now widely accepted insight that the standpoint and status of a thinker or observer are implicated in the processes of thought or observation, predisposing both thought and observation towards bias. This naturally raises the question of whether any particular standpoint may be regarded as normative or privileged. The assumption of privileged observer status is a significant aspect of the orthodox Marxian notion that the normative standpoint for a radical critique of capitalism is that of the proletariat; the decisive rejection of this notion by Jürgen Habermas and other members of the Frankfurt School of Critical Theory is of considerable significance, in that this rejection entails the quest for what Habermas terms 'adequate normative foundations for a critical social theory'.[65]

It is perhaps not unfair to suggest that sociology has, in the past, tended to arrogate to itself the virtual monopoly of a process of critical and analytical thinking, in much the same way as theology and philosophy once advocated similar claims to privileged status. Thus Fortes, in his study of the West African religion of the Tallensi, insists that it is only the outside observer who can perceive the *real* meaning of its symbolism – a meaning which is denied to the Tallensi, who do not have the necessary 'cultural resources' for its sociological analysis.[66] This assumption of privileged observer status was especially evident within the sociology of religion in the 1960s, which tended to treat religious beliefs as erroneous and irrational, perhaps reflecting the fact that the discipline as a whole was then effectively committed to a set of more or less anti-religious assumptions. The proliferation of sectarian studies may have reflected the desire to study something manageable and amenable to social explanation, as much as something distinctively eccentric (and hence obviously erroneous in its beliefs).[67] It is thus interesting to note that in his cult novel *The History Man*, Malcolm Bradbury has his sociological anti-hero Howard Kirk cut his historicist teeth on a study of Christadelphianism in Wakefield.[68] It is much easier to give an account of the origins of a sect in terms of purely social explanation than it is of the parent ecclesial body from which it derives; there is thus a certain irresistable temptation to extrapolate from a study of the origins of a sect such as Christadelphianism to the origins of Christianity, as if the two were totally analogous.[69]

There is, however, increasing recognition in recent sociological analyses that the difficulties raised by the existence of religious belief systems points to a more fundamental difficulty concerning *all* systems of belief, whether religious or purely secular. How does *any* system of belief arise? It is on the basis of the assumption that religious belief is non-obvious, even irrational,[70] at least to certain secular sociologists, that it is held to require sociological explanation. The early domination of the sociology of religion by secularism and anti-religious attitudes in general may go some considerable way towards explaining this observation. What is 'problematic' is what is often assumed to require sociological analysis: what is obvious, it is suggested, requires no such explanation.[71]

What is 'obvious', however, depends upon the presuppositions of the analyst: thus Freud feels obliged to give an explanation of forgetting, but not remembering, on the basis of his presupposition that remembering is obviously rational.[72] (We are not here concerned with noting the obvious difficulties faced by some sociologies of religion – for example, the relation between religion and society, as superstructure and substructure, is more generally asserted than demonstrated. Particularly in the Durkheimian tradition, we are left with the assertion that social structure and religion are related, basically as cause and effect – but with little illumination as to *how* this causal sequence is to be articulated and verified. The two ends of this causal chain are well defined; the links between them, and the manner in which these might be verified or falsified, remain elusive. What we are primarily concerned with is the question of why some beliefs should have been regarded as requiring sociological 'explanation', where others are self-evidently 'rational'.[73]) To the present writer (who makes no claims to privileged status), it seems as if sociology itself, or certain strands within contemporary sociology, had developed a notion of intradisciplinary 'common-sense', an inherited cluster of self-evident presuppositions, treated as axiomatic – whereas the social origins of these concepts of 'rationality' themselves required sociological explanation. The presuppositions of the observer effectively dictate what is regarded as 'rational' and what is 'irrational'. Commenting on the anti-religious attitudes of an earlier generation of religiously-alienated social anthropologists – such as Durkheim, Frazer, Malinowski and Taylor – Evans-Pritchard notes their obvious hostility towards the idea of a revealed religion.[74] 'Social anthropology has been the product of minds which, with very few exceptions, regarded all religions as outmoded superstition.'[75] Their religious presuppositions, he suggests, shaped both their anthropological questions, and the resulting answers. But how, it may be asked, are these presuppositions of the observer generated and maintained? The anti-religious attitude of what I shall term old-fashioned (and thus open myself to the charge of relativism) social anthropology actually requires to be explained as much as the religious attitude of the subjects of their studies.

The recognition of the importance of such questions is ample evidence of the development of a more mature perspective within sociology in general, and sociology of religion in particular: *all* belief or value systems – whether religious, secular or agnostic – are recognized as being equally open to sociological investigation. The disturbing questions which sociology addressed in the past primarily to religious belief systems are those which it now realizes it must address to all belief and value systems, its own included.

For John Henry Newman, religious faith was the paradigmatic instance of the whole problem of epistemology: the question of how we know *anything*.[76] It represents a particularly critical challenge to think through how we know anything about anything else. In many ways, religion is posing a similar challenge to sociology: the demand to consider how any belief system, religious or otherwise, arises, and how its truth- and value-claims may be investigated. Far from being an exception, religion is proving to be a particularly luminous rule for belief systems. The epistemological problems raised by sociology of religion are seen to pervade sociology in general, relativizing the privileged position the discipline once claimed for itself. There is a growing recognition that sociological theories of explanation are not themselves value-free. The explanations offered derive from and express some prior understanding (whether this is explicitly stated or not) of the nature of human existence and destiny.[77] Underlying a particular sociology of knowledge may be an unacknowledged ideology, seeking to undermine the plausibility of alternative ideologies by 'explaining' their origins.

This point has been stressed by such theorists as Peter Winch and Charles Taylor, who have drawn attention to the *Standsortgebundenheit* of social scientific understanding.[78] The direction of research within a given field, the standards by which hypotheses are generated and tested and the criteria for the relevance of data – all refer to a normative framework of assumptions, conventions and purposes. In that it is conditioned by this framework, such theorists argue, it cannot be considered to be value-free. There is a cluster of prior questions concerning the framework of rationality employed by the social sciences, which require to be addressed. Recognizing this point, Anthony Giddens argues persuasively that sociology has the structure of a 'double hermeneutic'.[79] Sociology, in addition to interpreting a given social phenomenon (let us say, religion) is obliged to recognize that its own criteria of interpretation have themselves been formulated in a definite social situation. Social theory cannot be detached from the hermeneutic situation in which it is formulated, to assume the status of a universal framework of rationality. In effect, the sociology of knowledge is to be regarded as one social grouping assessing the ideas of another social grouping on the basis of the former's frameworks of rationality. The essential point made by the 'double hermeneutic' is that the frameworks of rationality of both the observed and the observer are socially conditioned, requiring social explanation – yet there is no way in which a third observer, detached from the hermeneutical situation, may assess them. The third observer, like all others, would be trapped within the flux of history, and subject to the same limitations.

In many ways, there are instructive parallels between an earlier preoccupation of theologians with the question of verification through the rise of logical positivism in its various forms,[80] and the more recent concern for perceived difficulties arising through the problem of cultural relativism. By raising questions concerning their validity, both illuminate the manner in which language and concepts are shaped, and the manner in which they articulate reality. For logical positivism, 'a formula which can be checked neither by observation of the world, nor by deduction from our definitions, has no meaning.'[81] This naturally evacuated theology, philosophy, moral and political theory and aesthetics of any meaning. It also demonstrated the same tendency to self-reference noted earlier (p. 85) in the case of the principle of historicization: the verification principle, as stated above, would appear to be meaningless, by its own criteria, in that it does not derive from observation of the world, nor is it a logical or mathematical statement deduced from definitions.[82] Nevertheless, by forcing discussion of the manner in which non-empirical and non-intratheoretic statements could be considered meaningful, logical positivism eventually may be regarded as serving the function of a stimulus to clarification.[83]

The concept of cultural relativism similarly obliges us to clarify how cross-cultural communication may occur at all. It does not cause us to abandon an appeal to the past; rather, it forces us to reconsider the situation of the present, using the past as a model. The genuine difficulties that we experience in understanding the past serve as a paradigm for investigating how we understand *any* situation which does not correspond exactly to our own as observers, whether the differences relate to space, time or culture. For relativism is not simply diachronic, relating to differences between the past and the present; it is synchronic, relating to pervasive cultural differences which exist at this very moment. The very language which we inherit shapes our understanding of our world, placing limits upon the range of alternative world-views which we can seriously expect to entertain. We are creatures shaped by an inherited language, placing limits upon the range of imaginative and conceptual possibilities open to us. Language is more than the 'dress of thought' (Johnson), in that it shapes as well as expresses that thought.

George Steiner, for example, is able to score some very important points against Noam Chomsky in asserting that there exists a certain degree of indeterminacy between modern languages.[84] A straightforward translation between languages is impossible, in that it is impossible to convey the totality of meaning of a given passage in another language. 'Meaning' is so culture-specific, so nuanced, that total comprehension of a piece of writing is virtually impossible. It is not just that certain words, certain ideas, will not translate; it is that certain levels of meaning, verbal cues, nuances of equivocation and so forth may be overlooked or misunderstood in the process of translation. Surrounding the lexical core of a sentence is a penumbra of nuances, threatening to turn language into ideolect, whose coincidence with public meaning is partial and unpredictable.[85]

There thus exist a spectrum of possibilities between the total commensurability and total incommensurability of cultures, recognizing that the term 'culture' cannot be taken to imply a monolithic ideology. Between these poles resides a space occupied by understanding which is at best partial, rather than total,[86] in which meaning is imperfectly rather than perfectly expressed and communicated, in which 'truth' is at least partly culture specific. It is, however, a space in which we are all, relativists included, obliged to live, think and communicate. The very fact that I can communicate my ideas with *anyone*, bridging the gap between myself and anyone who does not share my precise (although changing) linguistic, cultural and historical niche, is in itself a minor miracle, which relativism merely threatens to convert to epic proportions. The relativity of the past is paralleled by the relativity of the present, reminding us that we are all condemned to speak and think in history and in historical forms, which threaten to distort as much as to convey our ideas.

To recognize that we are obliged to speak and think in history and in historical forms thus in no way entails total relativism. It obliges us to acknowledge the difficulties associated with communication between one culture and another – indeed, between one human being and another. It obliges us to bid farewell to such notions as universal frameworks of rationality and modes of thought and discourse which are independent of time and place.[87] Past frameworks of rationality and modes of discourse are not totally commensurate with those of the present, just as they are not totally incommensurate: a partial (in the sense of less than total) appropriation of the past remains a real option. The recognition that we are linked with a specific historical situation does not oblige us to dispense with past beliefs on account of the fact that they are past; rather, it demands that we interrogate them closely concerning their plausibility, just as past beliefs and the frameworks of rationality which they presuppose or express challenge us to reappraise our own beliefs and frameworks of rationality.

The central question posed by the sociology of knowledge may thus be rephrased: how may the thesis of relativism be upheld, without degenerating into a radical and total tendency towards cognitive agnosticism?[88] By making everything unbelievable, relativism has – in effect, rather than intention – made everything believable, failing to articulate criteria by which the truth of belief systems or value judgements may be evaluated, or declaring that such criteria are meaningless in the first place. There is no privileged Archimedean point from which reality may be observed; there is no rock of universal truth in the raging sea of relativism. All human observers are locked into their relativized worlds, from which there is no privileged escape route. So how, then, may anything of interest, relevance or importance concerning the world – whether religious, sociological or metaphysical – be said to be 'true'? Or are we all to be permanently condemned to silence, lest we overstate ourselves?

The key to this problem would appear to lie in the search for the grounds of the plausibility of beliefs. In other words, what factors led or lead to a belief becoming credible? Why did, why *do*, people believe *that*?[89] Why do people believe in God? Why do others believe that this belief is irrational, and requires sociological explanation? This point has been stated clearly and succinctly recently by Barry Barnes and David Bloor:

> All beliefs are on a par with one another with respect to the causes of their credibility. It is not that all beliefs are equally true or equally false, but that regardless of truth and falsity the fact of their credibility is to be seen as equally problematic. . . . This means that regardless of whether the sociologist evaluates a belief as true or rational, or as false and irrational, he must search for the causes of its credibility. In all cases he will ask, for instance, if a belief is part of the routine cognitive and technical competences handed down from generation to generation. Is it enjoined by the authorities of society? Is it

transmitted by established institutions of socialization or supported by accepted agencies of social control? Is it bound up with patterns of vested interest?[90]

This approach allows the sterility of much older sociological analysis to be avoided, in order to account for factors of potential influence in the origination of ideas. To account for the genesis of belief, as much for the genesis of doctrine, it is necessary to identify the constraints under which they were formulated as much as the factors which led to their plausibility in the first place. It is necessary to ask, not merely *why* anyone should believe *that*, but *how* that belief came to be expressed, articulated or conceptualized in the specific form which it assumes.

The question which the sociology of knowledge thus requires us to examine is why Christian doctrine was or is credible. How are we to account for its plausibility? for its various historical shapes and forms? How are we to explain the emergence of patterns of rationality which lent it credibility and coherence? In turning to deal with these questions, we are obliged to deal with the past, leaving present patterns of rationality and styles of thinking aside for the moment. Are vested interests involved in the generation of religious attitudes (for example, towards the authority of the past)? Are these attitudes transmitted through agencies of social control? Do they reflect patterns of vested interests? In short, are there any reasons for suspecting that they may have been invented, through a deliberate process of fabrication or some form of 'wish-fulfilment' – to serve the needs of a specific social grouping?

A theological example of this problem may be noted, in order to illustrate the importance of this sociological approach to the genesis of doctrine. It is possible to interpret Nicene orthodoxy as the consequence of an age which was obsessed with a hierarchical political structure, originally derived from paganism. This political structure shaped the social structures of the age, which led to the construction of the Nicene Christology as an epiphenomenon.[91] The Nicene confession of faith thus arises from, articulates and legitimates a monolithic totalitarian social structure. In short: Nicene Christology is conditioned by an ideology, reflecting the vested interests of a specific power-group. This is clearly a suggestion which demands historical and sociological, as much as theological, inquiry, indicating the potentially important and illuminating role which the sociology of knowledge may have to play in the history of doctrine.

Beliefs are unquestionably conditioned by the social conditions of their formulations and the vested interests of those who formulated them; to suggest that they are necessarily determined by those conditions, however, is to move from the realm of the empirical to that of the purely speculative, verging on the dogmatic. The Nicene Christology may indeed be conditioned or influenced by a prevailing social paradigm. It may indeed reflect the vested interests of power groups. Identification of these possibilities naturally raises doubts concerning the intellectual credentials of such a Christology. Nevertheless, as sociologist Jon Elster stresses, 'there is no reason to suppose that beliefs that serve certain interests are also to be explained by those interests.'[92] When all is said and done, the basic question remains: is the Nicene Christology justifiable? Is it an adequate and accurate reflection of the identity and significance of Jesus Christ? How may we account for the genesis of this Christology? How may we account for its plausibility? And to ask this sort of question is to move towards an examination of the history of Jesus of Nazareth, in so far as this is accessible to us. To fail to do this is to assert the authenticity or inauthenticity of a doctrine such as the Nicene Christology as a matter of principle, without regard to what it purports to interpret.

Nevertheless, the suggestion that certain theological attitudes, methods or doctrines may reflect the needs of specific social groups within the church or society remains intensely important. It creates a climate of suspicion, demanding that we interrogate such attitudes, methods and doctrines concerning their origins, in order to uncover possible ideological conditioning. Can it be shown that they serve the needs of some specific social grouping? We propose to examine this question in some detail in the chapter which follows, focusing on a major theme of this study – the authority of the past in relation to the criticism and appropriation of the doctrinal heritage of the past. As I shall suggest, it seems clear that modern theological attitudes to this crucial question are far from immune to influence, overt or covert, from ideological considerations. Modern Christian attitudes to the past appear to reflect certain quite definite patterns of vested interests, and serve specific social functions as a consequence of their social rootedness.

5

The Authority of the Past in Modern Christian Thought

It is impossible to engage with the question of the authority of the past without considering the broader question of ideology. The term 'ideology' is here defined purely phenomenologically, as 'an integrated system of beliefs, assumptions and values, not necessarily true or false, which reflects the needs and interests of a group or class at a particular time in history';[1] or as involving 'a distinctive and more or less coherent agglomerate of assumptions, attitudes, sentiments, values, ideals and goals accepted and perhaps acted upon by a more or less organized group of persons'.[2] The attitude of an individual or group to the *religious* authority of the past generally mirrors their stance towards the more general question of the *cultural* authority of the past. Any attempt to document modern attitudes to the theological authority of the past (and in particular the heritage of doctrinal formulations) must engage with the network of beliefs, assumptions and values of the society (or social grouping) to which that theologian belongs. This point is of particular importance in relation to the Enlightenment, when ideological considerations assume decisive importance.

The question of when the 'modern' period may be regarded as having begun remains intensely controverted, reflecting prior disagreement concerning the notion of 'modernity' itself. For the purposes of the present study, the modern period is assumed to open with the Italian Renaissance, which brought with it a new consciousness of the historically situated character of knowledge. In that the Reformation itself is now increasingly regarded as an integral part of the Renaissance, rather than a separate movement in its own right,[3] it is essential to discuss the general features of the Renaissance attitude to the past before considering their modification within the Reformation movement. The primary object of the present chapter is to ascertain what criteria were used in evaluating the theological legacy of the past, and identifying what factors led to the adoption of those criteria.

The Renaissance

The social context of the Italian Renaissance has been the subject of considerable attention in recent years, with a view to illuminating the relation of the cultural programme of the Renaissance to the changing political, social and material conditions of the period. Particular attention has been directed towards the cultural outcome and expression of the tension between the conservative feudal aristocracy on the one hand, and the more sobre and rational upper middle classes on the other.[4] On the economic front, it has been suggested that the economic prosperity of the Italian city states lay behind its cultural expansion, allowing capital to be channelled into the arts;[5] others, however, argued that the period of the Renaissance was characterized by economic recession, disrupting the view of the economic preconditions of the Renaissance found in Adam Smith's *Wealth of Nations*.[6] As indicated below, the political situation of the Florentine republic in the early fifteenth century may have conditioned an ideology favourably disposed towards classical Rome. As I shall stress throughout this work, ideas cannot be divorced from the social context in which they emerge. The Renaissance is no exception to this rule, in that we are required, not merely to document its attitude to the past, but to indicate what social factors may account for its appeal and plausibility.

According to Claude Lévi-Strauss, the absence of a sense of historical perspective is a characteristic feature of *la pensée sauvage*. By this criterion, the medieval period was thoroughly primitive, giving every indication of a total lack of awareness of any differences between its own period and the past.[7] The medievals saw the past in terms of a retrospective extension of the present, projecting themselves into and onto that past. Early medieval portrayals of the classic period, for example, frequently depict Roman citizens wearing costume of the Middle Ages – not on account of some sophisticated theory of historical empathy, but simply on account of a lack of awareness of any fundamental difference between the past and present in this respect.

Many reasons may be given for this near-total absence of any sense of historical perspective in the Middle Ages. In a society in which development occurred but slowly, there was no cumulative awareness of radical change within an individual's lifetime which might point to comparable change in the more extensive past.[8] The paradigm employed for envisaging the past was an individual's experience: in that relatively little change was experienced during this period, it was assumed that a similar pattern of constancy characterized the past. More significantly, the technology for measuring time had yet to be developed.[9] Mechanical clocks first appeared in the fourteenth century; prior to this, vague and task-orientated conceptions of time prevailed. Thus in sixteenth-century rural France, the habit of measuring time in 'Aves' (the amount of time it takes to recite one 'Hail Mary') was widespread. Societies that lacked the means to measure time as an absolute concept (as opposed to a task-orientated parameter) appear to have been unaware of the very idea of the passing of time. If there was one society in which mechanical clocks proliferated, however, it was Renaissance Italy[10]. Clocks appeared on the town hall at Bologna around 1450, on the Castello Sforzesco in Milan in 1478, and in the Piazza San Marco at Venice in 1499. The astrologer Giacomo da Piacenza had an alarm clock by his bedside in Milan in 1463.[11] As a study of the paintings of the period reveals, a new sense of both historical and pictorial perspective appear to have developed side by side in the Italian Renaissance: as Francastel has pointed out, a new sense of awareness of history, time and space becomes evident in the art of the fifteenth century.[12] While we are not suggesting that this new sense of historical perspective is necessarily the consequence of a technological innovation, it is clear that a new awareness of the notions of time and space developed alongside a new sense of historical location. The growth of historical consciousness during the Renaissance, along with the attending development of a new attitude towards historical evidence and documents, may be regarded as precipitating an historical crisis which inevitably entailed the end of the medieval understanding of history, and necessitated a sustained reconsideration of the manner in which the past relates to, and impinges upon, the present. The past, it seemed, could no longer be viewed as identical to the present. With the dawn of this insight, modernity may be said to have arrived.

With the development of a sense of historical perspective,[13] a new awareness of the distinction between past and present became the foundation of the Renaissance attitude to the past. The past, however, was not seen as defunct, as dead on account of its pastness, but as a paradigm, not merely for the comprehension of the present, but for its creative refashioning. The past disclosed present possibilities. Perhaps the most eloquent exponent of this widespread attitude is Coluccio Salutati, Chancellor of Florence (1331–1406). 'Believe me', he wrote, 'we create nothing new, but like tailors we refashion garments from the oldest and richest garments, which we then present as new.'[14] A certain irresistable parallel suggests itself in addition to this: Renaissance architects frequently used the ruins of ancient Rome as a quarry for raw material, especially marble, for their own designs: once more, ancient materials were being incorporated into modern constructions. (So widespread was this practice, incidentally, that the somewhat gullible fourteenth-century traveller Ludolf von Südheim actually believed Genoa to have been built from the ruins of Athens, and Venice from those of Troy.[15]) The same principle employed in the making of clothes and the construction of buildings may also be detected in the formation of world-views. The fundamental principle contained in Salutati's neat analogy is that of the critical reappropriation of the past: the 'oldest and richest' ideas are reappropriated and reworked, only to be presented as ideas of relevance to the present. The criterion of antiquity is implicit within the analogy, while the notion of 'richness' requires clarification. I shall return to these criteria presently.

We seriously misrepresent the thought of the Renaissance if we suggest that a new awareness of the 'pastness of the past' led to the past being discarded as unusable. There is no sense of the total impermeability of the past, or of the total incommensurability of cultures (despite the new sense of historical awareness). Rather, the past is viewed as displaying patterns of human (and, it must be added, divine) behaviour which, while not exactly corresponding to the present, nevertheless possessed an inherent capacity to illuminate it. A significant degree of isomorphism is perceived between past and present, allowing the discerning historian to appropriate elements of the past in the course of a search for understanding the present. Salutati states this principle as follows: 'If one were to search diligently throughout history, one would plainly see the same cyclical pattern in human affairs, where although nothing recurs which is exactly the same, nevertheless every day we see a sort of image of past events renewed (*videmus tamen quotidie quandam preteritorum imaginem renovari*).'[16] Hints and traces of events of antiquity are discernible in present events.[17]

Perception of parallels and a significant degree of phenomenological isomorphism between the historical situations of Florence and republican Rome fostered the genesis of an ideology, which provided a symbolic universe which gave both political and social legitimacy on the one hand, and historical dignity on the other, to Florence's internal and external struggles in the late Renaissance. Like a classical Greek city-state, Renaissance Florence developed a culture which has been the subject of intense scrutiny by historians.[18] The Florentine city-state was primarily characterized by gross political instability, which Dante compared to the situation of a bedridden invalid who twists and turns, only to find herself uncomfortable in every position.[19] Around 1400 Giangaleazzo Visconti, duke of Milan, had successfully seized a group of cities ringing Florence: Bologna, Padua, Perugia, Pisa, Siena, Verona and Vicenza.[20] The Florentines felt themselves to be faced with extinction as an independent city- state; however, where the other city-states chose to capitulate, Florence opted for resistance. Baron has argued that the serious threat posed to republican liberty by Visconti made the Florentines aware of their collective identity, and of the distinguishing characteristics of their society. The perceived need to defend their ideals led to an enhancement of a communal awareness of these ideals. While it is controversial to suggest, with Baron, that the year 1402 is of decisive importance in the shaping of the Florentine self-consciousness,[21] there is ample evidence to suggest that the general events of the period 1390–1420 shaped the attitudes of a generation of thinkers, and made certain age-groups aware of their common location in the social and historical process.

The later calamity of 1494, as Charles VII invaded Italy and threatened to destroy much of what humanism had achieved, did more than merely inspire the political theories of Machiavelli (one of Florence's embassies to France); it brought home to many the essential fragility of the cultural values of the Florentine republic, and reinforced the perception of parallels between ancient and modern times. The Renaissance appeal to the past was perceived to possess 'objectivity', precisely on account of its constant reinforcement by historical events on the one hand, and the internal structures and external relations of the Italian city-states on the other. The sack of Rome in 1527 was thus widely perceived to bear an ominous resemblance to a similar event more than a millenium earlier, with a renewed threat of the extinction of culture and the establishment of a new Dark Ages.[22]

The awareness of this communal self-identity in the face of various threats led the Florentines to perceive a certain similarity between their situation and that of the great republics of the ancient world – Athens and Rome. Although the historical links between Renaissance Florence and republican Rome were somewhat tenuous (and those with Athens virtually non-existent), a distinct and well-documented tendency to identify with these ancient cultures developed. It was an invention, governed by the social and historical needs of the period – but, as inventions go, it was highly plausible. In his funeral oration for the patrician Nanni Strozzi, Leonardo Bruni explicitly identified Florence with classical Athens. Even Bruni's funeral oration appears to be modelled on that of Pericles. Throughout this oration, there is constant appeal to classical Athenian culture as a model and inspiration for Florence. Through the editorial and educational endeavours of humanist scholars, Bruni asserted, it is now possible to encounter the writers of ancient Greece directly in their original language, instead of indirectly through mediocre translations. Using a Pauline turn of phrase, Bruni asserts that no longer is anyone obliged to see them darkly, through a distorting glass of inept translation, when they may be encountered face to face through the original text.[23] For Bruni, the end of the Roman republic spelled the end of Roman culture; it was only through defending the liberty of republican Florence that its cultural heritage could be safeguarded. The Florentine perception of continuity between the situations and ideals of their own city-state and the great classical republics led to a growing tendency to shape the culture and political and social institutions of fifteenth-century Florence after its classical forebears.[24]

Thus, although increasingly aware of the historical differences between past and present, writers of the Italian Renaissance felt at home in the classical period, as they had reconstructed it. During his first visit to Rome in the spring of 1337, Petrarch took the opportunity to wander among the ruins of the ancient city with his travelling companion Giovanni Colonna, apparently armed with the best guide-book available (the *Mirabilia Romae Urbis*). In a letter written to Colonna a few weeks later,[25] Petrarch re-lived the wonder and awe that he felt in the presence of ancient Rome, his imagination stirred by memories of Virgil and Livy. Petrarch's sense of historical and cultural empathy with ancient Rome captured the imagination of many in the fourteenth century, as may be seen from the paintings of the Paduan school of the period.[26]

The importance of ancient remains in Italy in evoking a sense of respect for antiquity should not be allowed to pass overlooked. The writers of the Middle Ages treated ancient remains chiefly as convenient landmarks to guide travellers on their search for famous churches or collections of relics, or as a cheap source of high-quality building materials. In the fourteenth, and supremely in the fifteenth century, a new sense of historical empathy can be seen developing:[27] ancient remains provided a point of contact with classical civilization and culture, a concrete stimulus to reflection on the continuity of the historical process and the possible present value of the past. The spirit of Rome could be recaptured, by walking through its ruins, by reading its literature and by mastering its language. The growing interest in historical investigation of both artefacts and documents and awareness of the importance of evidence in historical reconstruction led to a growing interest in the exploration of the past, and contains the germs of modern archaeology. The fifteenth- and sixteenth-centuries' debates over which modern Italian river corresponded to the Rubicon crossed by Caesar – the Fiumicino, the Pisciatello and the Uso being the most frequently mentioned possibilities[28] – illustrates this development. The past was physically present, whether in the ever-present ruins of classical Rome, or in the ancient artefacts unearthed by builders, treasure-hunters and amateur archaeologists (such as the practically intact body of a Roman girl found in a sarcophagus on 19 April 1485).[29]

It may be emphasized that the Italian humanists were not disposed to treat the present and past as identical. It was the spirit, rather than the letter, of classical Rome, that was pursued. 'Antiquity' was understood primarily as a spiritual or cultural entity.[30] The past was believed to have a moral and aesthetic presence. The influence of the 'Hellenic ideal' in early eighteenth-century German neoclassicism is another illustration of this phenom-enon,[31] as is the partial reappropriation of the cultural idiom of the Renaissance in the Risorgimento.[32] Although a perception of historical distance existed, there was none the less a belief that the standards and values of an earlier period could be echoed within the culture of a later period, without the necessity of reproducing the precise socio-historical location of those earlier values. While there might be significant parallels between, for example, the Florentine and Roman republics, the thinkers of the fifteenth century were aware of significant differences which precluded their direct identification. A critical partial reappropriation of the past was thus indicated by an awareness of the different historical location of past and present.

Alongside the historical insight that the past *could* not be totally reproduced, however, was an additional consideration of taste, which laid down that the past *should* not be reproduced. The debate between Pietro Bembo and Angelo Poliziano illustrates this point perfectly: while Bembo argued that contemporary literature should imitate Cicero (at least in the sense of taking his style as a model for emulation), Poliziano dismissed this as uncreative, turning artists into parrots and magpies.[33] Yet throughout this debate, the primary question was the extent to which the past should serve as a model for the present; the fact that it had assumed such a paradigmatic function could not be denied. But on the basis of what criteria was the heritage of the classical period to be reclaimed?

The predominant answer may be stated in a word: eloquence. The underlying principle which gives unity to the remarkable diversity evident within the humanist movement is its common agreement concerning ends (the pursuit of written and spoken eloquence) and means (the study of the classics, both Greek and Latin).[34] Renaissance humanism was not a philosophical system, nor even a system characterized by certain philosophical tendencies (and it was certainly not an anti-religious movement, as might be supposed if the word 'humanist' is understood in its twentieth-century sense, rather than allowed to bear its proper Renaissance sense): it was essentially a cultural programme which gave the received tradition of *studia humanitatis* a new sense of direction by pointing to classical standards as the end to be achieved, and classical studies as the means by which this end should be pursued. We do a serious injustice to Renaissance humanism if we treat it simply as a movement devoted to classical scholarship and philology, failing to understand why humanists should have wished to study that period in the first place. The Renaissance humanists understood themselves as the literary heirs of the classical period, men who were charged with the historic responsibility of restoring to the modern period the eloquence denied to it by the cultural barbarism of the Middle Ages. The slogan *ad fontes!* summarized both their programme, and the means by which it might be achieved: a return to the written and spoken eloquence of the classical period, through the study of the classics in their original languages. This programme necessitated the production of new editions of the classics, and a wider familiarity with both Latin and Greek – needs which were rapidly met by a newly confident publishing industry, and given added impetus through the development of printing in the late fifteenth century.

In adopting this programme, the Renaissance consciously marginalized the culture and presuppositions of the Middle Ages. Both the term and the concept of the 'Middle Ages' are the product of the ideology of the Italian Renaissance. Using a technique later commended by Hegel, the Italian humanists wished to don 'seven league boots' in order to allow them to step directly from the glories of antiquity to the rebirth of its culture in the fifteenth century. The 'Middle Ages' was thus invented chiefly on the basis, not of historical analysis, but of ideological conditioning. The very criterion of 'eloquence' is profoundly ideological, in that it encapsulates the notion of social and cultural acceptability. It is certainly true that even as early as the 1430s, Flavio Biondo had developed a general theory of the historical development of Italy which involved the interposition of a *media aetas* between antiquity and his own times;[35] nevertheless, the general Renaissance tendency was both to define and devalue the medieval period primarily with reference to a *cultural* criterion (its *ineloquentia*, according to the somewhat vague criteria employed by Renaissance writers). Writing in the early sixteenth century, Vadian and Beatus Rhenanus used terms such as *media aetas* or *media antiquitatis* to designate the cultural and literary dark ages interposed between antiquity and modernity.[36] The medieval period was effectively stigmatized as pre-modern, in that it did not share the presuppositions and methods of the new age.

The slogan *ad fontes* demands more careful attention that it usually receives, particularly in relation to its relevance to Christian theology. Implicit in the slogan is more than a programme of a direct return to the original sources in their original languages, with a deliberate evasion of later commentaries and translations. Three major presuppositions may be identified as of relevance to our study.

1   A stream is purest at its source. The medieval view of tradition – evident, for example, in the development of complex glosses upon the scriptural text, as each commentator added his ideas to those already present[37] – as an accumulation of insight and wisdom is called into question. For the Renaissance, medieval additions to the stream of tradition were inelegant and obscure, concealing rather

than revealing the meaning of scripture. Glosses and commentaries, whether upon scripture or upon the Justinian *Pandects*,[38] were to be set aside as an impediment to interpretation, in order to engage directly with the sources of the Christian faith.

2 Truth is historically located, rather than universal. The new sense of being located in history, characteristic of the later Renaissance,[39] led to a growing unease with the notion of universal truths. The irreducible particularity of human existence was considered to be more suitable to historical description, rather than to logical analysis. The New Testament was not to be read as a logical presentation of Christian theology, but as a record of the foundational Christian experience, given in a specific literary and historical form. By the judicious use of appropriate literary, philological and historical techniques, it was believed that the vitality and immediate experience of the apostolic period could be restored to a period which had degenerated into a form of religion which was largely external and superficial.

3 The original sources were to be read in a new spirit. Virgil's *Aeneid*, for example, was read with a new sense of historical empathy. The experience of Aeneas, recounted by Virgil, in setting out to sea to discover new and strange lands, was one which could be recaptured in the late fifteenth century. The discovery of the Americas in 1492 brought to a climax a series of voyages of discovery which would continue into the following century, making a deep impression upon the consciousness of Renaissance Europe. The past was seen to be relevant to the present, in that it recorded experiences which could be reproduced as a present possibility. History was read as the recurrence of the possible, of genuine possibilities of experience and existence. In much the same way, the New Testament was read with new interest, as recounting the experience of those who encountered the risen Christ – an experience which was a present possibility, not one which was trapped in the historical particularities of the first century.

The past, then, was treated as the source and archetype of a present possibility – what we might define, for want of a better term, as the Christian experience. The New Testament contained, in a specific literary form, an account of the shape of this possibility and the means by which it might be appropriated. It is this grasping of the experience described by the New Testament, rather than the New Testament itself (considered as a literary document of antiquity) which constitutes its significance for the Renaissance. Traces of this attitude may be discerned at a very early stage in the Renaissance. For example, Coluccio Salutati, in considering the concept of 'fame', made the point that it originates 'not in the famous themselves, but in the witness of their celebrants, just as the moon glows not by its own, but by an alien light'.[40] It is the fact that the present is able to value and appropriate the past – rather than the mere quality of 'pastness' itself – that gives it its present significance.

It will be evident that there are obvious difficulties with and inconsistencies within the Renaissance attitude to the past.[41] Two examples may be noted. In the first place, there seemed to be an obvious tension between the religious views of republican Rome and of the New Testament. In employing the criteria of antiquity and eloquence, how could the totally different religious claims of classical mythology and the New Testament be evaluated? In practice, writers such as Boccaccio, Petrarch and Salutati tended to interpret classical myths as 'poetic theology',[42] illustating moral values. Perhaps, if the anachronism may be allowed, we might suggest that they were demythologized to yield a moral core. Salutati's *de laboribus Herculis* (*c.*1391) is perhaps the most impressive early Renaissance work to adopt this approach, thus defusing any potential tension between Christianity and pagan mythology.[43] Marsilio Ficino suggested that each of the gods of antiquity might be treated purely as symbols of moral or physical qualities – for example, Venus symbolized humanity, and Minerva wisdom. The iconography[44] of the Renaissance lends little support to the suggestion (frequently put about by irritated contemporary northern European critics of the Italian Renaissance) that it reclaimed the myths of Rome as much as the gospel of Jesus Christ. It is certainly true that Botticelli's Venuses bear a disquieting resemblance to his Madonnas, while Michelangelo's Christ in the *Last Judgement* has clearly been modelled on a classical Apollo: nevertheless, this reflects classical taste, rather than conscious paganization. Pagan myths and the gospel might both be associated with the same paradigmatic period: the two were never, however, treated as possessing equal authority. Curiously, however, the criteriological difficulties this raised for the ideology of the Renaissance were never fully explored. Erasmus pointed out the tension, noting how the central insights of the Christian faith could not be accommodated within a Ciceronian framework:[45] nevertheless, the tension appears to have been perceived as potential, rather than actual; theoretical, rather than practical.

A second difficulty concerned the criterion of eloquence. For most Renaissance writers, the dual criteria of antiquity and eloquence served to identify the New Testament as taking priority over its medieval interpretations without any difficulty. Paul was singled out as a particularly eloquent writer by many fifteenth-century writers, despite the fact that most lacked the ability and the means to study him in the original Greek, and based their literary evaluation upon the rather inadequate Latin translation contained in the Vulgate. But what of the patristic period? Most Renaissance theologians appeared to rest content with investing the writers of the 'patristic period' (a conveniently ill-defined notion) with a collective authority on account of their corporate antiquity and eloquence. Erasmus, however, initially (1503) identified Origen, and subsequently (1515) Jerome, as supreme among the fathers on account of their eloquence.[46] Augustine was given no position of priority; indeed, Erasmus' editorial activity suggested that early critics of Augustine (such as Arnobius) were to be given equal weighting with the sage of Hippo. Given the significant doctrinal differences between Jerome and Origen (or Augustine and Arnobius), a certain hesitation concerning the viability of Renaissance theological criteria may be registered. However, this was not perceived as a problem by most Renaissance writers.

For the Renaissance, Christianity was primarily a mode of living, and doctrine was perceived as being of little significance. As we noted earlier (pp. 48–51), medieval Christendom (to which the Renaissance was heir) was essentially a social unity. The writers of the Renaissance – who, it must be stressed, were generally religious in their inclinations – had little interest in matters of doctrine, which tended to be regarded as the preserve of scholasticism, with its barbarous Latin, its obsession for logical niceties, and its monkish lack of engagement with the real world of social existence. If one concern may be identified as of primary concern to Renaissance humanists, it was the need to interiorize religion. Doctrine (in common with most matters of church order and structure) was regarded as concerned with externals; what was of central importance was the recapture of the interior dynamics of the Christian faith, of its subjective vitality. Medieval religion was widely perceived as an empty shell; with the outward shape of that shell, there was no particular quarrel (although other shapes were certainly possibilities). It was the fact that it was empty that was the cause for concern: the shell required to be filled. It did not matter that Origen and

Jerome differed on matters of theology; they were at one in bearing witness to the early vitality of the Christan faith, which the medieval church appeared to have lost. That vitality was regarded by the Renaissance as a historical possibility open to present recovery, and as in no way linked with the specific historical circumstances of the first century.

There is an irresistable parallel here between the Renaissance attitudes to the ruins of Rome and to the Christian church. Petrarch, happily wandering through the ruins of Rome, wondered what it was like to live in the days when those ruins were inhabited edifices. What would it have been like to meet Livy? What would Livy have wanted to say to Petrarch and his contemporaries? Was there any way in which the past could be brought to life, and transferred – in however partial a fashion – to the present? Would not the present be stimulated and enriched by its contribution? To many writers of the fifteenth century, the medieval church was like a ruined building, a present testimony to past vitality. But could that vitality not be recovered by the present? Could not the New Testament serve as a guide to the rebuilding, or at least the reinhabitation of that ruin? In fact, could not the New Testament serve as a quarry for more acceptable approaches to religion than that offered by the medieval church? Could not the apostolic period be brought back to life and transferred to the present, in order to challenge and renovate it?

The humanists of the late Renaissance were not concerned to identify the New Testament and the writers of the patristic period as models of written eloquence, in the manner in which Cicero, Horace and Virgil were treated. Nevertheless, they were regarded as assuming a paradigmatic function. The New Testament disclosed patterns of human existence associated with the foundational period of the Christian faith, which were still present possibilities; the patristic period demonstrated the art of eloquent and simple exposition of the New Testament, which contrasted with the tortuous and uncouth logical speculations of the medieval period. The New Testament thus assumed classic status, with the Renaissance being regarded as the recovery and renovation of this classic, which the action of time had eclipsed, and which now reappeared in a new relationship with the present.[47] Just as the classic period served to shape the Renaissance concept of 'taste',[48] so the New Testament was understood to shape the internal contours of Christian existence.

One of the most significant Renaissance contributions to the genesis of doctrinal criticism was its insistence that 'scripture' was not to be equated with the text of the Vulgate, but with the Old and New Testaments in their original languages, as ascertained from the best manuscripts available.[49] The phenomenon of doctrinal criticism may be observed in operation in the critical writings of Lorenzo Valla. Valla noted that a significant number of medieval doctrines – particularly relating to Mariology and the theology of the sacraments – rested upon Vulgate passages which were now to be recognized as erroneous translations of the Greek of the New Testament.[50] The publication of Valla's work in 1505 by Erasmus, complemented by the latter's *Novum instrumentum omne* of 1516 (which made available the first complete Greek text of the New Testament, with a new Latin translation, differing significantly from the Vulgate) created a climate of suspicion concerning many medieval theological developments. Western medieval theologians, unlearned in Greek, based their theological speculations upon the Vulgate text: the recognition of the inadequacies of this text added further to the widespread demand to return to Christian antiquity, bypassing the spurious doctrinal developments of the Middle Ages. Not only did the fathers write with elegance, and due attention to the New Testament – they had access to and were capable of handling its Greek text. Erasmus was scornful of the attitude of the medieval church to the fathers: it venerated their relics, he wrote, but ignored their books.

In assessing the significance of the Renaissance attitude to the past to the present study, several potentially conflicting strands must be identified. In the first place, the dawn of a genuine sense of historical consciousness drew attention to the differences between the past and the present. Classical Rome belonged to the past, and could not be treated as if it were fifteenth-century Florence. In the second place, however, certain aspects of the past were invested with cultural, moral, religious and political authority, on account of their antiquity. To Renaissance humanism of the fifteenth century, the ideas of Cicero, Horace and Virgil were considerably more significant and relevant than those of modern writers, such as William of Ockham. On account of the presuppositions of humanism, the temporal gulf separating the classical period from the Renaissance thus simultaneously *diminished* the correspondence of past and present and *increased* the authority of the past for the present. In a remarkable act of empathetic solidarity, the Renaissance aligned itself and its values with the classical period. This attitude extended to first-century Palestine as much as to republican Rome: the paganism of the latter was creatively reinterpreted within the framework of Christianity, as noted earlier. The methods of modern history, which emerge during this period of exceptional creativity, were not perceived to be laden with a demand for the revision of Christian doctrinal formulations. The spirituality and morality – perhaps even the structures of authority – of the late medieval church were certainly called into question, in the light of the new paradigms of Christian identity; doctrine, however, was not the subject of criticism, if only because humanists regarded doctrine as something of an irrelevance.[51] Nevertheless, the seeds of doctrinal criticism had been sown; it was not long before they germinated.

The Reformation

Intense scholarly activity has been devoted to the clarification of the origins and subsequent development of the Reformation.[52] It is unquestionably true that the Reformation was not concerned solely with religious ideas, but rested upon and reflected political, social and economic developments central to the shaping of early modern Europe. Intense critical study of the social setting of the Reformation has clarified the appeal of Reformation ideas to urban populations in the early sixteenth century, and the manner in which they were transmitted and modified in the period which followed. Nevertheless, the *origins* of those ideas have not yet been explained satisfactorily upon ideological grounds,[53] largely on account of the social and cultural heterogeneity both of early sixteenth-century Europe in general and of those individuals who would exercise such an influence over the intellectual shaping of the various components of the movement we designate 'the Reformation'. For example, studies on popular religion in the Renaissance and Reformation periods demonstrated considerable variation between geographical regions on the one hand, and social strata on the other, within which such views were influential. The contrast with the Enlightenment, which lends itself particularly well to explanation at the ideological level, is significant.

Despite this general difficulty, a broad distinction may be drawn between the magisterial and radical wings of the Reformation.[54]

The former was socially and politically conservative (in the sense of endorsing the political systems already prevalent in the local situation: in the cases of Luther, Zwingli and Calvin, these happened to be rather different), whereas the latter were radical, often associated with primitive communist beliefs and a negative attitude to existing social and political structures of authority. These broad differences in ideology are reflected in their attitude to tradition: the magisterial reformers adopted a positive approach to tradition, particularly the *testimonia patrum*, whereas the radicals adopted a generally negative approach.[55] To most of the radicals, the fathers were an irrelevance: every individual had the unfettered right to interpret scripture in whatever manner seemed right to him or her. We shall consider these divergent tendencies within the Reformation movement individually.

The Magisterial Reformation

The complex intellectual origins of the magisterial Reformation render generalizations concerning the movement hazardous.[56] Nevertheless, it is helpful to distinguish two broad components within the movement during the second decade of the sixteenth century, which would later develop into the Reformed and Lutheran wings of the Reformation. The evangelical faction at Zurich, centring upon Huldrych Zwingli, was concerned with the formulation of a programme of social, political and religious reform reflecting the wider concerns of the Swiss humanist sodalities of the period, and the socio-political realities of the Helvetic Confederation. On account of underlying shifts in political power structures within the region, the programme of reform associated with Zwingli was subjected to significant modification, with the centre of gravity of the movement subsequently becoming Berne, and finally Geneva.[57] The evangelical faction within the university faculty of theology at Wittenberg, centring upon Martin Luther and Andreas Bodenstein von Karlstadt, was initially concerned with little more than the restructuring of the university theological curriculum. On account of a number of significant historical accidents, this faction came to serve as a nucleus for a programme of social, political and religious reform extending considerably beyond the somewhat narrow confines of the Wittenberg theology faculty, making deep inroads into German society and beyond.

In turning to deal with Zwingli, it is impossible to evade the conclusion that we are confronted with an individual who has been deeply influenced by *Quattrocento* humanism, in the specific form associated with the universities of Vienna and Basle at the turn of the century.[58] Among the subtle modifications introduced to Italian Renaissance attitudes to the past as they migrated north of the Alps was a gentle downplaying of the significance of the religious views of antiquity. The Greek and Latin classics jostled for space alongside the fathers in Zwingli's library at Einsiedeln in 1516–18, along with his treasured new possession – a copy of the Greek text of the New Testament.[59] Always appreciative of the eloquence of classical pagan writings, and mindful of Augustine's dictum that 'all truth is from God', Zwingli nevertheless subordinated the writings of antiquity to scripture, even to the point of interpreting the religious views of those writers in the light of scripture. Thus Pindar's polytheism is reworked in the light of the gospel affirmations of monotheism.[60] The works of Erasmus – all heavily annotated, indicating that they had been thoroughly read – were the most significant component of Zwingli's personal library in the 1520s, despite his increasing interest in Luther. Zwingli met Erasmus at Basle in 1516, as the latter was engaged in putting the final touches to his edition of the Greek New Testament, and appears to have been deeply influenced by him.[61] He had already learned Greek in 1513; from 1516 he mastered the New Testament in that language, and, like so many others, became acutely aware of the deficiencies of the Vulgate text. Nevertheless, Zwingli was not moved to become a *doctrinal* reformer as a result. Zwingli's stress upon the sufficiency of scripture at this stage is probably best understood in terms of spirituality, rather than doctrine: the pious individual who reads the New Testament has access to the fundamental resource of Christian spirituality.

In his early period as a reformer, Zwingli also reflects Erasmus' attitude to the heritage of the patristic period. Augustine is not regarded as endowed with particular significance: for Zwingli, it is Jerome and Origen who vie for the title *summus inter theologos*. Furthermore, when Zwingli began to employ Augustine seriously in relation to his programme of doctrinal reformation in the 1520s, it is not in connection with the doctrine of grace (there is not a trace of any interest in the questions which gave rise to Luther's doctrine of justification by faith alone);[62] Zwingli found Augustine's theory of signification useful in articulating his theory of the real presence (which for Zwingli is more of a real absence) in the mid-1520s.

In the 1510s, Zwingli's attitude to the past parallels that associated with Renaissance humanism in general, and (from 1516) Erasmus in particular.[63] An appeal is made to the past in order to disrupt contemporary religious theories and practices to which Zwingli took exception. Using historical methods and theories of evidence paralleling those associated with Valla, Zwingli undermined contemporary religious practices (for example, clerical celibacy and communion in one kind) by recording the counter-factual. He argued that the tradition concerning priestly celibacy had clearly been falsified at points, and that there was evidence that Swiss congregations had been served by married priests in the past, just as they had once been allowed to receive communion in both kinds.[64] History was a weapon to be employed in discrediting practices to which Zwingli took exception. What criteria did Zwingli employ in evaluating the received traditions and doctrines of the church?

For Zwingli, the primary criterion is the New Testament. Although hints of the Renaissance justification of an appeal to the New Testament with reference to its antiquity and eloquence may be found in his early writings, the primary grounds on which this appeal is justified by Zwingli is theological: the New Testament is the Word of God. This assumption is treated as axiomatic, requiring no demonstration. It is significant that Zwingli appears to follow the common outlook of the Renaissance, treating religion as a matter of practical existence rather than intellectual formulations. Ernst Ziegler, commenting on the Reformation in eastern Switzerland in general, and Vadian's city of St Gallen in particular, writes persuasively of the Reformation as 'a Reformation of life and morals'.[65] It was the practices, spirituality and structure of the church (and, Zwingli would subsequently add, society) which required reformation in the light of the New Testament. Following Erasmus, a hermeneutical method (based partly upon Origen) which places considerable emphasis upon the moral sense of scripture is adopted: the New Testament is not treated primarily as God's promises of mercy and salvation to his people (Luther's characteristic position), but – in a manner reminiscent of Wycliffe – as a source of *lex divina*, which might be contrasted with the *lex humana* of canon law and later ecclesiastical tradition.[66] Scripture lays down norms for conduct, defining practice rather than theory. No explicitly theological criteria are formulated by which the *doctrinal* heritage of the past may be critically reappropriated, however, even though it would appear that such a criterion is implicit in his identification of the New Testament as the Word of God. In his early period, Zwingli is significantly silent on the question of doctrinal criticism, reflecting the common humanist belief that the thrust of reform was directed elsewhere. During his first year at Zurich (1519), Zwingli appears to have preached a programme of moral and spiritual reform – similar to that contained in Erasmus' *Enchiridion* – from the pulpit of the Grossmünster, apparently concerned with orthopraxy rather than orthodoxy. The practices of clerical celibacy, communion in one kind, praying for the dead and worshipping images are open to criticism in the light of the paradigm of scripture – but Zwingli is reluctant, at this stage, to move beyond criticism of practices to the theories which undergirded them, or were generated by them (the causality involved being a matter of dispute, then as now). The genesis of Zwingli's vocation as a *doctrinal* reformer is to be dated from some point after 1520,[67] and may probably be put down to the influence of Luther. It is thus possible that Zwingli's move towards a programme of doctrinal reform may be derivative, rather than original.

A very different attitude towards doctrinal criticism – and, it may be added, that which would rapidly become the common currency of the Reformation – is associated with the evangelical faction at Wittenberg in the 1510s. Modern scholarship has tended to lay stress upon the corporate nature of the reforms within the theological faculty at Wittenberg in the period 1513–19, attempting to redress the balance of those accounts focusing solely upon Luther. Whereas Zwingli was initially concerned with a programme of social reform which subsequently included doctrinal criticism, the Wittenberg theological faculty was initially concerned with a programme of academic reform, centring upon the theological curriculum at Wittenberg.[68]

The very different social contexts of these early reforming movements must be recognized: Zwingli set out to reform a major city, which had only recently ousted Lucerne as the *Vorort* of the Helvetic Confederation, while Luther *cum suis* had as their initial objective the reform of the theological faculty of one of the most insignificant universities in Europe. The near-total difference in the social contexts in which Luther and Zwingli began their programmes of reform goes some considerable way towards explaining why Zwingli was initially so disinterested in theological criteriology, while such considerations were close to the centre of Luther's concerns. Where Zwingli had no need to concern himself with matters of theological criteriology in the 1510s, Luther's objective demanded that attention be given to precisely this question: the essential prerequisite to the drawing up of a new theological curriculum was the formulation of explicit criteria by which subjects and texts might be evaluated, with a view to their elimination from the existing curriculum or incorporation into its successor. The importance of the criteria selected for this revision of the curriculum would have been of purely academic interest, were it not for the fact that precisely the same criteria came to govern the theological stance of the Lutheran Reformation, and would thence exercise considerable influence over other wings of the movement. (The growing influence of Luther over the Swiss reformation, and the gradual shift in power away from Zurich to Geneva and its doctrinally aware reformer John Calvin should be noted here).

The Wittenberg reform itself dates from March 1518, when members of the theological faculty met at the lodgings of its dean, Karlstadt.[69] The reforms adopted reflect the emergence of a growing consensus on sources and methods within the faculty over the period 1513–18. The first major element of this consensus concerns scripture: theology is based upon scripture, read in its original languages. The establishment of a trilingual college at Wittenberg parallels developments elsewhere in European universities, and may be taken as a reflection of the growing influence of humanism.[70] The virtually total elimination of works of medieval theology from the curriculum, and the new interest in the patristic period[71] reflect the humanist conviction that the *media aetas* was something of an intellectual lacuna. In May of the previous year, Luther had sketched the contours of (and indicated the initial success of) such a curriculum in a celebrated letter to Johann Lang:

> Our theology and St Augustine prosper and, by the work of God, reign in our university. Aristotle is in continual decline, perhaps to his future permanent ruin. Lectures on the *Sentences* are treated with disdain, and nobody can hope for an audience unless he puts forward this theology, that is, the Bible or St Augustine.[72]

The influence of humanism upon the reforming faction within the Wittenberg theological faculty is evident at every point, reflecting similar developments taking place at much the same time at other European universities.

The criteria employed by the Wittenberg evangelical faction in reappropriating the theological heritage of the past differed from those of humanism at a number of points, however. The authority of scripture resided, not in its antiquity and eloquence, but in its being the Word of God. Luther and Karlstadt, like Zwingli, regarded this identification as self-evident, requiring no further demonstration. It may, however, be pointed out that some such identification, along with an assertion of the material sufficiency of scripture for Christian doctrine, was the common heritage of medieval theology, within whose ample girth both Luther and Karlstadt were once contained.[73] The use of this explicitly theological criterion served to identify scripture as the *sole* foundation of Christian theology.[74] Alongside this, however, was a new emphasis upon the importance of the anti-Pelagian writings of Augustine. Whereas humanist writers tended to employ the criteria of eloquence and antiquity in assessing the relevant merits of the fathers, Luther and Karlstadt used an overtly theological criterion in identifying Augustine as *summus theologus*.

How may Luther's criteriology be accounted for? The central concern which governs Luther's attitude to sources is the affirmation of the possibility of a personal transformative encounter between the individual and Jesus Christ. This theme is a commonplace in late Renaissance thought, particularly in northern European humanism of the period 1490–1520. John Colet at Oxford and Jacques Lefèvre d'Etaples at Paris may be noted among its proponents. Throughout his career, Luther placed emphasis upon the ability of justifying faith (*fides apprehensiva*) to lay hold of Christ. The content of scripture is nothing other than Jesus Christ: Christ is the *punctus mathematicus sacrae scripturae*.[75] Scripture constitutes 'the swaddling clothes and manger in which Christ lies.'[76] Scripture is canonical in so far as it inculcates Christ.[77] Underlying such affirmations is the consistent belief that it is through scripture that the believer encounters Christ.

The New Testament is thus the means by which an encounter with Christ may take place. Two themes may be discerned within Luther's cluster of affirmations concerning the Christological content of scripture: on the one hand, scripture establishes the conditions under which this encounter may take place; on the other, it describes the shape of this encounter, sketching the outlines of the Christian existence which results. Luther's hermeneutical scheme, employed in the exegesis of the Psalter over the period 1513–15,[78] is fundamentally directed towards the identification of the effects of Christ upon the believer (the tropological sense of scripture, regarded as primary by Luther at this point, and interpreted in a manner very different from that associated with Erasmus and Bucer),[79] and clarification of the manner in which this transformative encounter may be precipitated. Luther's favourite image to describe this encounter is that of a spiritual marriage between Christ as bridegroom and the Christian as bridge,[80] with faith as the bond of union between them.[81] At this point, Luther is able to exploit a distinction, originating with Lefèvre d'Etaples, between the historically situated meaning of scripture and its existential significance. Luther's hermeneutical scheme is directed towards a deliberate and systematic disengagement with the historically situated content of scripture (designated the *sensus literalis historicus* by Lefèvre, and subsequently by Luther) in favour of the present-day relevance of that history (the *sensus literalis propheticus*).[82]

The function of scripture, therefore, is to mediate Christ to posterity, and hermeneutical schemes are to be evaluated on the basis of their ability to detach the essential Christ from the accidents of history (if I may be excused for using the Aristotelian terms which Luther so detested). The basis of Luther's theological criteriology thus has virtually nothing to do with such matters as antiquity or eloquence, despite any superficial similarities that may be discerned. In declining to adopt this strand of Renaissance criteriology, however, Luther appears willing to endorse another – the characteristic notion that scripture mediates, in a specific literary and historical form, the experience of Christ, the recovery of which appropriate literary and historical techniques may permit.

At this point, a highly significant difference between the Wittenberg reformers and Zwingli should be noted. For Zwingli (who here follows Erasmus), the medieval period was an irrelevance, an obstruction inhibiting access to the foundational period of Christianity. It was something which could and should be avoided and by-passed, en route to the classic period. For Luther, however, it was essential to engage in critical dialogue with the medieval period. Luther's interaction with late medieval thought was regarded with something approaching astonishment by the Swiss reformers, whose humanist presuppositions dictated that the theology of the medieval period compounded inelegance and irrelevance. Nevertheless, Luther's sustained engagement with the more prominent writers of the *via moderna* expresses an important element of his theology: the need to engage in dialogue with the present concerning the heritage of the past. Luther incorporates a surprising number of 'modern' ideas (particularly in the fields of logic and epistemology) into his thought, while insisting upon the paradigmatic character of the past.

Luther's understanding of Christian theology identifies the New Testament as the necessary starting point for doctrinal reflection. Explicitly rejecting the idea that theology deals with general principles, Luther insists upon the grounding of the Christian faith and Christian doctrine in a particular historical event. Theology is concerned with the significance of *Deus pro nobis*, rather than *Deus in se* – and for Luther, 'God' is defined Christologically. *Nullum Deum scito extra istum hominem Iesum Christum.*[83] God can be fully known (in both the cognitive and personal senses of the word) only through Jesus of Nazareth.[84] The proper subject of theology is thus 'God', as defined in the saving event of Jesus Christ.[85] Given Luther's theological premise that theology is obliged to wrestle with Jesus Christ rather than with general principles or universal *a priori* concepts of divinity, the priority of the New Testament is thus secured on historical and literary grounds.[86]

It remains, however, to explain the particular place of honour assigned by Luther and his colleagues (especially Karlstadt) to Augustine. That priority was given to Augustine is not a matter of dispute. From 1513 onwards, patristic texts became available at Wittenberg in large numbers,[87] encouraging a new interest in Christian antiquity. Nevertheless, it is Augustine who is singled out for especial attention within the Faculty of Theology. Lying behind this development may be discerned a late medieval Augustine renaissance, which made available both texts (especially the anti-Pelagian writings) and new approaches to such texts.[88] The celebrated debate of September 1516 between Luther and Karlstadt, which centred on the interpretation of Augustine's views on grace, highlighted the importance of Augustine interpretation to the shaping of the corporate views of the faculty. Karlstadt's action in defending 151 Augustinian theses in May 1517 (after having conceded the accuracy of Luther's interpretation of Augustine) firmly stamped the impression of the African bishop upon Wittenberg's emerging reforming theology, a process which was consolidated through Karlstadt's justly celebrated lectures on *de spiritu et littera* the following academic year. Although it is possible to argue that the influence of Augustine over Luther's personal formation may be less than decisive,[89] it is clear that his influence over the corporate theological reflections of the faculty as a whole was nothing less than decisive. But was this nothing more than an historical accident, reflecting peculiar local circumstances at Wittenberg?

This question may be answered in the negative. The importance of Augustine to the Wittenberg faculty may be appreciated by drawing out further an aspect of Luther's thought. As noted above, for Luther the essence of the Christian faith concerns the appropriation by the individual believer of the living Christ. The question of how and under what conditions this transforming encounter takes place, which Luther articulates with particular reference to the image of justification, thus assumes a position of considerable importance. Christology may define who Jesus Christ is – but soteriology defines how who and what he is may be made relevant and available to those who stand at a distance from him in the historical flux. Augustine's importance to the Wittenberg theology resides chiefly in his anti-Pelagian writings, in which he criticized inadequate understandings – both Manichaean and Pelagian – of how the individual is able to (or, perhaps more accurately, is *enabled* to) orientate himself or herself correctly towards the Christ-event.

It will be clear that significantly different attitudes to the past, and more specifically to the history of Jesus of Nazareth, underlie the theological reflections of Zwingli and Luther. For Zwingli at Zurich and Vadian at St Gallen, the past defined primarily a paradigm of existence; for Luther and Karlstadt at Wittenberg, it served not merely to define such a paradigm of existence, but as the means by which that existence might be established in the first place. There is thus a strongly moral atmosphere associated with the early Reformed attitude to the past, which is taken to indicate and define contemporary possibilities of moral action or existence. The Wittenberg faction, however, regarded Christian existence as something which had to be achieved or effected, prior to any structuring or orientation of that existence in terms of the paradigm of the past. Luther's attitude to good works summarizes this belief well: transformation of one's personal existence through a creative encounter with the risen Christ brings with it a predisposition towards the paradigm of existence indicated by Jesus of Nazareth himself.[90] It is the encounter which makes possible the new existence – whereas for Zwingli and Vadian, the suggestion is clearly implicit that it is the new existence which makes possible the encounter.

Or, to express this in the language suggested by the prevalent image of justification: for Luther, personal righteousness is possible on account of justification, whereas the early Zwingli suggested that justification was possible on account of personal righteousness.

The importance of Augustine to the Wittenberg faction (and his relative depreciation by Zwingli and Vadian) thus derives from the Wittenberg reformer's belief that the *doctor gratiae* had correctly articulated the framework which made possible the encounter between the believer and Christ. Even in his earlier phase in the period 1513–14, Luther persistently addresses the question of what the believer must *do* if he or she is to encounter the living God through Christ. Similarly, Melanchthon's first edition of the *Loci Communes* (1521) is little more than a presentation of the chief points of the narrative of salvation, particularly as presented by Paul. As Melanchthon stressed, the important thing was to 'know Christ (*Christum cognoscere*)', more specifically, to 'know his benefits', rather than indulge in flights of theological fancy.[91] Doctrine is not understood as naked intellectual belief, but as a means of generating an atmosphere of expectation, of removing obstacles, of orientating oneself in an appropriate manner, in order that the risen Christ may be encountered and known, and his benefits appropriated. Doctrine is belief orientated towards action, in order that Christ may be 'grasped'. It is something of existential significance, in that it functions as a channel, as a skeleton, through which and onto which something greater may be directed. Augustine's authority for the Wittenberg reformers thus rests upon his reliability as an exponent of the New Testament, especially Paul.

This insight also allows us to understand the characteristically contradictory approach of the magisterial reformers to Augustine. For Augustine's theology, as has often been observed, is not appropriated by the reformers in its entirety, with equal enthusiasm being manifested for its several components. The Reformation may, for example, justly be regarded as the victory of Augustine's doctrine of grace over Augustine's doctrine of the church.[92] Augustine's doctrine of grace was perceived to be of crucial significance by the reformers, at least in part on account of its importance in relation to the centrality of the encounter of the individual believer with the risen Christ to Reformation spiritualities. No other aspect of Augustine's thought had quite the same significance for the reformers; indeed, where another aspect of his theology was felt to be at odds with this (at least, on account of the sixteenth-century situation), the reformers felt at liberty to set the former to one side. The criterion which led to Augustine being so highly prized in the first place by the Wittenberg reformers led also to him being received selectively and critically.[93]

There is, however, a second reason for the priority attached by Wittenberg to Augustine. The Wittenberg reformers, particularly Melanchthon, noted a certain similarity between their own situation and that of Augustine. For Melanchthon, Augustine's assault on Pelagianism in the early fifth century presaged the Lutheran Reformation in the sixteenth – both in regard to the issue involved, and the means by which it might be handled.[94] According to Melanchthon, the first four centuries were marked by a gradual defection from the *primum et verum*, particularly on account of Origen's allegorizing method (so highly valued, incidentally, by the early Erasmus and Zwingli). The restoration, at least in part, of the true gospel was due to Augustine, just as the more recent restoration of the true gospel and the elimination of the distortions of the medieval period is due to the Wittenberg faction. This perception of historical isomorphism allows Melanchthon to draw significant parallels between the story of Augustine and the story of Wittenberg, lending dignity, purpose and theological credibility to the latter on account of the reputation of the former, and evoking a sense of historical empathy (rather than identification *tout simple*) on the part of the latter for the former.

On the basis of this brief analysis of the early Wittenberg reforming theology, it will be clear that a broadly consistent set of criteria underlie its characteristic approach to the past (and, indeed, its perception of its own historical role, which is consciously modelled upon that of Augustine at points by its image-makers and propagandists, such as Melanchthon). The reformers (whether Lutheran or Reformed) had no quarrel with the patristic dogmas of the hypostatic union or the Trinity, which they regarded as adequately justified on the basis of scripture.[95] The real point at issue was the theoretical framework by which authentic Christian existence might be achieved, which was articulated by the New Testament and at best adumbrated and at worst contradicted by the teachings of the medieval church. For the Wittenberg reformers, doctrinal reformation was essentially doctrinal renovation, returning directly to the foundational event of the Christian faith and its earliest interpretations in the New Testament. Where patristic or medieval writers were faithful to the New Testament, they were to be respected; where they were not, they were to be criticized. Thus both Luther and Melanchthon felt able to criticize Augustine in relation to aspects of the doctrine of grace,[96] while retaining those aspects of his theology which they consider to be justifiable interpretations of the New Testament.

The history of Jesus of Nazareth, as presented and interpreted in the New Testament, functions as the ground and goal of most early Reformation thought. This past event is understood to be authoritative, in that it both establishes the possibility of Christian existence and indicates its contours. It is both the foundational event and the paradigm of Christian life. The authority of scripture, and the manner in which scripture is to be interpreted, rest on its perceived ability to mediate the experience of the risen Christ to posterity. Calvin's theology, for example, has as one of its central concerns the establishment of a personal union between Christ and the believer.[97] The concept of *fides apprehensiva*, central to Luther's Christocentric spirituality, finds its place in Calvin's more rigorous exposition of the same theme: saving faith is ingrafting faith, which effects a union between Christ and the believer.[98] It is through being incorporated into Christ that the believer is conformed to Christ. Faith is thus directed towards Christ,[99] as the substance of scripture, with scripture being viewed as the channel through which Christ is transmitted to the present.[100] Faith provides the means by which the present may encounter the past, appropriately interpreted, in order to be transformed by it.[101] Using appropriate hermeneutical tools, and subject to the guidance of the Holy Spirit,[102] the reader of scripture and those hearing the proclamation of the gospel (in so far as this is based upon scripture) may expect to encounter the risen Christ.

There is thus a clear and consistent attitude to the past evident within the writings of magisterial reformers such as Luther and Calvin. The foundational event of the Christian faith is understood to be the history of Jesus Christ. Access to this history, and a legitimized range of interpretations of its significance, is provided by the New Testament. In addition to this, however, is a tradition of reading the New Testament, a particular way of approaching and interpreting it, which facilitates access to the Christian experience. The core is to be approached through outer concentric circles.

Although it is often suggested that the reformers had no place for tradition in their theological deliberations, this judgement is clearly incorrect. While the notion of tradition as an extra-scriptural source of revelation is excluded, the classic concept of tradition as a particular way of reading and interpreting scripture is retained.[103] Scripture, tradition and the *kerygma* are regarded as essentially coinherent, and as being transmitted, propagated and safeguarded by the community of faith.[104] There is thus a strongly communal dimension to the magisterial reformers' understanding of the interpretation of scripture, which is to be interpreted and proclaimed within an ecclesiological matrix. It must be stressed that the suggestion that the Reformation represented the triumph of individualism and the total rejection of tradition is a deliberate fiction propagated by the image-makers of the Enlightenment.[105]

In stressing the centrality of the history of Jesus of Nazareth, culminating in his death and resurrection, for Christian faith, the reformers thus did not neglect to indicate how access to that history might be gained. A series of concentric circles is perhaps the most helpful way of envisaging this approach: a central core represents the history of Jesus of Nazareth, with two outer circles representing in the first place the New Testament interpretation of that history, and in the second the communal way of approaching and interpreting the New Testament.[106] Access to this core cannot be gained directly,[107] but only through the outer circles. In the first place, the believer stands within a corporate tradition (characterized by its language, liturgy, traditions and its structures of authority), which adopts a particular stance (or restricted range of stances)[108] to the New Testament. In the second place, the New Testament, approached and read within this matrix of expectation, allows encounter with and experience of the risen Christ. The Reformation itself may be regarded as a radical interrogation of the corporate tradition of the western church concerning its foundations in scripture and the early church, in order to ensure that the communal matrix of expectation and interpretation (upon which considerable hermeneutical weight was laid) was both adequate and authentic. The outcome of this process was not intended to be, and was not in fact, the *elimination* of a corporate tradition, nor the generation of a *new* tradition, but the renovation and reformation – where necessary – of the corporate tradition of the western church. The contrast with the radicals, to which we now turn, could hardly be more pointed.

The Radical Reformation

The opinion of Bernhard Rothmann summarizes neatly the prevailing radical view of the past in the 1530s: 'for fourteen hundred years there have been no Christians on earth.'[109] For influential radicals such as Thomas Müntzer and his followers, the notion of reformation of existing ideas or institutions was an absurdity only equalled in magnitude by the suggestion that it was possible to restore some past condition as normative: what was required was a complete social and theological revolution *ab initio*, which would bring about the immediate rule of God upon earth, and the establishment of peace and freedom.[110] The notion of the 'authority of the past' was viewed as at best an irrelevance, and more realistically as a burden perpetuating the unjust social conditions of the present. It is difficult to read the radical pamphlets of the late 1520s and early 1530s without being reminded of aspects of the Enlightenment critique of the past.

The ideological roots of the radical Reformation seem to lie predominantly with radical-bourgeois elements in society; indeed, it is significant that the movement occasionally appears to lack an autonomous theological base, reflecting primarily social attitudes and expectations widespread within alienated sections of German society. The strongly anti-authoritarian views of Sebastian Franck were warmly received within this section of the community, which saw in them the possibility of establishing the theological legitimation of radical social views. The late medieval social order and its attending ideology received its legitimation largely from theological ideas;[111] a social revolution thus required some form of theological legitimation for revolutionary changes within the structures of society. The perception of this need appears to have been prior to the formulation of the theological principles implicated – such as the right of every believer to interpret the bible as he or she pleased, and the stress upon apocalyptic imagery which enhanced the expectation of imminent social change. Initially, this took the form of a set of specific and concretely articulated social, legal and political demands at the time of the Knights' Revolt (1522) and Peasants' War (1524–5); subsequently, the pursuit of comprehensive social change dissolved into a cluster of vague expectations and demands, having little in common other than a demand for radical change and a break with the oppression of the past.[112]

The specifically *theological* views of the radical Reformation, in all their glorious diversity, thus cannot be separated from a complex prevailing network of social attitudes and expectations within an alienated section of society. There is a significant degree of ideological conditioning to the thought of the radical Reformation. The radical emphasis upon the immediacy and individuality of divine revelation through the Holy Spirit eliminated any necessity for an appeal to the past: even scripture itself was subjected to interpretation on radically subjective lines, without reference to traditions or communities. God speaks directly to his elect, through the spirit rather than the letter. The intensely apocalyptic tone of much of the radical writings points to the belief that the past order is not merely an irrelevance, but is about to be overthrown altogether, with the establishment of a new economic and social era.[113] The past *cannot* have authority, in that it is proclaimed to be on the verge of destruction, rather than renewal or reformation.

The German Enlightenment

The American and French Revolutions of the eighteenth century may be taken as symbols of the dominant ideology of the Enlightenment – the perceived need to break free from the oppression of the past.[114] The past was experienced as something corrupt and dead, serving the vested interests of outdated structures of authority – political, moral and intellectual. The Enlightenment may be regarded as a concerted attempt to overthrow the hegemony of the past, to break free from its stranglehold, to break asunder its chains. Outmoded political structures and the ideas upon which they were based were to be swept aside, and a new age ushered in.

The German Enlightenment, or *Aufklärung*, is of particular importance to this study, in that it engaged in a dialogue, however critical, with the doctrinal legacy of the Christian church. The theological potential of the new methods of the Enlightenment were explored with a seriousness which contrasts radically with the monolithic hostility to religious ideas associated with the movement in France. It must be stressed, however, that it is impossible to discuss the ideas and methods of the *Aufklärung* without reference to the social context of the movement,[115] which served to foster and condition, and perhaps even (on the basis of more than one materialist reading of intellectual history) to engender, its leading ideas.[116]

The tendency of many theologians to evaluate such ideas purely in terms of their ideational structures and antecedents, without any reference to their *social function*, must be resisted. It is in no way to cast aspersions upon the Enlightenment commitment to the search for truth to suggest that, at one level, its methods and ideas may also have served to express and legitimate the social attitudes and expectations of the movement, supremely its negative attitude towards the question of the authority of the past. It will be recalled that ideology may be defined as 'an integrated system of beliefs, assumptions and values, not necessarily true or false, which reflects the needs and interests of a group or class at a particular time in history'.[117] By identifying the needs and interests of those social groupings collectively referred to by the phrase 'The Enlightenment', it is possible to give a sociological account of the genesis of the 'integrated system of beliefs, assumptions and values' associated with it – including its religious views. I therefore propose to include in the present section material of a social-historical nature, which indicates how the Enlightenment ideology was perceived to possess 'objectivity' in that it was reinforced by the social structures of the society to which it was specific. The Enlightenment ideology provided a symbolic universe which gave legitimacy to its prior social and political programme.

The closing decades of the eighteenth century witnessed a serious crisis in the professional stratum of society throughout many of the German territories. A rapid rise in population in the second half of the century was not matched by an increase in professional positions within the church, government or the academic world. The resulting social dislocation, fragmentation and loss of cultural legitimacy of the professional classes, which became acute in the 1780s and 1790s, served to create considerable discontent within the ranks of intellectuals,[118] who developed a considerable vested interest in the overthrow of the *ancien régime* and its tradition-ridden outlook as a result. An ideology which fostered a break with the past and an emphasis upon personal merit and autonomy expressed the outlook of many disgruntled intellectuals and other professionals in this period of crisis. In the religious field, these attitudes were expressed in a rejection of the religious (and, more specifically, the *doctrinal*) authority of the past, a rejection of the notion of original sin (which called into question the adequacy of human moral, epistemological and soteriological resources), a rejection of the doctrine of justification by grace (in favour of a notion of justification by personal merit, whether moral or religious),[119] and a marked tendency to respect Jesus of Nazareth to the somewhat limited extent which reason endorsed his teachings and actions.

This ideology found its expression in the intellectual sphere,[120] as well as in the sphere of political action. In eighteenth-century Germany, where the possibilities for political action were decidedly limited, the Enlightenment found its expression primarily in intellectual forms (the contrast with France is again significant). One of the more striking features of the social structure of eighteenth-century Germany is the strictly limited impact of capitalist modes of production and market relationships on social structures. For much of the century, the economy was essentially agrarian, regulated by the state and its functionaries. The universities were generally seen as the means to social mobility and advancement within the state apparatus, with the result that the political and social tensions of the German *ancien régime* were prefigured, if not actually generated, in the academic struggles within the universities of the period.[121] A radical challenge to the intellectual *ancien régime* was laid down within the German universities of the period, as an intellectual expression of the freedom denied at a more overtly political level. The assertion of the autonomy of the individual was seen as the essential prerequisite for political and social emancipation. The baleful influence of the past was to be abolished, by an appeal to the enlightened reason of the individual. The overthrow of the intellectual *ancien régime* was, given the social function of the universities, seen as the precondition for political and social change.[122]

A comparison with the heady days of student life in May 1968 suggests itself in attempting to capture the spirit of the age at the height of the *Aufklärung*. The critical phase of the German Enlightenment may be regarded as 1789–1796. When the news of the French Revolution reached the universities of Germany, a sense of standing on the threshold of a new era appears to have dawned.[123] Europe had come of age. The ideas of the Enlightenment seemed about to be transformed into social and political action. A collective historical transformation seemed possible. The war between France and the German princes of 1792 seemed poised to effect this transition for once and for all. No longer were children obliged to resign themselves to the authority structures and outlooks of their parent's generation. The age-old theme of son rebelling against father (cf. Luke 15.11–24) assumed a new significance: in the 1790s, sons did not merely rebel against their fathers, but against the world-order which their fathers' generations represented. Hölderlin, von Hardenberg, von Humboldt and Schlegel[124] – to name but four – saw a direct correlation between their personal crises with their fathers, and the great crisis now facing European civilisation: both were pregnant with transformative possibilities, as the minority of childhood gave way to the freedom of adulthood. Europe, like these wayward sons, was about to come of age, and enter into its inheritance.

Rationalism was thus not seen as a movement restricted to a narrow academic world, but as being intimately connected with the consolidation of a centralized state and the process of modernization and liberalisation from the interests and values of the traditional estates and power structures.[125] A large and amorphous group developed within German society in the second half of the eighteenth century, consisting of professionals – such as journalists, lawyers, physicians and writers – and an embryonic capitalist bourgeoisie. This group was impatient with the petty restictions and inhibiting conventions of the past. At a purely social level, the Enlightenment may be regarded as a manifestation of the growing influence of this class. It was a thoroughly bourgeois movement, reflecting the response of the German professional classes to the social and political crisis of the late eighteenth century, culminating in the 1780s and 1790s. Indeed, the wide support for the *Aufklärung* among Lutheran theologians reflects both their membership of the opinion-shaping academic community and their support for the associated programme of political and social modernization.[126] The *Aufklärung* was seen as a general programme of modernization, centring upon academic institutions but extending from there to influence those in positions of social and political authority, which could not be appropriated in a partial and piecemeal manner: theological conservatism and political radicalism were thus thought to be mutually opposed within the complex political situation of the period. An apparent exception to this might at first seem to be provided by the duchy of Württemberg, where most theologians were markedly hostile to the Enlightenment: this, however, reflects the particularly conservative links between the church, universities and the *ancien régime* in this region, leading to modernization being perceived as a threat to the vested interests of the professional classes.[127]

The importance of the intellectual aspects of the German Enlightenment to its cultural, social and political components is thus largely due to the social structures (such as the role of the universities and the professional classes) in late eighteenth-century Germany. However, it is possible to explain the role of the *Aufklärung* intelligentsia on the basis of other models. For example, Hegel's conception of the philosopher as one who gives expression to the objective or universal self-consciousness of his or her age allows him to think of the intelligentsia as a directive group which raises the collective practice of the community to the level of self-consciousness (a notion remarkably similar to Gramsci's concept of 'organic' intellectuals).[128] The intellectual elite serve to enhance the self-consciousness of the cultural community by *expressing* (rather than imposing) its ideology, and exploring its consequences.[129] On this model, the philosophers and theologians of the *Aufklärung* would be expected to give systematic expression to an already existing ideology, reflecting the prevailing culture of the bourgeoisie. Hegel's temporal proximity to the *Aufklärung*, in addition to his concern for the integration of philosophy and culture, lends weight to this interpretation of the role of the intelligentsia in giving directive expression to an ideology.

The German Enlightenment, then, may be regarded as the expression of a quite definite outlook upon life, an ideology, firmly grounded in and directed towards the prevailing social and political situation in Germany.[130] More specifically, it may be regarded as a response conditioned by the experience of, and perspective on, the world particular to members of a specific social group within a specific historical generation within a specific socio-political and cultural system. The remarkable ability of the movement to cross national boundaries (such as those of Germany and France) and oceans (evident in the influence of French rationalism upon North America before, during and after the Revolution of 1776) reflects the general atmosphere of political crisis and revolutionary expectation of the closing decades of the eighteenth century in many parts of western Europe and elsewhere, as the 'old order' seemed to totter on the brink of its final destruction. The seriousness with which the German Enlightenment took doctrinal formulations has no direct parallel in England or France, and is largely due to the specific religious situation in Germany, arising partly from the influence of forms of Pietism (such as Moravianism),[131] which gave religion relevance to personal experience, and also of Lutheran Orthodoxy, which gave it a coherent intellectual framework. The new Enlightenment emphasis upon the individual found a convenient point of contact with Pietist spirituality, while the doctrinal formulations of Orthodoxy were suitable intellectual grist for the Enlightenment mills.[132]

A less than fully attentive reading of the intellectual output of the Enlightenment might suggest that the intellectual legacy of the past was not rejected in its totality, but merely subjected to rigorous critical scrutiny on the basis of the criterion of autonomous human reason. In practice, however, the dialogue which this metaphor suggests never really took place. The past was treated as redundant and defunct. Human reason was fully competent to establish what was right *de novo*, eliminating the need to engage in any dialogue with the legacy of the past, or, indeed, to take any notice of it whatsoever. The suggestion that the past had any authority was seen as a poisoned chalice, laden with potentially heteronomous consequences. The legacy of the past might occasionally endorse present-day beliefs – but those beliefs were established without reference to the past, and their credentials rested upon their inherent rationality. To put it bluntly, the past was an irrelevance which could be, and generally was, ignored.

The distinctive contribution of the Enlightenment to two of the questions addressed in this work – the genesis of doctrine, and the authority of the past – may be summarized as follows:

1 Doctrinal formulations are to be regarded as historically conditioned, perhaps appropriate to their own period, but of questionable modern relevance. While historical criticism is an appropriate tool for the evaluation and correction of doctrinal formulations, history is incapable of disclosing rational truth.

2 The truths of reason are autonomous, and may be ascertained without any appeal to history in general, or any specified component in particular (such as the history of Jesus of Nazareth).

3 The past can only be known in a fragmentary, relative and corrigible manner; it is never anything more than, to anticipate Kierkegaard's luminous phrase, 'approximation knowledge'.

Each of these matters is of major importance to our theme, and will be discussed individually. It will, however, be clear that they express a more general set of values and attitudes, which are prior to the specifically religious propositions outlined. The Enlightenment attitude to the specifically religious questions of the nature of doctrine and the authority of the past is a consequence – and not the cause! – of a more general set of values and attitudes, assumed as self-evidently correct within Enlightenment circles, given the socio-political situation of the day and age.

It is tempting to suggest that the decision to reject the past was the outcome of an accumulation of empirical and theoretical evidence which suggested that the past *could not* be used by the present; in fact, however, it appears that the decision that the present *should not* use the past appears to have taken chronological and logical precedence over the formulation of strategies by which the past might be discredited. It is axiomatic for the *Aufklärung* that nothing from the past may be considered as an essential point of reference, a controlling paradigm, or a normative statement: everything must be capable of establishing its authority *derivatively*, in the light of reason and experience, wherein the ultimate grounds of its authority are to be located. The decision to wage war upon the heritage of the past thus seems to have been prior to the forging of intellectual weapons by which this struggle might be prosecuted.

The Historical Criticism of Dogma

'The history of dogma', wrote Loofs, 'is a child of the period of the German Enlightenment'.[133] From its beginnings, the history of dogma has been written by those concerned with its elimination. Historical research into the origins of doctrine, it was believed, would disclose that doctrinal formulations were a response to a definite set of cultural and historical circumstances, which could be dismissed as outmoded. Although these insights would be developed with particular force within liberal Protestantism, their origins are to be traced to the close of the eighteenth century. It is important to set the origins of doctrinal criticism within its social setting in late eighteenth-century Germany, and avoid the error of treating it as a purely intellectual development. 'Dogma' was regarded as instantiating ecclesiastical authoritarianism, as perpetuating the outmoded systems of the past, and as posing a threat to individual autonomy (in that the individual was being asked to accept such dogmas on the authority of another, rather than being able to establish and verify them independently). Doctrinal criticism was part and parcel of the *Aufklärung* ideology, and cannot be treated as an independent entity. From its beginning, the 'history of dogma' was written by those who, for well-defined ideological reasons, wished to eliminate the phenomenon altogether.

This programme of doctrinal criticism was not inconsistent with the principle of the omnicompetence of human reason, as might at first seem to be the case. Why bother to criticize the past, it might be asked, when most Enlightenment writers chose to ignore it? The intended audience for doctrinal criticism was, however, Orthodoxy, which generally declined to accept the intensely rationalist world-view of the age, retaining an outlook which the *Aufklärung* designated 'supernaturalist'. By criticizing doctrinal formulations on the basis of their historical development, it was believed that the Orthodox attitude to them could be discredited. The historical criticism of doctrine served two purposes: the consolidation of the 'religion of reason', and the discrediting of 'supernaturalism'.

This early programme of doctrinal criticism may be illustrated from Steinbart's *Glückseligkeitslehre* (1778), in which a number of classic Protestant doctrines drawn from the sphere of soteriology are 'explained' in terms of their historical context. The Augustinian doctrine of original sin is to be accounted for as a vestige of his Manichaeism, Pelagius having a far surer grasp of the authentic and older view of human nature; the idea of the imputation of Adam's guilt to his posterity arises through logical confusion, and has no direct connection with scripture; the notion of vicarious satisfaction arose through a later development of Augustine's ideas by Anselm of Canterbury, on the basis of very questionable presuppositions.[134] Throughout, Steinbart suggests that, once the origins of a belief are accounted for, it may be set to one side as spurious. Crude though his methods and conclusions may seem, a significant new historical tool for the criticism of doctrine may be seen in the making. Nor must the ideological significance of this criticism of soteriology be overlooked: the cluster of doctrines subjected to criticism in this manner were all perceived to be linked with the notion of a human deficit – for example, an inability to understand a situation, an inability to respond to something, or a lack of moral righteousness. The implicit threat posed to human autonomy by these beliefs was thus eliminated by criticism of their historical origins.

Similar developments may be seen in the field of Christology, where doctrines such as that of the 'two natures' are increasingly put down to historical misunderstandings which Enlightenment historiography has been able to identify and eliminate. The celebrated 'Quest of the Historical Jesus' has its origins in English Deism of the seventeenth century, in a concerted attempt to eliminate the dogmatic view of Christ in favour of a more historical and modest view of his significance.[135] A disjunction exists between Jesus himself, and the elevated dogmatic views concerning him entertained and propagated by his first followers: a critical historical approach allows the latter to be discarded, and the former to be reappropriated. Once more, the ideological function of this criticism must be stressed: criticism of the 'two natures' doctrine eliminated the potential threat to individual autonomy posed by Christ's divinity. Christ's authority thus came to rest upon his moral and religious teaching, which could be evaluated and appropriated by the autonomous individual, on the basis of whether it coincided with already existing rational beliefs. Indeed, some have suggested that the 'historical Jesus' which later rationalism discerned behind the gospel narratives was fundamentally a projection of rationalist values,[136] disarming any threat Jesus might pose to the programme of the Enlightenment.

The Necessary Truths of Reason

A pervasive and characteristic feature of Enlightenment thought is its rationalism. Human beings are understood to possess the necessary epistemological capacities to uncover the rational structure of reality by autonomous exercise of the faculty of ratiocination. Supplementation of this faculty by external sources (such as divine revelation) was regarded as not merely unnecessary but as a potential threat to the autonomy of human reason. 'Revelation' possessed strongly authoritarian overtones, which the spirit of the age found unacceptable, in that it was perceived to be binding upon the individual in a potentially heteronomous manner.[137] Rational truth, it was asserted, possessed the vital characteristics of eternity, universality and necessity. A religious message, such as that of Christianity, commended itself in so far as it 'chimed in' with ideas already present in the rational individual, thus posing no threat to his or her intellectual autonomy.

Given this understanding of reality, it will be clear that Enlightenment thinkers had little time for the idea that truth could be mediated through historical forms. How could the narrative of a series of accidents, of the contingencies of history disclose universal and necessary truths? Lessing's famous dictum expresses this point lucidly: 'the accidental truths of history can never become the proof of the necessary truths of reason.'[138] The notion of historically mediated rational truth was effectively treated as a contradiction in terms, given the Enlightenment understanding of the nature of rationality. Lessing, for example, had no decisive difficulty with the idea of 'historical truth': the crux of the problem lay in relating such truths to universal frameworks of rationality. How, asked Lessing, can we make the transition from one class of truths to another? How, for example, can one move from the historical statement 'Christ rose from the dead' to the rational truth that 'Christ is the Son of God'?[139] There is considerable epistemic distance between historical claims (assuming that they may be verified) and universal rational truth; Lessing suggested that the distance was such as to render them incommensurable.

The significance of this point is considerable, and outweighs any perceived difficulties concerning establishing the history of Jesus of Nazareth in the first place. Suppose the crucifixion and resurrection were to happen in Lessing's back yard, in front of a judiciously selected audience as witnesses. What would the religious significance of this event be? Lessing's arguments allow us to suggest that he would respond as follows: 'I am prepared to accept as historical truth that Jesus Christ was crucified and that he rose again from the dead. However, I fail to see that this possesses any *metaphysical* significance, or that it gives access to any universal and necessary truths of reason.' The difficulty does not concern the historical facts; it concerns the metaphysical status of history, or perceived lack of such status at the time of the Enlightenment.

In the summer of 1780, Friedrich Heinrich Jacobi accused Lessing of being a Spinozan. Although this was generally taken to mean little more than that Lessing was an atheist, the comment demonstrates considerable theological insight.[140] Spinoza – in common with other great idealistic system builders and panlogists, such as Hegel – envisaged the whole of reality as one great logically coherent system, capable of being grasped by the autonomous human reason. Truth was only to be attained in a single, logically integrated theory of reality: it was possible to ascertain the general relation between ideas ('common notions') in order to discern their universal, inherent necessity ('intuitive knowledge'). In his *Ethica ordine geometrico demonstrata*, Spinoza used the analogy of mathematics to illuminate how such a system might be constructed and conceived. Similarly, Lessing appears to envisage reality as a rational system accessible to human reason. God is thus to be approached and conceived in terms of universal and general ideas, rather than contingent historical specifics. Underlying this approach is a belief in a universal framework of rationality, which may be echoed in historical events, but which has a totally independent existence. A similar point is made in the fragments of Reimarus' *Schutzschrift* published by Lessing during the period 1774–8. The very concept of revelation is to be regarded as untenable, in that its historical character would necessarily be inconsistent with the universal and necessary character of rational truth.[141]

The Knowledge of the Past

The rationalist presuppositions of Enlightenment thinkers such as Lessing and Reimarus deny universal significance to historical events on account of their particularity. The contingencies of history cannot bear the epistemological weight required of the necessary truths of reason. An event, whether present or past, can at best corroborate what is established through reason. An appeal to history is thus precluded from possessing any potential theological significance.[142] Having made this point, however, both Lessing and Reimarus stress that, in any case, our 'knowledge' of past events in general, and that of the history of Jesus of Nazareth in particular, is fragmentary and corrigible, dependent upon the testimony of the dead.

Reimarus draws a distinction between an historical event (which might conceivably be regarded as divine revelation) and the historical reports of this event upon which subsequent generations are obliged to rely. How can we be sure that these reports are reliable?[143] Lessing's approach to this question demonstrates the same emphasis upon the immediate data of sense experience: the past cannot be experienced directly, save through potentially unreliable and fragmentary second-hand reports. Lessing's individualism, characteristic of the Enlightenment in general, leads him to assign priority to first-hand personal experience of the world. First-hand personal experience of, for example, the resurrection is one thing; to be dependent upon second-hand evidence mediated solely in the form of human testimony is quite another.[144] A corporate tradition concerning a past event is of little moment, unless that event can be verified in the present.

Underlying Lessing's discussion of knowledge of the past is the implicit assumption that present-day experience serves as a criterion for correcting reports concerning past events. 'I live in the eighteenth century, in which miracles don't happen any more'[145]: therefore, Lessing suggests, reports which suggest that miracles did happen in the first century are to be corrected in the light of the present data of experience. Present-day experience of the world is to be given greater weight than reports concerning the past. It is qualitatively superior to corporate traditions concerning the past. Furthermore, to suggest that something of significance happened *uniquely* in the past is to become the victim of heteronomy, compromising the axiom of the autonomy of human reason. The implicit assumption is that of the homogeneity of history and the universalizability of religion, in which radical novelty is excluded. Nothing can happen in the past which lacks present-day analogues.[146]

The authority of that past moment of history we designate 'Jesus of Nazareth' thus cannot be grounded in anything such as his resurrection, for which there is no present analogue. His authority resides in his teaching.[147] That teaching, however, is evaluated in the light of general rational principles: its authority is not inherent, but derives from its correlation with already existing moral principles. Throughout, Lessing upholds the autonomy of individual reason, which evaluates Jesus according to the rationality of his teaching. Whatever authority he possesses is derivative, rather than inherent. To suggest that an individual is bound to receive Jesus' teaching on account of who Jesus is, or what status he possesses, is tantamount to an assertion of intellectual heteronomy. Jesus does not possess authority in that he *establishes* religious or moral values, but to the extent that he *reflects* what reason endorses as acceptable religious or moral values. Reason is in itself authoritative: Jesus possesses a derivative authority, to the extent that his words and deeds are perceived to reflect universal human patterns of rationality. It is the autonomous rational individual who is the criterion for the validity of the teaching of Jesus. In this, Lessing demonstrates the attitude to history particularly associated with the *philosophes* of the French Enlightenment, soon to become the common currency of the *Aufklärung*: history is a convenient vehicle for the illustration of non-historical truths, the validity of which is *independent* of the means of their historical disclosure, while totally *dependent* upon their conformity to the human faculty of reason.

This emphasis upon the rational autonomy of the individual has significant consequences for the discipline of doctrinal criticism. The *primary* criterion by which a doctrine is to be judged is human reason. A doctrine which fails to satisfy such criteria as human autonomy and Lessing's requirement that authentic religion do justice to the autonomous self is to be rejected. This is particularly clear in the case of the doctrine of original sin, which was held to compromise both these requirements. Whilst Voltaire and Rousseau criticized the doctrine on account of its socio-political consequences (it encouraged a spirit of docility and submission), many writers of the *Aufklärung* objected to its implication of a human moral or epistemological deficit (the Kantian notion of radical evil being a significant exception to this general rule).[148] Given the unacceptability of such a doctrine as original sin, the question of its historical origins could be pursued, with a view to showing that such unacceptable doctrines were the consequence of certain specific historical circumstances which were not binding upon posterity. In other words, the *primary* criteria were those of pure reason; the *secondary* criteria were those of history. Where it could be used to enhance the religion of pure reason, history was used for purely tactical purposes, in a supporting role; where it could not, it was marginalized.

This analysis of the Enlightenment attitude to the doctrinal heritage of the past allows us to raise a significant question at this point for discussion later. The religious views of the Enlightenment reflect the ideology of the movement, particularly its concerted move to break with the structures of authority and frameworks of rationality of the past, in order to establish the autonomy – political and intellectual – of the modern individual. Those views, the methods upon which they rest and the attitudes which they express, cannot be taken in isolation, in that they are part of a broadly coherent world-view, engaging directly with the social, political and intellectual realities of the late eighteenth century. The perceived need of certain social groupings to break free from the past gives rise to the formulation of intellectual strategies by which this objective might be attained. These views served a definite social function, and are rooted in the specific social situation of late eighteenth century Germany.

But what happens if there is a significant shift in ideology? What happens, for example, if the paradigm expressed in Oliver Wendell

Holmes' Phi Beta Kappa address (the need to break free from the intellectual and spiritual colonialism of the past) is replaced by that found in Alex Haley's novel *Roots* (the need to establish continuity with the past)? Can the religious views of the Enlightenment, including the frameworks of rationality and values which they presuppose and express, be maintained when the ideological matrix within which they arose is itself part of an allegedly defunct (given the presuppositions of the Enlightenment) past? Furthermore, insights (however controverted) from the discipline of the sociology of knowledge (see pp. 90–102) cast serious doubt upon whether 'reason' and frameworks of rationality are as universal and eternal as Lessing and others appear to presuppose. Patterns of rationality are now recognized to be shaped by such factors as social existence and by language, so that the 'autonomous rational individual' – the criterion upon which so much weight is laid by the epistemology of the Enlightenment – may possibly have to be recognized as a social construct. We shall return to a fuller discussion of the ideological conditioning of attitudes to the past in a later section; our attention is now claimed by a fuller examination of the contribution of *Dogmengeschichte* to our theme.

The Historians of Dogma

As we noted earlier, the origins of the 'history of dogma' (to use the traditional English rendering of the German term *Dogmengeschichte*) date from the period of the Enlightenment; the consolidation of the discipline dates from the period of Liberal Protestantism, especially during the second half of the nineteenth century.[149] Perhaps surprisingly, Lessing had no particular interest in the history of dogma;[150] the discipline is generally regarded as having been initiated in the eighteenth century by Johann Friedrich Wilhelm Jerusalem, who argued that dogmas such as the doctrine of the two natures and the Trinity were not to be found in the New Testament. If anything, these arose through confusion of the Platonic *logos*-concept with that found in the Fourth Gospel, and the mistaken apprehension that Jesus personified, rather than exemplified, this *logos*.[151] The history of dogma was thus a history of mistakes – mistakes, however, which were in principle reversible, were it not for the monolithic hostility of the institutional churches to any such reconstruction.

Initial attempts at writing histories of dogma were somewhat unpromising, often being little more than disorganized lists of quotations and pieces of information which appealed to their writers. Among these may be noted Bertholdt's *Handbuch* (1822), Ruperti's *Geschichte der Dogmen* (1831), Lenz' *Geschichte der christlichen Dogmen* (1834), Engelhardt's *Dogmengeschichte* (1839), and Baumgarten-Crusius' *Compendium der christlichen Dogmengeschichte* (1840).[152] The first serious attempt to give structure to this enterprise, and discern general principles of development within the history of dogma, is due to Ferdinand Christian Baur.[153] While the nature and extent of Hegelian influence upon Baur's understanding of history remains contested,[154] it is clear that he views the development of doctrine through an idealist prism. Baur evidently regards the development of doctrine as a unity, rather than a series of unrelated episodes. The histories of dogma influenced by Enlightenment rationalism tended to treat history as a web of irrationalities, interspersed with depressingly few rays of light. The Enlightenent historian of dogma tended to regard himself as rational, and his subject as irrational. Baur's studies – such as *Die christliche Lehre von der Versöhnung* (1838) and *Die christliche Lehre von der Dreieinigkeit und Menschwerdung Gottes* (1841–3) – were, however, able to draw upon Hegel's philosophy of history in an attempt to discern continuity and development within history, rather than perpetuate a wooden tradition of monolithic hostility towards the rationality of the past. History was going somewhere, and the discerning historian could grasp its unity and dynanism, while at the same time attempt to comprehend its meaning and thus illuminate his own present situation.[155] Retaining the Enlightenment view that the doctrinal legacy of the past was unusable in the modern period, he held that the development of doctrine nevertheless afforded insights into the manner in which modern views developed.

The culmination of the discipline is generally held to rest with Adolf von Harnack, whose *Dogmengeschichte* represents a pillar of Liberal Protestant historical scholarship. On the basis of his historical studies of the development of Christian doctrine, Harnack argued forcefully that the transition of the gospel from its original Palestinian milieu, dominated by Hebraic modes of thought and rationality, to an Hellenistic milieu characterized by radically different modes of thinking represented a decisive turning point in the history of Christian thought.[156] The notion of dogma, Harnack argues, is due to the specific historical location, characterized by

Hellenistic modes of thought and patterns of discourse, within which the dogmatic statements of the early church were formulated.

> What Protestants and Catholics call 'dogmas' are not only ecclesiastical teachings, but also (1) conceptually express theses which, taken collectively, form a unity. These theses establish the contents of the Christian religion as knowledge of God, of the world, and of sacred history as demonstrated truths. Furthermore, (2) these theses have emerged at a definite stage in the history of the Christian religion. Both in the manner in which they are conceived and in many of their details, they demonstrate the influence of this stage (the Greek period), and they have preserved this character in all subsequent epochs, despite qualifications and additions.[157]

Harnack's historical documentation of this process is formidable. He is, however, adamant that this is not an insight for which he, and he alone, is responsible. Mosheim's eighteenth-century *Platonisme des pères dévoilé* is cited as a pioneering work in demonstrating the covert influence of Greek presuppositions upon patristic theology.[158] Harnack explicitly states that his studies on the nature and development of early catholicism are foreshadowed in the writings of Richard Rothe.[159] In his analysis of the doctrine of God and the person and work of Christ, it is clear that Harnack both draws upon and extends the researches of Albrecht Ritschl.[160] Harnack's distinctive contribution to our themes resides in the monumental character of his researches, and his willingness to draw significant and far-reaching theological implications from his historical researches.

For Harnack, the gospel is nothing other than Jesus Christ himself.[161] 'Jesus does not belong to the gospel as one of its elements, but was the personal realization and power of the gospel, and we still perceive him as such.'[162] Jesus himself *is* Christianity. In making this assertion, however, Harnack implies no *doctrine* of Jesus; the basis of the assertion is partly historical (based on an analysis of the genesis of Christianity), and partly a consequence of Harnack's personalist religious assumptions (Jesus' significance resides primarily in the impact he has upon individuals). Nevertheless, the transmission of the gospel within a Hellenistic milieu, with its distinct patterns of rationality and modes of discourse (which, curiously – given the weight which he attaches to it – Harnack never defines with any great precision) led to the attempt to conceptualize and give metaphysical substance to the significance of Jesus. In the first edition of the *Dogmengeschichte*, Harnack illustrates this trend with particular reference to Gnosticism, the Apologists, and particularly the *logos*-Christology of Origen.[163] To a certain extent, the development of doctrine may be likened, in Harnack's view, to a chronic degenerative illness.[164] In the case of Christology, for example, Harnack detects in the shift from soteriology (an analysis of the personal impact of Jesus) to speculative metaphysics a classical instance of the Greek tendency to retreat into the abstract.[165]

Nevertheless, Harnack does not regard this as an historically irreversible process: Athanasius is viewed as correcting the Hellenistic excesses of Origen; Augustine is seen as a reformer of Greek speculative theology in general; and Luther is declared to be the reformer of the post-Augustinian western theological tradition. The role assigned to Luther by Harnack is of particular interest, in that the German reformer is viewed as directing fundamental criticism against speculative and moral conceptions of God, Christ and faith.[166] Harnack clearly saw the science of the history of dogma as performing a comparable task in the modern period. In a letter of March 1879, Harnack stated the object of his programme of historical investigation as the reversal of the trend towards 'philosophical evaporation of our saviour.[167] Dogma is to be corrected by history.

Many criticisms have been directed against the 'history of doctrine', which must lie beyond the scope of this brief account.[168] Nevertheless, one decisive criticism, of immediate relevance to this study, must be made. Harnack appears oblivious to the epistemological consequences of his own specific historical location. For example, his own profoundly anti-metaphysical presuppositions concerning the nature of knowledge make it impossible for him to enter into dialogue with a world-view which accepted as axiomatic a rather different understanding. Kantian assumptions concerning the nature of knowledge – part of Harnack's inherited cluster of 'self-evident' presuppositions[169] – inevitably tend to cause those entertaining them a certain degree of scepticism concerning those of Hellenism. Modern values and norms effectively control Harnack's assessment of the concept of dogma. Harnack's own view of the nature of Christianity, as well as his historical methods and understanding of the nature of knowledge, are distinctly located in nineteenth-century Germany. Harnack here appears to fall victim to the naive tendency of individuals to regard their specific historical location, including its associated modes of discourse and frameworks of rationality, as providing a privileged standpoint from which others may be evaluated.

The difficulty here noted concerns the 'double hermeneutic' (see pp. 97–8), by which both the *interpretandum* and *interpretans* are recognized by an external observer as being equally open to covert cultural conditioning, despite the assumption on the part of the *interpretans* that an objective assessment of the *interpretandum* is actually being offered. 'Objectivity', as I have stressed, is an historically conditioned concept. Although Harnack does not consider the question in any detail, presumably regarding it as of scant importance to his programme, it must be asked whether the theories of knowledge and representation associated with what Harnack loosely designates 'Hellenism' can be set aside as historically outmoded, or whether they represent a genuine option in modern theological reflection. The notion of *philosophia perennis* is certainly vulnerable to criticism from the standpoint of the sociology of knowledge; nevertheless, there exists a long-standing tradition of adopting metaphysical approaches to Christian theology which continues to find patristic Christological speculation a valuable contemporary resource, rather than an outmoded liability. Harnack occasionally appears to suggest that, since 'Hellenistic' frameworks of rationality have been historically eroded, dogma can serve no useful purpose in the modern period. A more reliable judgement would be that, for those who find such frameworks plausible, dogma continues to be a helpful and legitimate means of articulating the significance of Jesus of Nazareth, and does not occasion the anxieties noted by Harnack.

As I argued earlier (pp. 52–66), the transition between narrative and an interpretative framework must be regarded as an historically inevitable and theologically intelligible and legitimate development. The proclamation of the gospel cannot be confined to those cultural units prepared to think only in narrative forms, as if other frameworks of rationality were invalid or incapable of expressing, at least in some form, the significance of Jesus of Nazareth. The transition is not, however, historically irreversible; Harnack's identification of Luther as a pivotal figure in the history of doctrine is correct, in that Luther may be regarded as asserting the priority of the Christian narrative over the interpretative metaphysical framework which it engendered.

Nevertheless, Harnack's insistence that history should be the critic of dogma remains significant in one major respect. If it can be shown, on historical grounds, that an element in the interpretative framework does not legitimately arise from the narrative which underlies it, that element may reasonably be regarded as of questionable validity. For Harnack, the idea of incarnation was a direct result of Greek metaphysics, and had no place in the gospel itself.[170] The reliability of this particular judgement is questionable; nevertheless, Harnack must be considered correct in his demand that we interrogate the Christian doctrinal tradition closely concerning its intellectual pedigree, with a view to eliminating those components which are clearly reiterations of Greek metaphysical axioms rather than evangelical insights.

In a perceptive study, Maurice Bévenot notes the general tendency to think of the process of doctrinal development 'as a kind of *expansion* of elements that were entrusted to the Church from the beginning, an expansion or fructifying of seeds of Christ's own planting'. Bévenot, however, notes that development may also take another form, which has generally been overlooked. 'Instead of being an expansion, the fructifying of a scriptural plant, it can on the contrary be the *pruning* of some too vigorous growth'.[171] The biological analogy is not without its difficulties; nevertheless, it serves to make a point familiar to the historian of doctrine, who is aware of the possibility of retraction of previous doctrinal formulations in the light of their perceived inadequacies. History, through establishing the intellectual pedigree of certain notions current in Christian theology, is in a position to suggest that these notions should be eliminated from Christian doctrinal formulations as spurious growths.

An excellent example, unfortunately not given full weight by Harnack, is the patristic axiom of the divine *apatheia*.[172] The notion of the absolute unchangeableness of God resulted from the fusion of certain selected, but far from representative, biblical insights with axioms of divine perfection associated with what Harnack designated 'Hellenism'. As a result, the Christian tradition became committed to a view of God which placed severe limits upon his activity, omnipotence and omniscience, and exercised a decisive influence over traditional discussions relating to Christology (did the incarnation involve God in change?) and the problem of suffering (can God be said to suffer?)[173]. The recognition that this axiom did not originate from the scriptural narrative itself, but from pagan notions of divinity subsequently given fuller expression in Greek metaphysics, may be regarded as liberating Christian theology from a self-imposed bondage to Hellenism at this point. Luther's concept of *Deus crucifixus*, central to his theology of the cross, may be regarded as a deliberate challenge to this development.[174] A similar situation arose through the interpretation of the scriptural phrase 'the righteousness of God' in terms of Ciceronian conceptions of distributive justice, whereby the imposition of an alien framework of rationality caused a radical alteration in the meaning of a fundamental theological concept: once more, credit for the exposure of this distortion may be given to Luther.[175] The application of Harnack's critical historical methods into the intellectual pedigrees of doctrines also serves to expose the Cartesian origins of many contemporary theological axioms. For example, Alasdair MacIntyre points to the fundamentally Cartesian concept of God implicated in modern discussion of the problem of evil, when he notes that 'the God in whom the nineteenth and early twentieth centuries came to disbelieve had been invented only in the seventeenth century'.[176] The historico-critical identification of intrusive Cartesian elements in recent Christian doctrinal debates and theological reflection is necessarily prior to their elimination and reformulation, perhaps on Wittgensteinian lines.[177]

While the suggestion, implicit within much *Dogmengeschichte*, that doctrine is an outmoded form of articulating Christian insights must be regarded as implausible, the assertion that history must be permitted to criticize doctrine remains valid, to the point of being of crucial importance in the contemporary task of evaluating and reappropriating the doctrinal heritage of the Christian tradition. The intellectual and historical credentials of this heritage must be investigated, with a view to ascertaining how and why a given doctrine gained its plausibility within the community of faith, with a view to eliminating those found to be deficient. The ecumenical and apologetic implications of this process are potentially considerable: how many doctrines which divide the churches from one another,[178] or which cause bewilderment to outsiders, owe their origins to presuppositions alien to the gospel? Theology needs its Harnacks, if it is to address such questions.

The Authority of the Past: The Covert Influence of Ideology

The present chapter has documented the attitudes to the doctrinal heritage of the past encountered in the modern period, and the criteria employed in evaluating this legacy. Without wishing to reduce Christian theology to an ideological epiphenomenon, an ideational superstructure erected upon a socio-economic base, the history of this discipline suggests that ideological factors are a major consideration in shaping a theologian's attitude to the past; questions of 'truth' concerning attitudes to the past may thus ultimately reduce, at least in part, to the question of whether a conservative or progressive ideology happens to be dominant in a given situation. (I use the terms 'conservative' and 'progressive' as defined in Marx's *German Ideology*, accepting the inevitable conceptual limitations which result).

In that there is no universally valid or specifically privileged framework of rationality, the question of which of a variety of competing rationalities is to be adopted becomes of acutely pressing importance. Neutrality or absence of commitment in this respect is an impossibility: a decision to adopt one of a considerable number of rival conceptions is inevitable. As Alasdair MacIntyre stresses, the frameworks of rationality associated with liberalism and fundamentalism are equally open to challenge, despite the naive assumption of the superiority of the former by those with liberal precommitments.

> To the readership of the *New York Times*, or at least to that part of it which shares the presuppositions of those who write that parish magazine of affluent and self-congratulatory liberal enlightenment, the congregations of evangelical fundamentalism appear unfashionably unenlightened. But to the members of those congregations that readership appears to be just as much a community of prerational faith as they themselves are but one whose members, unlike themselves, fail to recognize themselves for what they are, and hence are in no position to level charges of irrationality at them or anyone else.[179]

There is unquestionably a general trend among theologians, from the Renaissance onwards, to adopt an attitude to the past consonant with the experience of, and perspective on, the world particular to their specific social group within their specific historical generation within their specific sociopolitical and cultural system. For example, it is evident that the Renaissance attitude to the theological preoccupations and conclusions of the medieval period is conditioned by ideological, rather than historical, considerations. As a matter of deliberate policy, the medieval period was declared to be devoid of cultural value. A pervasive climate of suspicion concerning its intellectual credentials was generated, on the basis of ideological criteria, which still persists even in the closing decade of the twentieth century. This ideological approach to the Middle Ages is reflected in the writings of early Reformed theologians, such as Zwingli and Vadian, who assume – as a self-evident truth – that there is nothing to be gained by entering into dialogue with theologians of the period. This serves to highlight the ideological tensions between the early Lutheran and Reformed factions, in that Luther – who declined to adopt the ideology of the Italian Renaissance and its theological implications – insisted on entering into a dialogue (however critical) with the representatives of late medieval theology. Both these, of course, were opposed to the radical ideology which advocated a total break with the past, and whose theological transposition involved the rejection of the authority of the past in favour of direct individual revelation. These three divergent strands within the Reformation movement represent a fundamental clash of ideologies, rather than mere differences of theological method or susbtance.

It is therefore necessary to register a certain degree of hesitation concerning the image of 'selecting' criteria for evaluating the authority of the past, in that this image suggests an active choice on the part of the agent. A more nuanced account of this process would suggest that a certain outlook on the authority of the past is (possibly unconsciously) *presupposed* within the group to which the theologian belongs, reflecting its social needs and aspirations, and that this is received and assumed as self-evidently correct. There thus is no evidence, for example, to suggest that Zwingli consciously determined to marginalize scholastic theology, on account of its unacceptable methods or doctrines; he appears simply to have assumed that medieval theology was irrelevant, on the basis of the general intellectual climate of the peer group to which he belonged (the Swiss and Austrian humanist sodalities of the 1510s). Such attitudes were part of the intellectual furniture of a social grouping, and were subsequently transposed into theological affirmations.

Attitudes to the past appear to function as theological premises, rather than conclusions, reflecting the extent to which modern theology is subject to ideological conditioning.

In noting that there is a significant ideological component to the attitude of an individual or group to the authority of the past, I am not suggesting that, for example, a conservative political attitude is *necessarily* linked with a traditionalist approach to the doctrinal inheritance of the past. Rather, I am drawing upon a cultural analysis similar to that found in Nikolaus Monzel's neglected study of doctrinal traditionalism, in which the phenomenon was investigated at both the phenomenological and sociological level. Although perhaps unduly reliant upon Mannheim's idiosyncratic notion of ideology, Monzel was able to demonstrate a significant degree of correlation between religious (more specifically, *doctrinal*) and political conservatism.[180] Whatever sociological explanation may be advanced to explain this (and the equivalent correlation between political and religious radicalism), the phenomena unquestionably point towards the existence of such a correlation.

The significant parallel between specifically *religious* and more general *cultural* attitudes to the past suggests that at one level modern Christian theology may be treated as doing little more than reflect one aspect of more general cultural trends. If this is correct, the importance of Hegel's insights concerning the relation of philosophy and culture (and, more specifically, the cultural role of the intellectuals: see p. 136) must be conceded. Conservative and progessive ideologies tend to find their appropriate theological expression. Certainly exceptions exist – but the general trend is decisive. Tensions which might be represented as a quest for 'truth' might more properly be described as the inevitable outcome of conflicting foundational ideologies. To illustrate this point, we may consider the modern conflict between university theologians and the ecclesiastical establishment.

The tension between academy and church has often been portrayed as that of academic freedom and integrity on the one hand, and of consciousness of standing within a corporate tradition on the other.[181] On this view, academic theology is unfettered by such restricting factors as tradition or a sense of corporate loyalty, and is free to explore reality without precommitments; whereas the church tends towards uncritical and unreflective affirmation of the doctrinal heritage of the past, which it jealously guards as a matter of principle. A responsible account of the development of doctrine should therefore marginalize the contribution of the church (in that it is uncritical, uninformed and backward looking), and concentrate upon developments within academic theology (which is radically open to the future, without precommitment). While there is unquestionably some truth in this characterization, it is potentially seriously inadequate in that it fails to pay due attention to the significantly different social roles assumed by university and church at crucial periods in intellectual history, such as 1770–96, the 1830s or the 1960s (to name but three). Limitations on space make it impossible to discuss this point in full detail; to illustrate the factors I have in mind, I shall consider the social role of the German universities and intelligentsia in two of these formative periods.

In the *Aufklärungszeit* the universities, for reasons already indicated, generally fostered the progressive and modernist ideology of the Enlightenment, in conscious opposition to that of the *ancien régime*. Part and parcel of this ideology was a critical attitude to the religious past, with prioritization of present religious experience and rational reflection. The perceived need to deprive the old order of its intellectual and cultural weapons led to a sustained assault upon the notion that the past was endowed with any authority or insights currently denied to the individual thinker. A conscious decision to disarm the past of intellectual authority thus *preceded* the devising of academic strategies by which this goal might be acheived. With occasional exceptions, on the other hand, the German Lutheran church was usually regarded as sharing the vested interests and prejudices of the established order, generally retaining a high regard for doctrinal formulations of the past as part of that order. To a certain extent, the Lutheran church justified its social position and religious views by an appeal to tradition – a Gordian knot which the Enlightenment felt able to cut. A clash of ideologies thus conditioned the theological disagreements between the academy and church of the period, which were seen as one specific conflict in the more general confrontation between the orders of the past and the future – a confrontation in which neutrality or inconsistency were generally regarded as unthinkable.

This tension did not disappear with the waning of the Enlightenment; it was, however, modified to a significant extent, in that the criticism of the established church and its doctrinal formulations extended beyond the universities. The post-Napoleonic period seemed to many merely to restore the same reactionary state of affairs as that which had existed in the mid-eighteenth century. The social unrest accompanying the new political activism of the 1830s led to a polarization between cultural and political radicalism on the one hand and conservatism on the other developing in the 1830s and 1840s, reflected in the emergence of right- and left-wing Hegelianism. The strong cultural affiliations of Hegel's system (whether viewed from an idealist or materialist stance) inevitably meant that 'Hegelianism' was prone to echo cultural tensions. Karl Rosenkranz' comic drama of 1840 (in which the problem of succession within the Hegelian school was to be settled by a shooting match at Berlin)[182] hints at the seriousness of the social and political divisions within German society at the time, echoed in the tensions within Hegelianism following Hegel's death. The sensation accompanying the publication of Strauss' *Life of Jesus* (1835) was partly due to its appeal to socially and religiously alienated progressive elements, who recognized it as a useful propaganda weapon in their concerted attack on each and every aspect of the German establishment.[183] An important contemporary witness to this polarization is W. H. Riehl, who argued that the period witnessed the emergence of a new 'intellectual proletariat' which had broken with the old social and intellectual order, and saw themselves as the new *ecclesia militans*.[184]

The evidence for this suggestion is impressive, and is particularly so in the specific case of theology. Of the total graduate output of German universities in the 1830s, two in every five were theologians.[185] Ecclesiastical positions of any kind became increasingly difficult to find: despite the sharp increase in population which is so significant a feature of German social history in the 1830s, the number of ecclesiastical posts available decreased over the period 1815–40.[186] Perhaps three or four theological graduates in every ten might hope to find employment of this nature.[187] The situation in the universities was even more bleak, with contractions, moratoria and salary cuts becoming a regular feature.[188] Simultaneously, however, establishment figures (such as the landed aristocracy) were given particular preference in obtaining positions in the civil and ecclesiastical administration, causing intense anger among those outside this privileged section of the community. As a result, there were many disaffected and unemployed graduate theologians who saw themselves as members of the new 'intellectual proletariat', prepared to assault the civil and religious establishment. The emergence of a socially alienated, theologically literate, anti-establishment lay intelligentsia is one of the more significant consequences of the social history of Germany in the 1830s.

Earlier, I drew attention to the importance of establishing the grounds of plausibility for attitudes and beliefs, on the basis of the dictum of Barnes and Bloor (p. 100):

> All beliefs are on a par with one another with respect to the causes of their credibility. It is not that all beliefs are equally true or equally false, but that regardless of truth and falsity the fact of their credibility is to be seen as equally problematic. . . . This means that regardless of whether the sociologist evaluates a belief as true or rational, or as false and irrational, he must search for the causes of its credibility. In all cases he will ask, for instance, if a belief is part of the routine cognitive and technical competences handed down from generation to generation. Is it enjoined by the authorities of society? Is it transmitted by established institutions of socialization or supported by accepted agencies of social control? Is it bound up with patterns of vested interest?[189]

The two general attitudes to the past we have identified in eighteenth- and early nineteenth-century Germany are both susceptible to explanation upon sociological grounds.[190] The grounds of their plausibility are linked with their social function, and the manner in which they are associated with institutions and agencies which have vested interests in their propagation. The credibility of an affirmative attitude to the past is linked with the perception of the threat posed to the vested interests of certain social groups by radical change; that of a negative attitude towards the past is linked with a set of patterns of social alienation, culminating in the perception that the vested interests of specific socially alienated groups are best served by a total break with the *ancien régime*. Both attitudes are fostered and transmitted (at a range of levels, including that of religion) within their respective social groupings, in the service of their patterns of vested interests.

While it has become a commonplace to assert that a conservative attitude to the past reflects vested social interests, there has been an undue lack of attention paid to the ideological aspects of the Enlightenment attitude to the past. By insisting that this latter attitude is ideologically conditioned, I do not intend to dismiss it *tout court*: ideological conditioning is a perennial feature of the history of ideas, and discredits the Enlightenment attitude to the past as little as it does a more conservative attitude. Rather, I am insisting that the allegedly 'objective' programme of the

Enlightenment is not immune from the common pattern of ideological conditioning and legitimation of patterns of rationality and social structures. It reflects an integrated system of beliefs, assumptions and values, not necessarily true or false, which reflects the needs and interests of this specific social group or class at a particular period in history. It is 'objective' only in the sense that it is constantly reinforced by the structures of the social groupings to which it is specific;[191] it is not objective in the sense that it is detached from and independent of the interests and precommitments of the Enlightenment.

A further development of relevance here is the sociologically significant theme of professionalization. The growth of the university sector in the Enlightenment era led to the professionalization of most academic disciplines. For example, the academic development of *Historik* (that is, discussion of the nature and practice of historical writing, research and thinking) in German universities over the period 1750–1900 can be shown to reflect this social development,[192] as can the development of academic philosophy in the twentieth century under the influence of Russell and Husserl.[193] As a result of this development, certain intellectual pursuits were detached from their original context within the community as a whole, and localized within specific institutions, especially universities. Philosophy and theology, once held to be activities open to all in the community (a presupposition reflected in Renaissance concept of the intellectual), increasingly became isolated from that broader community as they became concentrated upon the narrower academic community and its associated institutions.

In part, this development may be discerned as underlying the perceptible trend towards social marginalization of these academic disciplines. An academic's professional status was increasingly held to be open to compromise through association with non-academic institutions (in the case of theology, the church). The professionaliz-ation of academic theology is reflected in a growing tendency for university theologians to distance themselves from the life of the churches, lest their professional status might be thought to be compromised. A similar professionalization is evident within church structures, leading to the growing perception that 'academy' and 'church' (to employ what is probably an over-worked distinction) defined different professional groupings with relatively little in common. The origins of this rupture between the community of faith and academic theology may be traced to the growing professionalization of both academy and church since 1750, reflecting a significant general social development of the period affecting academic life in general, rather than theology in particular. While the sociological concept of a 'profession' may require revision (perhaps along the lines of Michel Foucault's notion of a 'discipline'),[194] the point I wish to make is that the growing trend in the modern period to professionalize both academic theology and ecclesiastical direction led to the emergence of a growing hiatus between the universities and the community of faith (especially evident in modern New Testament scholarship)[195] for fundamentally social reasons.

A direct comparison of the attitudes of academic and ecclesiastical religous writers on the theme of the authority of the past at the time of the Enlightenment thus cannot be held simply to represent academically neutral and informed opinion on the one hand, and inherent and blind conservatism on the other, as if the former were totally free of vested interests and bias. The outlooks of both parties are conditioned by their respective ideologies, by their distinctive patterns of social *rootedness* and vested interests, and by the different (and increasingly professionalized) social functions associated with (and, to a certain extent, imposed upon) both the academy and the church. Both a radical and a conservative attitude to the past may be 'explained' on sociological grounds. Both ideologies and theologies are constantly reinforced by the social structures to which they are specific. It is perfectly proper for the historian to chart the rise of the progressive ideology of the *Aufklärung* in its various forms, correlating the rise of the religious component of the movement with its political, social, scientific and moral counterparts.[196] This procedure often demonstrates the close relationship between academic theology and developments in intellectual history in general, itself a significant conclusion. The questions of the nature of doctrine and the authority of the past were not, however, debated solely in academic circles but can be shown to be a widespread concern within ecclesial bodies in general, and leading thinkers within those bodies in particular. The community-orientated character of doctrinal formulations requires us to insist that these cannot be ignored.

Considerations such as these lead us to register considerable hesitation in the traditional pattern of writing historical theology.[197] In dealing with the period 1750–1850, for example, it is customary to centre upon the theologians of the Enlightenment, followed by

Schleiermacher and Hegel, along with those who orbited their respective theological suns (in orbits of varying eccentricity), such as Baur, Strauss, and Feuerbach. In doing this, one is recording what is predominantly an academic movement, centring upon German universities in a period which saw those institutions assuming a quite definite social role, which is in turn reflected (to set aside for one moment the question of causality) in their religious ideas and methods. It is potentially to concentrate upon one ideological strand in society, exercising a sociological selectivity which, to a certain extent, predetermines perceived patterns of development over the period. While the present writer is acutely aware of the deficiencies of the notion of *histoire totale*, the insistence of the *Annalistes* (such as Gerard Bouchard) upon the need for comprehensive analysis of the totality of phenomena (rather than those which happen to interest the historian, or fit in with predetermined schemes) has important consequences for the writing of the history of doctrine, the evaluation of trends in doctrinal development, and the contemporary appropriation of the doctrinal heritage of the past.

Thus – to give one example – the *Repristinationstheologie* (similar in its appeal, presuppositions and methods to the roughly contemporaneous Oxford Movement) of the period 1830–60 was occasioned by factors which had no direct bearing upon the German universities: it was precipiated by the Kiel pastor Claus Harm, and given added impetus through the 1830 anniversary of the Augsburg Confession, and the publication of the Erlangen edition of Luther's works. The movement was concerned with a recovery of the past legacy of Lutheranism, and a reassertion of the authority of the past in the present – a significant reversal of a general trend. Yet, as this movement originated outside an academic context, was largely influential only in ecclesiastical circles, reflected a conservative ideology, and to a marked extent diverged from trends in academic theology, it is generally marginalized in accounts of nineteenth-century religious thought – especially those which are concerned to portray the history of Christian thought as a uniformly evolving entity.

Repristinationstheologie is thus not to be seen as a reversal of a trend within a progressive ideology, but the reassertion of an older, more conservative ideology. Similar remarks apply to the Oxford Movement in England. But why should this latter ideology be marginalized in any account of our themes? It is true that it is not dominant in the academic sphere, but it nevertheless exercises considerably greater influence in ecclesiastical circles. A total account of the history of doctrinal formulations and attitudes to the authority of the past – which lies far beyond the scope of this work – would not be restricted to any one ideology or social grouping (such as academic theology), but would attempt to document attitudes to these questions across the entire spectrum of Christian opinion, from popular religion on the one hand to academic theology on the other. The writing of such an *histoire totale* is an essential prerequisite for an informed discussion of the future of the past. Equally, a theory of the 'development of doctrine' (to which I propose to return in a later work) would have to give a fully nuanced account of the relation of doctrinal developments *at every level of Christian articulation* to ideological shifts, obliging a more serious and sustained engagement with social history than anything seen in the sociologically deficient accounts of Harnack, Overbeck or Werner.

What might such an *histoire totale* of doctrine look like? On the basis of the ample quantitative analyses available, a sketch of the situation in the United States of America in the closing decade of the twentieth century would probably reveal that most Christians see no difficulties whatsoever with reappropriating the doctrinal heritage of the past; that many even see little difficulty in recreating (or 'restoring', to use their term) the New Testament Christian communities in modern America; that the pertinent questions addressed to the academy and church by academic theologians find their audience largely in the increasingly isolated academic theological community itself (now generally regarded as something of an irrelevance by most Christians and by most other university faculties.) The value-laden judgement (characteristic of much nineteenth- and twentieth-century *Dogmengeschichte*), to the effect that it is the opinions of academic theologians, and not those of ordinary individuals within Christian communities, which are the proper subject of the 'history of doctrine' is countered by *histoire totale*, which refuses to impose such qualitative judgements upon its quantitative analysis.[198] The criticism which modern social history has directed against the methods and presuppositions of 'history from above' – which have been characteristic of much *Dogmengeschichte* from its inception – has yet to penetrate the discipline.

Perhaps there are some who will feel moved to censure the ideas developed within this study because they might seem to endorse a 'conservative' thrust in theology.[199] I have to confess that I have a certain degree of scepticism concerning the value of such a precommitted stance, which criticizes allegedly conservative positions precisely because they are conservative.[200] If the ideas developed in this study are conservative, they represent a chastened conservativism, alert to the potential vulnerability of such an approach. In any case, the hardened categories of 'conservative' and 'radical' or 'liberal' now seem quite inappropriate for the needs of the contemporary theological debate, which requires reformulation of the theological problem rather than its crude restatement within an already archaic framework of polarities. It is by no means only 'conservative' theologians who insist on ascribing authority to the past, just as the demand to *criticize* the past in order to construct the future is by no means restricted to 'radicals'.

But, in the end, it is appropriate to ask whether this criticism has any particular merit. Viewed at the ideological level, conservative approaches to doctrine are clearly incompatible with the values and rationalities of liberalism. This is not, however, to suggest – still less, to conclude – that such conservative approaches are unjustified or unjustifiable; it is merely to note that they contradict and subvert the network of values and precommitments of liberalism. In view of the increasing willingness of liberal thinkers to recognize that their theory and practice are, after all, those of 'one more contingently grounded and founded tradition, in conflict with all other rival traditions'[201], it would seem fair to suggest that this contradiction and subversion of liberal values and rationalities cannot be numbered among the arguments advanced *against* a conservative understanding of the authority of the past.

Equally, conservative approaches to religion cannot be dismissed on account of the fact that they are 'value-laden', 'tradition-bound', or 'precommited'. That they are precommited in this manner is beyond dispute; but the implication would seem to be that alternatives (such as liberalism) are not, and are thus to be preferred. It is one of the many virtues of MacIntyre's *Whose Justice? Which Rationality?* that it disabuses us of the idea that liberalism represents a privileged and disinterested vantage point from which other doctrinal or religious traditions may be evaluated. Rather, liberalism entails precommitment to liberal values and rationalities; it is as value-laden and precommited in its judgements, and as tradition-bound in its approach, as its conservative rivals.[202] 'Like other traditions, liberalism has internal to it its own standards of rational justification. Like other traditions, liberalism has its set of authoritative texts and its disputes over their interpretation. Like other traditions, liberalism expresses itself socially through a particular kind of hierarchy.'[203] In part, the liberal distrust of conservative approaches to doctrine resides in its inherent distrust of substantive conclusions, and its precommitment to continuing debates for their own sake.[204] Doctrinal formulations are seen as premature foreclosures of debates which, by their very nature, ought to be declared permanently open. The conservative emphasis upon the provisional and fragmentary character of Christian doctrine is, in liberal eyes, vitiated on account of the concomitant stress upon its authoritative and identity-giving nature, which is viewed by some liberals as tantamount to authoritarianism. The conservative approach to doctrine is dismissed as static and rigid, seriously out of line with liberal values. Nevertheless, this amounts neither to a justification of liberal values, nor to a criticism of conservative approaches. Both conservative and liberal approaches may be treated as 'integrated systems of beliefs, assumptions and values, not necessarily true or false, which reflect the needs and interests of a group or class at a particular time in history'.

In that ideological shifts are virtually impossible to predict, grand theories of future attitudes to the past within the Christian church are somewhat hazardous. The theologian, after all, is not a clairvoyant. What may be said, however, is that a study of past attitudes to this question leads one to suppose that social groupings – whether ecclesial bodies or theological faculties – in which a conservative ideology is already dominant, or comes to be dominant, will regard the past as continuing to shape the present; whereas those in which a progressive or modernist attitude dominates will assign priority to present experience and reflection according to socially-legitimated frameworks of rationality. Individuals are predisposed to such attitudes by ideological considerations, often unconsciously assimilated at a pre-theoretical level. Criticism and evaluation of these theological attitudes to the past cannot therefore realistically be undertaken in isolation from the cultural systems which they reflect, nor that of the culture to which the critic belongs. A 'double hermeneutic' (see pp. 97–8) is implicated, in which the respective ideologies of proponent and opponent alike condition the resulting debate. There is no reason for suggesting that theological controversies represent nothing more than the clash of ideologies; nevertheless, this conflict is unquestionably a largely unacknowledged major component of many recent religious debates in western Europe and North America. The sterility of most of these debates derives in part from the failure to recognize that they cannot be isolated from the much broader debate concerning the contemporary cultural attitude towards the past.

If this analysis is correct, it may be predicted that the doctrinal legacy of the past will continue to be regarded as authoritative, in varying ways and to varying extents, within the Christian church throughout the world, to the extent to which a conservative ideology is dominant in society. If the present rapid decline in a liberal ideology continues from its zenith in the 1960s, the proportion of the Christian community which treats the past with high regard may be expected to increase accordingly. The theologian may be reduced to despair by the fact that it is ideological considerations, rather than a precise theoretical analysis, which tend to govern attitudes to the past, in however pre-theoretical a manner; nevertheless, the importance of ideology in shaping attitudes and conditioning outlooks can hardly be ignored, especially by those committed to the notion of religion as a cultural system.

A new respect for the past does not dispense those sympathetic to a conservative ideology from engaging with the difficulties which the notion of 'the authority of the past' raises. Indeed, the material presented in the present chapter may be regarded as setting the agenda for the remainder of this work, in that the questions raised by the Enlightenment and its successors cannot be ignored. In this respect, it is not of *decisive* consequence that the Enlightenment criticism of the past may arise, in part, from a deliberate and systematic attempt to discredit a conservative ideology, or that it is rooted in a specific socio-historical situation which cannot be recreated today: the objections raised and difficulties noted have academic merit, and demand at least a provisional response. One's attitude to the past may be conditioned by cultural considerations – but the viability of this attitude cannot be maintained without engagement with the critical questions it raises. An ideologically conditioned attitude to the past – whether positive or negative – cannot be maintained in the face of massive empirical and theoretical difficulties, in which ideological presuppositions are called into question.

I have already suggested that, on account of the nature of Christian doctrine, an appeal to the past is inevitable. The memory of the generative event of Christian doctrine imposes itself upon contemporary doctrinal reflections. I have also suggested that a growing trend towards a conservative ideology lends added weight to this observation. It may, however, be objected that the past is, as a matter of fact, dead. The 'pastness of the past' should, it might be suggested, be explicitly recognized. A provisional response to this point would include drawing attention to its obvious phenomenological inaccuracy, in that the memory of the past is of foundational significance in many areas of human existence, particularly in cultural spheres. It is, however, the *theoretical* aspect of the objection which is of greater importance. In what manner may a theoretical framework be constructed which lends philosophical credibility to the obvious cultural tendency to remember – and value – the past?

The Recollection of the Past: A Theoretical Model

'Complexity' is a word which necessarily recurs in assessing the manner in which the doctrinal heritage of the past has actually been evaluated and appropriated by the present. The critical historical analysis of the development of Christian doctrine disrupts neat biologically inspired theories of the evolution of doctrine by recording the counterfactual. Karl Löwith has documented how a belief in divine providence gradually came to be replaced within nineteenth-century thought by a belief in human progress: both were as attractive to their proponents as they were phenomenologically deficient, prompting the supporters of both to exercise a selective approach to the data, consistent with their belief in providence or progress. Doctrine does not, however, evolve in a linear progression, although by judicious preselection of the data, such a pattern may be imposed upon the historical phenomena by the theologian precommitted to this paradigm. In fact no single paradigm may be identified which adequately accounts for the phenomena with which the 'total history of doctrine' is encountered. The Renaissance appeal to antiquity; Luther's fascination with Augustine in the 1510s; the new interest in seventeenth-century Anglicanism on the part of the Oxford Movement of the 1830s; Barth's preoccupation with the period of Reformed Orthodoxy; the reappropriation of Luther's 'theology of the cross' by Jürgen Moltmann and Eberhard Jüngel in the 1970s; all illustrate a recurring theme of the history of doctrine

– the continued interest in, and critical reappropriation of the ideational heritage of the past. An idea originally finding its place within one framework of rationality or conceptual scheme may be imported to another,[205] with any resulting shifts in meaning considered to be acceptable; others – even those closely linked with reappropriated ideas – may be abandoned as of purely antiquarian interest. Two groups of thinkers, even those sharing much the same cultural situation, may adopt radically different attitudes to the past, and particularly the authority of its doctrinal formulations. The past may be treated by some as a quarry for theological resources, where others treat it as an intellectual charnel house for ideas now obsolete. Above all, prevailing secular attitudes to the past – whether positive or negative, whether academic, political or cultural – are transposed, often unconsciously, into theological affirmations by those sympathetic to those attitudes, with the result that labels such as 'conservative' and 'liberal' – originally designating specific political attitudes – came to be applied to theologians perceived to be linked with such attitudes and the ideologies underlying them. We shall return to a more detailed exposition of this theme in the following chapter. Our attention, however, is claimed by the need to give some form of theoretical foundation to the observation that doctrine does not develop in a linear manner. How are we to give an account of this observation?

Fortunately, such a theoretical framework is to hand in the 'Theses on the Concept of History' of Walter Benjamin (1892–1940) – possibly the most important cultural theorist within the Marxist tradition – reflecting disillusion with the Marxist notion of historical development in the aftermath of the trauma of the Nazi–Soviet Pact of 1939. Underlying the Marxist view of history (as expounded, for example, in Marx's preface to *A Contribution to the Critique of Political Economy*) is the notion of development within history, culminating in the inevitability of socialism, which may be explained upon the basis of such factors as the growth of productive forces.[206] Socio- economic evolution is thus identified as a force mirrored in both ideological (I use the term in a non-Marxian sense here) and political structures. History is thus not a blind anarchic process, but an evolutionary development, the unfolding of which may be accounted for by historical materialism.[207]

Commenting on the thought of José Ortega y Gasset, one of the more significant writers of the Spanish 'generation of 1898',[208] a modern scholar observes that 'an historical crisis' may be defined as 'a period in which the first principles that underlie a pattern of culture slowly die in the depths of collective consciousness. The relentless criticism of experience gradually reveals their inaptness to cope satisfactorily with the problems of life. The world built upon them is at the end of its tether.'[209] The rise of Nazi Germany in the fourth decade of the twentieth century may be regarded as precipitating an 'historical crisis' of considerably greater significance than the doubts concerning Spain's role in the modern world entertained by the 'generation of 1898'. At one level, Benjamin's 'Theses on the Philosophy of History' may be regarded as a cry of despair, in the face of the evident failure of historical materialism to account for the empirical data of history, prefiguring anxieties on a larger scale within Marxism in the closing decades of the twentieth century. The traditional Marxist assertion of the historical inevitablity of socialism seemed to some about as reliable as Dr Pangloss's declaration that this was the best of all worlds. In particular, the inadequacies of traditional Marxist approaches to the past[210] were intimated through the erosion of tradition by the rapid pace of events in Nazi Germany in the period 1936–9. In insisting upon the cultural and aesthetic importance of the past, Benjamin's central concern is to account for the persistence of 'remembrance' within intellectual activity, despite the theoretical prediction that evolutionary development *precludes* precisely this phenomenon.[211]

Benjamin argues that cultural history (as expounded by Dilthey and Ranke) covertly defines 'history' as 'history, written from the perspective of the victors', thus degrading the concept of progress to that of patterns of domination and oppression. Benjamin's theory of *Jetztzeit* attempts to break with this conception of 'progress' in order to establish a specific relation to the past, in which the images of the redeemed life – expounded in terms of *la promesse de bonheur* – are filtered out from the continuum of history, in order to assume their full trans-historical significance. Within history, certain moments are of genuinely trans-historical significance, capable of impinging upon the historical flux at later points, despite attempts by an oppressive present to suppress their memory. It is clear that Benjamin has the cultural programme of the Third Reich in mind at this point.

It is the fourteenth thesis which particularly concerns us. For Benjamin, it is a simple fact of history, obvious to anyone familiar with the history of culture, that the past is *not* universally perceived as dead and irrelevant. Although Benjamin's terse prose prohibits full historical illustration of this point, the few examples he provides are intensely significant. He notes that Robespierre regarded ancient Rome as charged with present-day significance for his own day and age, allowing it to stand out from the continuum of history for this reason. Similarly, he points out, the French Revolution viewed itself as a return to ancient Rome in this respect.[212] The Renaissance appeal to antiquity may be regarded as illustrating precisely the same point, although Benjamin does not exploit this. The basic principle which Benjamin identifies is that the present moment (*Jetztzeit*) involves the intermingling of the past and present, especially at the aesthetic level. The past injects an impulse into the historical continuum, which is appropriated at specific subsequent periods, if ignored by others. The present leaps like a tiger into the past. It is out of our history, as Marx remarked, that our new history is to be made. The historical continuum mediates the past to the present, in order that the latter may appropriate the former, however selectively.

It is not unreasonable to suggest that the influence of Marcel Proust's *A la recherche du temps perdu* lies behind Benjamin's reflections on the manner in which the past imposes itself within the present.[213] Throughout Benjamin's 'Theses on the Concept of History' is to be found the notion of recollection, occasionally tending towards a disjointed conception of time. The past is dead, in the sense that it is chronologically discharged – yet the present moment is able to salvage at least part of its heritage, and assimilate it. There is a sense of solidarity with the past. As Jürgen Habermas points out, this process of recollection is not necessarily aesthetically discriminatory, in that it can lead to the reappropriation of barbarism as much as culture;[214] nevertheless, Benjamin's point primarily concerns the *ability* – however aesthetically questionable it may be – of the present to spring into the past, like a tiger.

Benjamin's 'Theses on the Concept of History' thus provide a model which incorporates the notion of historical development (including the explicit recognition that the present is *not* identical with any past moment) with the pervasive and observable tendency of the present to 'recollect' – in the dual sense of 'remember' and 'pick up again' – the past. The present is able to reach back into the past, and appropriate – however selectively – what it finds there. The past is not regarded as dead; rather, it is viewed as a source of creative impulses, running parallel to the continuum of history, which may impose themselves upon that continuum. At times, Benjamin appears to envisage the present as active in appropriating the past; at others, to regard the past as active in imposing itself upon the present. Nevertheless, despite such unclarities, Benjamin's theoretical account of the manner in which the legacy of the past may fuse with the present allows important insights to be gained – perhaps the most obvious of which is the recognition that the phenomenon of reappropriation of the *doctrinal* heritage of the past involves no special claims for Christian theology; rather, it illustrates a general tendency of human historical and cultural reflection.

More important, however, is his demonstration that the notion of chronological historical continuity – that is to say, the unidirectional evolution of history – is not inconsistent with an appeal to the past, nor even with a creative reappropriation of the past. Benjamin's theoretical account of history allows *Historie* (history as that which is past) to become *Geschichte* (history as that which is existentially relevant and personally appropriated).[215] The evolution of the historical continuum does not involve leaving the past behind forever; the past (or at least part of it) remains part of the present, almost as if (to use Benjamin's model) it possessed a parallel existence, which occasionally broke into the present. 'Nothing which has ever happened is to be regarded as lost to history' (Thesis 3). In other words, the idea of 'pastness' implies neither forgetting nor losing, but rather the possibility of recollecting and reappropriating. The voices which we now hear are echoes of voices of the past, now silenced (Thesis 2) – yet, in some sense, still present and available. The present possesses the ability to recollect the *historisch* as the *geschichtlich*, setting to one side the associations of 'pastness' in order to disclose and illuminate present possibilities. The Enlightenment insistence that this *ought not*, indeed *cannot*, be done is set to one side as manifestly at variance with the empirical observation that it *is* done. Benjamin's model thus suggests that there are no overt historical contradictions implicated in the suggestion that the evolution of doctrine proceeds, at least in part, by the creative and critical reappropriation of the doctrinal heritage of the past – a heritage which is not experienced as dead, but as possessing potential vitality, should a theological tiger leap to reclaim it.

Of particular interest for our purposes, however, is Benjamin's covertly messianic understanding of history, which reflects significant strands in the Old Testament understanding of the nature of history.[216] Thesis 9 in particular draws upon prophetic imagery and expectations, which Benjamin focuses upon the image of 'the angel of history'.[217] (In 1921 Benjamin obtained a copy of Paul Klee's *Angelus Novus*, which served him as an object of meditation for the remainder of his working life.) The flight of the angel serves as an image both of continuity on the one hand, and the possibility of recollection of the past on the other, within the continuum of history, from its beginning to its end.[218] Benjamin uses the biblical image of Paradise to designate primal impulses within history, which are 'recollected' later in the continuum of history.

Benjamin's model is capable of being reworked Christologically, with the history of Jesus of Nazareth assuming the function which Benjamin assigns to Paradise. The memory of Jesus of Nazareth, embodied in certain specific historical forms and traditions, pervades the historical continuum, and is capable of being 'recollected' or 'remembered' throughout history. It is the generative event of the history of the communities of faith, in much the same way as Benjamin uses the image of Paradise and 'happiness (*Glück*)' to designate a fundamental impulse of general human history. The history of doctrine may therefore be approached as a process of recollection, of recalling the fundamental impulse of Christian faith and communal reflection. How that history and its mediating traditions may be reappropriated will vary according to the location within the continuum of history; nevertheless, the fundamental stimulus to and impulse of doctrinal reflection remains this generative event in history. On the basis of Benjamin's model, there are no fundamental difficulties raised by the suggestion that the memory of Jesus is a fundamental impulse to contemporary doctrinal reflection.

The importance of Benjamin's 'Theses on the Concept of History' lies in the fact that they originate within an interpretative tradition grounded in history (rather than in idealized abstractions). Benjamin is concerned with giving a theoretical account of the observable phenomena of historical development, especially its cultural aspects. Even though his approach to history represents a partial break with the main currents of Marxist interpretation, the seriousness with which he engages with history both reflects the strengths of this tradition, and exposes the shallowness of the Enlightenment approach to the subject. Far from laying down imperialistically what the present *may* do with the past, Benjamin attempts to give theoretical substance to what the present *does* do with the past, with a view to illuminating the form which the future might conceivably take. In view of the fact that Benjamin was writing as a leading Marxist theoretician in the 1930s, obviously thoroughly familiar with the historicist world-view, it is difficult to take seriously any suggestion that he is 'pre-modern', or insensitive to the realities of historical existence, in his outlook.

The full impact of Benjamin's theoretical account of the interaction of past and present has yet to be appreciated within the English-speaking world. Nevertheless, it is clear that his reflections on the nature of this interaction, especially as expressed in the 'Theses on the Concept of History', are of considerable significance to the theme of the contemporary reappropriation of the doctrinal heritage of the past, and reflection upon the significance of the generative event of the Christian faith. The Enlightenment dismissal of the past as dead and gone is, according to Benjamin's analysis, seriously inadequate, at both the phenomenological and theoretical levels. If Benjamin's theory is plausible, it may be argued that the doctrinal heritage of the past, and especially its generative and controlling event, will continue to impinge upon the present, and to be recollected – even by those who are not tigers by nature.

6

Tradition: Access to the Identity-Giving Past

A central theme of this work has been that the generative event of Christian doctrine is the history of Jesus of Nazareth. Prior to any attempt to articulate Christian doctrine is the community-generating and identity-giving history of Jesus of Nazareth. Christian doctrine is the response of the community precipitated by that history as it articulated its self-understanding in the light of that history. Whatever the ultimate external referent of doctrine may be, its proximate external referent is this history. Yet it is not simply facts about Jesus, but Jesus himself, who is passed on in the *actus tradendi*.[1] 'Christ is preached. And because of this I rejoice' (Philippians 1.18). What has been made known and made possible through the life, death and resurrection of Jesus of Nazareth is passed down to posterity, not as something which we are required to *imitate*, but as an enabling gift. The act of transmission is authentic, to the extent to which it is able to reproduce on the part of its present recipients the patterns of judgement and conversion evinced by encounter with Jesus of Nazareth.

But how is access to be gained to this fundamental generative and legitimizing resource of Christian faith and doctrine? The very word 'Jesus' designates an historical individual, and implies a past reference, an appeal to a moment of history which is no longer directly accessible. Historical and theological analysis concur: in so far as the significance of Jesus may be transmitted to posterity, that process of transmission necessarily involves kerygma, community, narrative and tradition[2] – a process by which the significance of Jesus of Nazareth to the human situation is proclaimed, retained and transmitted by a community. Henry Scott Holland summarized the situation with admirable clarity: 'we cannot now, in full view of the facts, believe in Christ, without finding that our belief includes the Bible and the Creeds.'[3]

The suggestion that there exists a polarity or tension between 'scripture' and 'tradition' – evident, for example, in the Decree of the Council of Trent, which seems to interpret both as independent sources of revelation[4] – is actually a somewhat recent development. The patristic period is generally characterized by an insistence upon the coincidence of scripture and tradition, and explicit rejection of the idea of extra-scriptural revelation as tantamount to gnosticism.[5] Tradition is not something which supplements the kerygma contained in scripture, but is the handing down of that kerygma within the community of faith. Recent studies of the concept of tradition in the Middle Ages have stressed the mutual coinherence of scripture and tradition:[6] tradition is an inherited manner of *interpreting* scripture and transmitting the kerygma which it contains, rather than a source of revelation in addition to scripture. This understanding of tradition poses no difficulties for theologians in the tradition of the magisterial Reformation, whether Lutheran or Reformed.[7] Indeed, as a matter of history it is fair to suggest that 'tradition' primarily designates *facienda* rather than *credenda* – practices rather than beliefs.

How, then, may tradition function as a theological resource?[8] In turning to deal with this question, we are obliged to consider more closely the manner in which the history of Jesus of Nazareth functions as a resource for the community of faith, and how access to this history may be gained.

The Inevitability of the Past

Characteristic of the historical Christian tradition is the view that, in the celebrated words of Ignatius of Antioch, 'God revealed himself through his Son Jesus Christ' (*Magn.* 8, 2). Underlying this assertion is a cluster of significant beliefs: that there is a God; that this God may disclose himself; that this self-disclosure is focused upon Jesus Christ. All these beliefs have, of course, been the subject of intense critical scrutiny, inside and outside the Christian tradition.[9] For example, as we have seen, Lessing argued that 'the contingent truths of history can never become the proof of the necessary truths of reason',[10] thus depriving the history of Jesus of Nazareth of any epistemic significance. This assertion, however, rests upon the prior assumption of an essentially Spinozan concept of truth,[11] called into question in the later eighteenth century through the rise of empiricism, in more recent times through the rise of interpretative philosophies of history such as Marxism,[12] and above all through the recognition of the social rootedness of patterns of rationality. The belief that God makes himself known to his people through his action in history, culminating in the history of Jesus of Nazareth, has also been called into question: it is suggested that the New Testament is innocent of the notion of 'revelation'.[13] However, as Pannenberg has perceptively pointed out, such criticisms seem to rest ultimately upon an improper imposition of modern concepts of revelation onto the revelational language of both the Old and New Testaments.[14]

The notion of revelation attempts to articulate and give substance to the pervasive Christian sense of the divine initiative which precedes, enables and demands a human response: before we speak, we are conscious of being addressed or called. At the soteriological level, this sense of the initiative lying with God is expressed in Augustine's concept of prevenient grace;[15] at the epistemological level, it finds its expression in the notion of revelation. The history of Jesus of Nazareth represents an initiative which is not ours (indeed, which takes the initiative away from us), and invites us to enter into a conceptual world which we ourselves did not fashion. As R. L. Hart has argued with some brilliance,[16] the very idea of revelation is inextricably bound up with the memory of the generative event which precipitates a 'hermeneutical spiral'. If the generative event, the primary *explicandum* of Christian theology is Jesus of Nazareth, it follows that we are invited to reshape our mental horizons and reconsider any prior understandings of God and human nature in the light of the story of Jesus of Nazareth. The history of Jesus of Nazareth once forced, and still forces, the redrawing of conceptual boundaries and mental horizons, demanding that we rethink and refashion our understanding of such matters as God, and human nature and destiny.

There is, however, a natural temptation to bring ready-made ideas of God (whatever their intellectual pedigrees) to the person of Jesus, and attempt to accommodate him to them. The uncritical rejection of the idea of incarnation as a 'philosophical impossibility' (Karl Jaspers)[17] is best regarded as an *a priori* assertion that it (and the view of God which it reflects) is inconsistent with a certain different preconceived idea of the nature of God. It is an unacknowledged assertion, not merely of a *conflict* of concepts of divinity – a conflict which requires resolution by inquiry concerning the intellectual pedigrees, frameworks of rationality and empirical justification of the conceptualities implicated – but of the need to clarify the manner in which frameworks of rationality are generated and transmitted. Jasper's assertion rests upon the assumption of a privileged pattern of rationality, capable of passing judgement upon others. Historical inquiry, however, would seem to indicate that Jaspers' presuppositions are historically conditioned, suggesting that his criticism might more appropriately be restated as follows: 'the idea of incarnation is inconsistent with the notion of divinity associated with a matrix of beliefs reflecting my specific historical location, conditioned to an ultimately indeterminate extent by covert ideological precommitments.'

If the idea of revelation is taken seriously, however, we must be prepared to revise, even to abandon, such prior ideas of God, and to refashion them in the light of who and what Jesus of Nazareth is recognized to be. The conflict of conceptualities implicit in Jaspers' uncritical rejection of the idea of incarnation is to be made explicit, with a view to clarifying how we know *anything* about God. Equally, his assigning priority to patterns of rationality raises the question of how such patterns are, in the first place, *generated*, and in the second place, *to be evaluated*. In common with all the inhabitants of the historical process, Jaspers has no privileged access to God which permits him to pontificate in this manner about what God can and cannot be like. Christology may thus be regarded as a permanent irritant to concepts of divinity, a theological corrective which obliges us to place question marks against even our most confident assertions concerning the nature and identity of God. The Cartesian principle of doubt may be operated at a Christological level, in that we may interrogate each and every concept of God according to its Christological credentials. Christianity is characterized by its tendency to insist that 'God' is Christologically specified, that we are constrained in our thinking about 'God' by the transmitted history of Jesus of Nazareth. The memory of Jesus is subversive, undermining our confident *a priori* assertions concerning God.

The past, then, is generative, in the sense that it precipitated lines of reflection and inquiry which continue within the historical community which arose in response to that past, centering upon a past event which is regarded as a central resource.[18] 'Truth', as understood within the Christian community, includes reference to an *event* – specifically, the 'Christ-event'.[19] Truth is something which *happens*.[20] Jesus *is* the truth (John 14.6), to note a characteristic insight of the Johannine circle.[21] The community of faith recognizes that, as a matter of history, its social and intellectual roots are to be traced back to a generative event in the past.

An analogous situation may be discerned within the Old Testament. Israel regarded herself as constituted in a dual sense by the exodus from Egypt: at the historical level, her origins were to be traced to this generative event, while at the ideological level, her social and religious structures (which we take to include both ideas and institutions) were grounded in and shaped by that experience.[22] Implicit within the exodus narratives was an quite definite specification of the form of life appropriate for the community whose historical existence was to be traced back to that generative event. The history of Jesus of Nazareth, mediated to us in narrative form through the New Testament, includes both historical and ideological elements, affirming certain patterns of belief and behaviour for the life of the community generated by that narrative. This revelation does not take an abstract or conceptual form. For example, the characteristic assertion that 'God is just' is devoid of significance unless the content of the abstract term 'just' can be substantiated.[23] In that the concept of 'justice' is contested within human societies,[24] a potentially meaningless statement concerning God is being made. Yet within the Christian tradition, the assertion that 'God is just' is associated with a quite definite pattern of behaviour and expectation, indicated by the Old Testament narratives, embodied in the history of Jesus of Nazareth, and echoed in the paraenetic literature of the New Testament. If human beings are constrained to live and think within history – with all the limitations that this imposes – then God has at least accommodated himself to our capacities (to use Calvin's memorable phrase)[25] by revealing himself in this history and in historical forms. As Karl Barth insisted, revelation demands historical predicates.[26]

An appeal to history, to the past, is thus inevitable, whether to discredit or confirm this belief (to the limited, but highly significant, extent made possible by historical inquiry). Christian doctrine arises through the attempt to engage with the history of Jesus of Nazareth, as it is transmitted to us through the New Testament tradition, in order to fuse the horizons of this history with our own history. 'A human being discovers his finitude in the fact that, first of all, he finds himself within a tradition or traditions'.[27] The theologian similarly discovers finitude through historicity, which limits modes of imagination and discourse. As Jean-Paul Sartre perceptively emphasized in his final interview prior to his death, his historicity limited his intellectual options.[28] We have inherited a framework of conceptualites and modes of discourse which simultaneously constrain the manner in which we think, yet make available insights denied by others.

The suggestion that historicity limits intellectual options raises a number of difficulties for Enlightenment rationalism (cf. p. 152). For our purposes, it is particularly important to stress that individuals (whether theologians, philosophers or natural scientists)[29] do not begin their quest for knowledge *de novo*, as if they were isolated from society and history. The Enlightenment emphasis upon knowledge gained through individual critical reflection, deriving from Descartes,[30] has been the subject of considerable criticism in recent years on account of its uncritical rejection of the corporate foundations of knowledge.[31] The specific historical situation of early Enlightenment thinkers may allow us to understand this rejection, and even to justify it on ideological grounds at that specific juncture: the *standsortgebunden* character of this criticism of the corporate foundations of knowledge, however, lessens – perhaps even to the point of vitiating – its present-day significance. The corporate memory of the community – whether scientific, philosophical or religious – passes on ways of viewing the world, of asking questions, of thinking, to each generation. Each succeeding generation is at liberty to criticize received views and methods, and pass on revisions to their successors. They do not, however, begin *de novo*, but from a received tradition.

The importance of this point is stressed by the historian of Marxism, Leszek Kolakowski, who points out that critical engagement with a tradition is an essential element of creative thinking. Although Kolakowski is primarily concerned with political theory and praxis, his comments are pertinent to most intellectual fields. 'The cult of tradition and the reaction against tradition are equally indispensable for social existence. A society in which the cult of tradition becomes all-powerful is condemned to stagnation; a society in which the revolt against tradition becomes universal is condemned to annihilation.'[32]

It thus involves no special pleading for the status of Christian theology to observe that the Christian faith does not come into existence in a conceptual vacuum, but is both generated and informed by a corporate tradition – the proclamation of the community of faith. The ideas, claims, symbols and structures of rationality of Christianity are not passed down in a random or stochastic manner: they are channelled, protected and directed in a more or less organized manner through the historical institutions of the Christian churches.[33] While the Christian tradition has tended to stress that it is none other than God himself who is the ultimate cause of faith, its more immediate cause is the proclamation of the community of faith. Indeed, underlying the affirmation, 'I believe in Christ', may be detected a latent 'I believe in the church': the transmission of the content of the tradition depends, to a limited but highly significant extent, upon the fidelity of the bearer of that tradition.

It is within this community that a tradition[34] is transmitted concerning the significance of the history of Jesus of Nazareth. Jesus is affirmed to provide a focus for the identity of the Christian community, in that this community discerns its identity with reference to nothing less and nothing other than Jesus of Nazareth. It is this community which retells the story of the great saving acts of God in history, culminating in the history of Jesus of Nazareth. It is this historical community which evokes the memory of the crucified Christ, and responds to it in worship and adoration. It is this community which insists that the paradigmatic shape of the redeemed life is to be discerned only in Jesus of Nazareth.[35] It is this community which recognizes the Bible as incorporating the formative and identity-giving traditions of the Christian faith, and insists that such scriptures be preserved, read and expounded in worship.[36] It is this community whose proclamation of the existential significance of Jesus has, directly or indirectly, led to the confrontation of those outside its historical bounds with the demand for faith, and subsequently informed the content of that faith. The generation of *fides qua creditur* and *fides quae creditur* alike is historically linked with the community of faith and its reception, interpretation and transmission of the tradition concerning Jesus of Nazareth. The Christian faith is made available to us through a historical tradition, transmitted and propagated through a community of faith, and shaped by the manner in which that community worships and prays.[37]

In dealing with the cluster of questions attending the genesis of doctrine, we are therefore obliged to deal with the communally transmitted authority of the past, supremely the history of Jesus of Nazareth, and the manner in which our knowledge of that past arises. The themes of the genesis of doctrine and the authority of the past interact as plot and subplot. For if Jesus is indeed the primary *explicandum* of Christian faith, the fundamental legitimizing resource of the community of faith, the question of how and what we know about him demands careful consideration. For, as the methodology of the natural sciences emphasizes, the manner in which knowledge derives decisively affects the nature of that knowledge itself.[38] In other words, how something is known determines what may be known concerning it. The manner in which we know about Jesus has a decisive effect upon *what* we know about him, thus restricting the manner in which we interpret him. In that Christian doctrine arises through wrestling with the tradition concerning Jesus of Nazareth, doctrine and history are inseparable.

The very idea of 'tradition', however, has been the subject of considerable criticism in the modern period, on account of the anti-tradition rhetoric of the Enlightenment, which we shall now turn to consider.

The Enlightenment Prejudice against Tradition

As indicated earlier, the Enlightenment attitude to tradition reflects its underlying ideology – the strategic break with the past (pp. 155–60), and the tactical appeal to the present-day resources of individual experience and reason. As a matter of principle, tradition is declared to be epistemically bankrupt, a source of intellectual enslavement rather than liberating knowledge. Jeffrey Stout summarizes this modern 'flight from authority' thus: 'Modern thought was born in a crisis of authority, took shape inflight from authority, and aspired from the start to autonomy from all traditional influence whatsoever.'[39] The Enlightenment axiom of the adequacy of the intellectual resources of the living individual had as its corollary the belief that the past could not give access to religious or moral information denied to this individual through immediate experience and rational reflection.[40] Michael Polanyi provides a neat summary of this negative attitude towards tradition:

> We were warned that a host of unproven beliefs were instilled in us from earliest childhood. That religious dogma, the authority of the ancients, the teaching of the schools, the maxims of the nursery, all

were united to a body of tradition which we tended to accept merely because these beliefs had been previously held by others, who wanted us to embrace them in our turn. We were urged to resist the pressure of this traditional indoctrination by pitting against it the principle of philosophical doubt.[41]

The notion that one should think for oneself, rather than be coerced into acceptance of existing patterns of faith or morals, clearly has much to commend it. Implicit in much of the anti-tradition rhetoric of the Enlightenment, however, is a tendency to blur the crucial distinction between *choosing* and *constructing* beliefs; between making beliefs one's own, and making one's own beliefs.[42] A 'prejudice against tradition', in its defensible form, demands that tradition should be evaluated critically; rhetoric, however, runs ahead of reality if it is suggested (or allowed to be understood) that traditional beliefs are untenable, simply by virtue of their being mediated by tradition. Four major criticisms may be directed against the general Enlightenment 'prejudice against tradition'.

First, it is sociologically naive. As I stressed earlier (pp. 152–60), frameworks of rationality are socially conditioned and historically located. Once accepted, this insight calls into question the Enlightenment concept of 'individual rationality'. Frameworks of rationality are social constructions, whether this is explicitly recognized or not. Human minds do not come into being in isolation but are shaped by the process of social living and shared corporate conceptions of rationality.[43] It is a sociological commonplace that the corporate memory of the community passes down ways of envisioning the world and asking questions concerning it, which condition the terms on which, and framework within which, knowledge grows and is subjected to criticism, at both the corporate and individual level.[44] Jeffrey Stout stresses that the modern 'quest for autonomy was also an attempt to deny the historical reality of having been influenced by tradition':[45] such a quest was thus doomed to failure, he observes, on account of its unacceptable a-historical presupposition. Thus, as Martin Heidegger stresses, we are thrown into a situation which predisposes us to certain interpretations: even before an individual begins to consciously interpret a text or grasp the meaning of an event, he or she has already placed it within a certain context (*Vorhabe*), approached it from a certain perspective (*Vorsicht*), and conceived of it in a certain manner (*Vorgriff*).[46] The individual is constrained by his or her historicity, which limits intellectual options by shaping given frameworks of rationality and accepted methodologies. You cannot escape from history by climbing into a stove – even when this process is dignified with the description of 'the principle of philosophical doubt'. The suggestion that you can is 'a kind of Robinson Crusoe dream of the historical Enlightenment, the fiction of an artificial island, as artifical as Crusoe himself for the alleged primary phenomenon of the *solus ipse*.'[47]

Individual reason is thus unable to begin speculation *de novo*, but is obliged to enter into dialogue – however critical – with a received tradition. Indeed, the individual reason has already pre-judged matters, precisely because it operates on the basis of unacknowledged pre-understandings of method, rationality and knowledge. It is this insight which underlies Gadamer's famous maxim: 'It is the tyranny of hidden prejudices that makes us deaf to the language that speaks to us in tradition.'[48] The recognition that all understanding involves pre-judgement is of central importance to responsible Christian attitudes to the authority of the past, as it is in any science concerned with understanding or interpretation.

It might be assumed that the natural sciences represent an obvious exception to this rule. This, however, is not the case. As theoreticians such as Thomas Kuhn and Michael Polanyi emphasize, the advancement and criticism of knowledge takes place within a growing framework of experience and knowledge, handed down by the scientific[49] community. Polanyi, for example, stresses the importance of adherence to a common tradition of investigation, shaped by the methods and presuppositions of the past.[50] The natural scientist stands within a tradition, which he simultaneously receives and criticizes. The manner in which natural science views problems, poses questions, and proceeds to investigate them, is conditioned by a communal tradition. It is, however, a *dynamic* tradition, in that his method of inquiry, although based upon past communal experience, is subject to criticism and development in the light of the manner in which it discloses reality. The tradition is not static, in that it is not committed to a permanent way of viewing problems or investigating them: it is open to self-correction in the light of experience, which in turn defines the communal tradition from that point onwards. 'Radical change' or 'new departures' are actually modifications to a tradition, which allow and propose new and unexpected ways of maintaining continuity with that tradition.

Kuhn points to the need for a 'paradigm',[51] or way of envisaging and investigating the world, which is the common tradition of the scientific community. The accumulation of experience and knowledge within the scientific community defines a way of approaching the natural world, a frame of reference which influences the way in which problems are identified as requiring solution, in which questions are asked and in which solutions sought. Every now and then, a 'paradigm-shift' occurs, as the inadequacies of previous frames of reference are disclosed through the accumulation of knowledge.[52] It is important to appreciate that Kuhn envisages a paradigm in a sociological manner (as a set of scientific habits) rather than philosophically (as a *Weltanschauung*): it is something concrete and pre-theoretical – a puzzle-solving device.

What is particularly significant concerning the views of both Polanyi and Kuhn on tradition is the manner in which corporate and individual knowledge are understood to interact. The inevitable outcome of the phenomenon of the accumulation of knowledge is tradition. Both stress that the corporate framework or paradigm of the scientific community may be challenged by an individual. The research of an individual – a Galileo, a Newton, or an Einstein – may call an entire paradigm into question. The work of others, however – destined to remain largely unknown outside the scientific community for this very reason – may *confirm* the reliability of existing paradigms. There is thus a constant questioning of the paradigm, of the traditional framework, which either serves to confirm its validity or demonstrate its need for revision. The tradition does not confront the individual as an oppressor, but as a catalyst, something which offers a starting point, a provisional way of envisioning and investigating the world, which points the way ahead, facilitating a process of inquiry which may result in its own modification.

Secondly, the phenomenological accuracy of the Enlightenment critique of tradition must be challenged. Gadamer argues that 'prejudice (*Vorurteil*)' and tradition are an integral and essential part of the human phenomenon of understanding, drawing on the phenomenology of Husserl to illustrate his point.[53] For Husserl, any understanding of an object involves the understanding of that object *as* something, projecting a meaning upon perception which may not strictly be included within that perception itself.[54] Husserl's phenomenological analysis of anticipatory perception and the preliminary projection of meaning within the process of perception is viewed by Gadamer as possessing significant hermeneutical insights. This 'anticipatory perception' goes beyond the evidence available; nevertheless, in order to gain any preliminary understanding of an object, I must make some initial judgement concerning it. This judgement is purely preliminary, and is open to modification as the process of understanding proceeds. For example, I might encounter a book entitled *Convictions* by one Donald Coggan, and make the preliminary assumption that it concerned his prison record. This preliminary judgement would, I think, be corrected as I read the book.

Gadamer thus stresses that 'prejudice' is simply a preliminary judgement (*Vor-Urteil*) made before the evidence in its entirety has been assessed. It cannot, therefore, be dismissed out of hand: 'prejudice' is merely a starting point, an anticipation of meaning, which is dynamic rather than static. Tradition may pre-judge a question – but this is merely to set up the dynamic interaction of individual and communal perception, essential to the advancement of knowledge. Tradition passes down a communal anticipatory perception as a 'preliminary judgement' for the individual to evaluate. In other words, it demands – rather than denies – the exercise of individual judgement and discrimination. The individual is asked to evaluate the judgements of others. Unless those judgements are to be denied to him, or to be dismissed without consideration, some framework for the transmission of corporate knowledge and understanding is essential. The individual must interact with corporate knowledge, this latter being viewed dynamically rather than statically, as open to criticism and development. Precisely the same interaction noted above within the scientific tradition occurs in other disciplines, to which Christian theology is no exception.

Developing this insight, Gadamer argues that there is no necessary antithesis between authority (or corporately based knowledge, mediated by tradition) and reason (or individual reflection).[55] If the Enlightenment operated with the model of the thinker as an isolated ahistorical individual, unshaped by history and society, Gadamer invites us to consider the thinker as a receptor, transmitter and evaluator of knowledge and understanding which are already part of the intellectual furniture of his world. Gadamer stresses the significance of *Wirkungsgeschichte* – the operative force of tradition over those within it, who remain conditioned by it, whether they accept or reject it.

A third difficulty arises through the observation that the Enlightenment attitude to tradition appears to be ideologically conditioned (see pp. 152–60). The 'prejudice against tradition' characteristic of leading Enlightenment thinkers is consonant with the experience of, and perspective on, the world particular to their specific social group within their specific historical generation within their specific socio-political and cultural system. The suggestion that tradition *could* convey relevant information to which access is otherwise denied is, in effect, excluded as a matter of principle, on account of its subversive implications. Earlier, I indicated that a central task set by the sociology of knowledge for the historian of ideas is to account for the *plausibility of beliefs* (pp. 100–2). For what socio-political reasons did a given belief gain plausibility? The negative Enlightenment attitude to tradition owes its plausibility, not to any formidable difficulties associated with the concept of corporate knowledge, but to the conservative attitude to society and politics which was perceived as being linked to this. The Enlightenment attitude to tradition is part and parcel of a total ideological package, reflecting the socio-political situation in eighteenth-century Europe, especially Germany. Its plausibility does not derive primarily from difficulties with the idea of corporately transmitted knowledge, but from fear of the social and political implications of this idea. This is not to say that the Enlightenment attitude to tradition may be dismissed as a total social construction, serving the vested needs and interests of the social groupings to which Enlightenment thinkers belonged; rather, it is to suggest that this attitude does not arise from any difficulties associated with, or inconsistencies within, the idea of corporately transmitted knowledge itself.

A fourth difficulty is raised by the suggestion that Christianity is not the 'republication of natural religion' (to use a characteristic and sociologically innocent Deist phrase),[56] but is a phenomenon whose ideas and outlook are shaped by the history of Jesus of Nazareth. The very use of the term 'revelation' challenges the suggestion of the autonomy or self-constitution of our understanding of ourselves or of God, and expresses the characteristically Christian idea of an initiative that does not lie with us. 'The mode of speaking of the Christian tradition,' writes Eberhard Jüngel, 'insists that we must be told what we are to think of the word God.'[57] Any suggestion of this sort was unacceptable to the Enlightenment, which saw in it an irrational appeal to superstition and authority (in the pejorative sense of the term). If, however, characteristically Christian concepts and values are in any sense determined, or even influenced, by the history of Jesus of Nazareth, as I argued to be the case in the previous section, the question of how we may gain access to his history becomes of considerable importance. For this history is mediated through the New Testament, which itself embodies a core of oral tradition. To ascribe authority to Jesus of Nazareth, to imply that we are in any sense authorized to ground our talk about God in his personal history,[58] is to acknowledge the importance of tradition in shaping our mental horizons. Information concerning Jesus is not scattered randomly throughout the universe, but is transmitted through certain definite social and literary channels. The formative traditions of the Christian communities, as we have them in the New Testament, both channel and protect information concerning Jesus of Nazareth which those communities felt it important to transmit. It is thus necessary, as a matter of theological pragmatism, to recognize that our knowledge of Jesus and his perceived significance for the first Christian communities are transmitted to us by tradition.

Tradition, then, may be regarded as the transmission, through certain quite definite historical institutions and social channels, of a cluster of interpretations of the significance of Jesus of Nazareth which, in principle, purport to be open to verification or falsification. The Enlightenment criticism of tradition is valid to the extent that it reminds us of the need to interrogate this tradition closely concerning its authenticity and reliability. The Enlightenment insistence that tradition cannot, as a matter of principle, convey relevant religious information unattainable by other means must, however, be regarded as vulnerable.

But how reliable is that tradition? How much historical weight may be attached to the memory of Jesus transmitted by the communities of faith? The psychology of human memory has important insights to offer in this context, which it is appropriate to consider at this point.

The Memory of the Past

The New Testament embodies the formative traditions of the Christian communities concerning the generative event both of those communities as social entities, and as bearers of an outlook upon life. Much attention has been paid to the possible social channels of transmission, with the needs and aspirations of the various early Christian communities being the subject of considerable speculation.[59] Inadequate attention, however, has been paid to the manner in which the past has been remembered – to the human memory processes underlying this transmission of tradition. While it is unquestionably true that social channels and communities are of considerable importance in the transmission of the memory of Jesus, the form in which that memory is encoded is of particular interest in relation to the historical validation of tradition. The psychology of human memory has significant insights to offer concerning the memory processes underlying the transmission of the tradition of Jesus, and in casting light on the historical reliability of the tradition concerning Jesus. In the end, the plausibility of that tradition is inextricably linked with the reliability of the memory processes involved in its preservation and transmission. Three points may be singled out as particularly important.

In the first place, the formative narrative traditions concerning Jesus of Nazareth must be regarded as having the psychological status and function of personal recollections, rather than of memorized data. Furlong suggests that a distinction may be made between retentiveness and retrospection:[60] retrospection includes as one of its major characteristic features a reference to context in time and space, with its attendant imagery. Similarly, Reiff and Scheerer draw a distinction between two primary forms of memory: those with an autobiographic index, and those without. The former are always accompanied by an experience of personal continuity through time, lacking in the latter.[61] A related distinction underlies Tulving's concepts of 'episodic' and 'semantic' memory:[62] episodic memory is concerned with unique, concrete personal experiences dated in the rememberer's past; semantic memory refers to a person's abstract timeless knowledge of the world, shared with others. The distinction allows us to understand the enhanced memorization of data with a personal reference – such as the narratives concerning Jesus of Nazareth.

In the second place, this information is transmitted in a narrative form. This is, in effect, the only literary form capable of expressing structurally time and history. The personal reminiscences embodied in the formative traditions of the New Testament demand expression in narrative form. Attention has, however, been drawn recently by psychologists to the facility of memorization associated with narrative structures. The facility with which epic narratives – such as the *Iliad* – were memorized in the ancient world is well-known. More recently, Bower and Clark have pointed to the particular value of narrative structures in memorizing data and subsequently recalling it: even unrelated lists of items can be memorized with enhanced facility if they are linked as elements in a narrative.[63] Narrative thus represents a literary form with enhanced possibilities for memory retention, even of unrelated events. The narrative structure of the synoptic gospels, and narrative substructures of certain key Pauline passages (such as Galatians 3.1–4.11), thus rest upon what was the most reliable form of memorization process then available.

In the third place, it is evident that the constituent elements of the formative traditions of the New Testament were passed down by a process of repetition. Once more, attention has been drawn by psychologists to the importance of the strategy of rehearsal for the memorization of complex data as a memory process unique to humans.[64] Rehearsal of data – essential to the process of corporate transmission by oral tradition – ensures its transition from short-term to the long-term memory of the individual, and hence of the community. The psychological and physiological basis of this strategy is not understood; its effectiveness is, however, undisputed.[65] The religious significance of this strategy for preserving the memory of Jesus is particularly enhanced through the importance attached to explicit public *anamnesis* of the culmination of the narrative of Jesus of Nazareth in his death and resurrection, even in the most primitive forms of eucharistic formulations (for example, 1 Corinthians 11.23–6).[66]

These three considerations do not allow extravagant conclusions concerning the historical reliability of the traditions concerning Jesus to be drawn. They do, however, point to such traditions being generated and remembered under the optimum conditions available to human memorization processes at the time. However, while the subject of the generation of the formative traditions of the Christian community remains a subject of considerable interest in its own right, it is the *function* of these traditions which particularly concerns us at this juncture.

The Hermeneutical Importance of a Community Tradition

It has already been noted that the study of intellectual history discloses a significant phenomenon: the present is able to empathize with, and even to selectively appropriate, the past. The use to which Renaissance Florence put classical Roman culture illustrates this point, as does the manner in which nineteenth-century Italian writers turned to the Renaissance for inspiration and example.[67] Neoclassical Germany found remarkably little difficulty in empathizing with classical Athenian aesthetics.[68] The fact that the modern Christian church has relatively little difficulty in appropriating the ideas and language of the New Testament fits this common pattern. These cases illuminate a common factor of central importance to the reappropriation of the past: *communal continuity with the past*. The past generated a tradition to which the present is heir. That tradition involves modes of discourse, ways of conceiving the world, and so forth, which it impressed upon the world, and which was perpetuated in a definite historical form, being mediated through both institutions and individuals. A community arises as the bearer of this tradition, thus establishing its continuity over extended periods of time. Those standing within this tradition detect a resonance of values, language and concepts with the past, in that their outlook has been shaped by a community tradition precipitated by the past. It is not, however, the past *in general* which assumes this status, but that specific cluster of events which precipitates the tradition within which the interpreter stands.

One of the most important reasons why I find it so difficult to understand the Azande or the Dinka tribes of Africa – who exist in my own day and age – is that their ideas and values have not been mediated to me as formative or identity-giving. I do not perceive myself as standing within a tradition precipitated by them, nor do I perceive us to share a common foundational tradition. The alleged strangeness of Jesus to many modern western persons is partly due to the fact that they do not stand within a community tradition oriented towards him, due to the secularization of their culture. Individuals sympathetic to the aims and objectives of an aggresively secular culture tend, as a matter of principle, to stand outside of and marginalize the Christian tradition; that the content and language of that tradition sound strange or irrelevant to such individuals cannot simply be taken as evidence of any deficiency or shortcoming within the Christian tradition itself.

As the history of Christian missions in Africa and on the Indian subcontinent suggests, the generation of a tradition which is orientated towards the foundational events of the Christian faith, and which is able to appropriate and empathize with its language and conceptualities, is of central importance in the embedding of the gospel in a culture. Once such a tradition has been established, and continuity with the past affirmed, the process of consolidation and expansion may begin. Cultural resistance to the foundation of such a community and tradition is considerable: nevertheless, the history of Christian missions – whether to Anglo-Saxon England or nineteenth-century East Africa – indicates that it can be done, and has been done. A community is generated, the outlook of which is shaped by reference to the past. Others joining this community take up its outlook, allowing its tradition to shape their worlds. Membership of the Christian community – proclaimed as a universal possibility – is recognized as entailing acceptance of the governing role of its traditions. The identity of the individual becomes linked with the history and story of the community.[69] It is therefore reasonable to suggest that a communal tradition is central to religious epistemology,[70] particularly in relation to the question of the relevance of the past. Kant's idealized fictional 'knowing subject' may be set to one side, and its place taken by an individual who is conscious of standing within a communal tradition. This latter is no idealized fiction, but a genuine historical existence.

A particular moment in the past thus assumes significance because it is held to be of historical and ideological importance for a community. Its historical importance may derive from its being the moment when the existence of the community was precipitated, thus ensuring that this moment remains part of the collective consciousness of that group. Its ideological importance derives from the possibility that this foundational event shapes and conditions the present perceptions of the community.

In the case of the Christian faith, the history of Jesus of Nazareth is regarded both as establishing the community of faith and shaping its outlook on life and mental horizons. That history precipitates and shapes the intellectual contours of the resulting community. A pattern of existence is disclosed, which is proclaimed to be a present possibility within the community. Zwingli perceived a significant isomorphism between the group memory of the foundational event of the Helvetic Confederation and that of the Christian community: both commemorated the foundational event which brought them into being, and both regarded their collective identity as being, to some extent, shaped by that event.[71] In the case of the Christian community, the memory (*anamnesis*) of that event is perpetuated in its eucharistic liturgy, which recalls and proclaims the present- day relevance of the foundational event. The *strangeness* of that event and its proclaimed meaning is diminished through a process of familiarization, as newcomers to the community learn its idiom. To become a member of any community – whether of pigeon breeders, software designers, or coffee blenders – is to learn its idiom, its mode of discourse, appropriate to its tasks and horizons. However strange it may appear initially, that idiom is subsequently discovered to be embedded in the situation of that community, and adapted for its needs and purposes.

We may be condemned to live in history – but that imprisonment does not take the form of solitary confinement. We exist within communal traditions, within the historical lives of particular social groups. To be, or to become, a member of the community of faith is to become part of the historical existence of that group. In that this community orientates its values and modes of discourse towards the history of Jesus of Nazareth, this past moment is perceived as part of the present. The strangeness of the narrative, language and symbols of faith diminishes through a process of exposure and familiarization. If the history of Jesus of Nazareth both makes possible and discloses the contours of Christian existence,[72] and if Christian existence is thought – at least by some – to be a good thing, then the continued relevance of Jesus of Nazareth to the community of faith is guaranteed.

Alasdair MacIntyre has persuasively argued that Cartesian foundationalism is to be set aside in favour of an historicist epistemology,[73] in that different traditions disagree concerning frameworks of rationality, the nature of evidence, and the conditions under which a truth-claim may be regarded as decisively proven. The interpretation of the significance of an historical event – whether Caesar's crossing of the Rubicon or the crucifixion and resurrection of Jesus of Nazareth – is to be determined by its historical context.

It is clear that such a contextual framework is provided by the narrative tradition of the Old Testament, and the manner in which this was perceived to interlock with the history of Jesus of Nazareth.

The framework of rationality employed in interpreting the history of Jesus of Nazareth was already present in the Palestinian cultural milieu, shaped by the Old Testament narrative of the activity of God in history and the expectations this engendered. The historical continuity of Judaism and Christianity is matched by continuity of modes of reasoning and evidence, which eventually conspired to force the historical and social bifurcation of the movements. This communal tradition defined the appropriate mode of reasoning and the framework of conceptualities to be employed in the interpretation of this history.[74] Within this communal tradition, the history of Jesus was perceived to have the range of significance now found in the New Testament; had other frameworks of rationality, such as that associated with the *Aufklärung* been employed, a different understanding of the identity and significance of Jesus would have resulted. Nevertheless, the fact remains that the historical community which identified Jesus as redeemer, Son of God, and so forth, employed a framework of rationality grounded in the Old Testament, which has been perpetuated by the New Testament community of faith, and reinforced by the historical events upon which that community is grounded. It is within the parameters employed by this community, and *only within these parameters and within this community*, that Jesus is perceived to have this identity and significance.

Perhaps, as the rise and fall of the 'life of Jesus' movement reminds us, there will always be a case for exploring what the significance of the history of Jesus of Nazareth within alternative frameworks of rationality (particularly those of the Enlightenment) might be. But what justification may be given for those alternative frameworks, and specifically for their use in such a Christological context? One of the most important contributions of the Enlightenment to the shaping of the modern world has been its aspiration to provide criteria and methods of rational justification, independent of the historical contingencies of time and place, by which beliefs and courses of action in every sphere of life could be evaluated. These criteria and methods could thus be applied to the history of Jesus of Nazareth as much as to any other event or idea. Yet, as Alasdair MacIntyre reminds us, the quest for a universal framework of rationality, independent of the vexatious contingencies of history, remains frustratingly unresolved:

Both the thinkers of the Enlightenment and their successors proved unable to agree as to what precisely those principles were which would be found undeniable by all rational persons. One kind of answer was given by the authors of the *Encyclopédie*, a second by Rousseau, a third by Bentham, a fourth by Kant, a fifth by the Scottish philosophers of common sense and their French and American disciples. Nor has subsequent history diminished the extent of such disagreement. Consequently, the legacy of the Enlightenment has been the provision of an idea of rational justification which it has proved impossible to attain.[75]

The legitimate demand that the insights of the Christian tradition be justified would therefore seem to face certain difficulties, given the evident lack of agreement over what criteria might properly be employed. This is not to evade the point at issue, but rather to stress the provisionality and historical contingency of all frameworks of rationality. There are no tradition-independent standards of argument or reason available by which the Christian tradition may be evaluated. All inquiry begins from some specific social and intellectual past – whether that of the Enlightenment or the New Testament – to which we have affiliated ourselves through a tradition of thought and inquiry.[76] A superficial reading of this section might seem to suggest that we are taking resort in 'fideism', in which rational criticism and intellectual justification of the Christian faith are declared to be improper as a matter of principle. A more careful reading, however, will indicate that we are registering an informed hesitation over the validity of the notion of some privileged 'universal rationality' which such criticism and justification presuppose. The Enlightenment belief that there exists a universal tradition-independent vantage point from which the 'rationality' of traditions may be evaluated is only marginally less indefensible than the assumption that the Enlightenment happened to occupy this position. This vantage point is not merely presently uninhabited; it is inherently uninhabitable, in that it stands outside the flux of human history and social existence. The Christian tradition may indeed be evaluated by the standards of another historically-contingent tradition; the notion, however, that it may be evaluated (presumably to be found wanting) by some universal rationality, purified of the contingencies of history, would seem to be a notion which is distinctly located in history, prior to the growth of historical insight.

Considerations such as this tend to suggest that the discipline of doctrinal criticism has its proper sphere within the community of faith, on the basis of those criteria which it recognizes as significant. Doctrine cannot be regarded as an isolable aspect of the Christian faith, as if it could be detached from the community of faith and treated as a purely ideational phenomenon. Christian doctrine belongs within the Christian tradition, inextricably interwoven within its various elements. The close interaction between the doctrines, symbols, values, patterns of life, and identity-giving narratives of a community is such that outsider perspectives would seem to be intrinsically incapable of making the judgements necessary to evaluate doctrine. This is not, however, to suggest that the phenomenon of Christian doctrine is immune from outside criticism and evaluation; it is to point out that criticism and evaluation presuppose agreement over the criteria thus to be employed.

All criteria have a history; for Christianity, however, history itself is a criterion. As has been argued throughout this work, Christian doctrine is a response to the history of Jesus of Nazareth. Its achievements and successes, its failures and weaknesses, are all to be judged with reference to that history. That history is mediated through a tradition, and socially embodied in a tradition-orientated community, whose *anamnesis* of its foundational and legitimizing event shapes its sense of identity, commitment and purpose. Doctrinal criticism finds its natural context within that community. Outside the community of faith, Jesus of Nazareth will continue to be interpreted according to rival theories of truth and reason; within the community of faith, however, Jesus of Nazareth remains the central object of worship, adoration and wonder. And in that sense of wonder lies the genesis of doctrine.

The Future of Doctrine

Throughout this work, it has been stressed that it is not merely individual Christian doctrines, but the phenomenon of Christian doctrine itself, which are susceptible to historical development and analysis. The historical circumstances and pressures leading to the genesis of doctrine may, within reasonable limits, be identified, as may those which contribute to the course of its historical development. The fact that the conditions under which doctrinal formulations came into existence and subsequently developed may be understood naturally poses a significant question: given what we know, or may reasonably infer, concerning the origins and history of doctrine, what is its future?

One of the more significant assumptions which may be detected as underlying the 'history of doctrine' concerns the historical location of doctrinal formulations. Doctrine, as a phenomenon, is primarily located in the past. It is something which may, in principle, be regarded as outmoded in a 'world come of age', a vestige of an earlier mode of thinking with which the modern period may dispense.[77] The vision of a 'Christianity without dogma' undergirded, at least to some extent, the discipline of *Dogmengeschichte*, especially as it culminated under Harnack. This notion has persisted to this day, partly on account of its attraction for those precommitted to liberal values, hesitant over the potential social divisiveness and apparent claims to particularity implicit in Christian doctrinal formulations.

In suggesting that the process of historical development has now reached the point at which the phenomenon of doctrine may be regarded as outmoded and superseded, writers sympathetic to liberal Protestantism and related movements were obliged to predict the future as much as describe the present and the more recent past. In order to do this, certain models of development had to be assumed, by which the past history of doctrine might be interpreted in order to yield predictions. It is of interest to note that the models which may be detected as influencing, at least to some extent, more recent attempts to predict the future course of doctrinal development in general, and the fate of Christian doctrine in particular, appear to derive from the life sciences.[78]

The model of biological evolution appears to have been particularly influential upon English writings of the late nineteenth and early twentieth centuries.[79] Here, doctrine appears to be envisaged as a primitive stage in the evolution of the human religious consciousness. Although an acceptable method of expressing human religious values in the past, doctrine has been overtaken by more advanced forms of religious symbolism and expression.[80] This model thus predicts that doctrine, like other less fit entities, will die out, as more developed forms of thought take its place.

A more sophisticated model might be Jean Piaget's account of the psychological development of children.[81] Although the importance of Piaget's views have been noted in relation to moral development,[82] their theological significance has yet to be fully explored.[83] Piaget distinguishes four stages in the development of the cognitive awareness and abilities of children: the *sensorimotor* phase (from birth to approximately two years, in which the child's world is dominated by sensations); the *pre-operational* phase (from two to seven years, in which the child acquires language and an enriched conceptual structure); the *concrete thought* phase (from seven to eleven years, in which inductive and deductive logic can be applied to concrete situations); and the *formal operational* stage (from eleven years onwards, in which the young person is able to think about thought itself). These four phases are hierarchical in that each stage incorporates its predecessors, building upon and modifying them.

This Piagetian model of cognitive development is considerably more appropriate to the discipline of doctrinal criticism than biological evolution, in that it is specifically concerned with the acquisition of cognitive abilities and methods, whereas biological evolution is concerned primarily with accounting for the existence of species (rather than the development of thought). If this model were to be applied by those sympathetic to the elimination of doctrine, it might be argued that doctrine represented a pre-operational or concrete thought phase, which was now superceded by more advanced forms of religious representation and symbolization in a formal operational stage.

Neither of these biological or psychological analogues, however, was developed with specific reference to human ideas. The notion that there may be direct parallels between the biological development of species or the cognitive development of a child and the overall history of human ideas may be attractive, and possess a certain degree of intuitive plausibility: nevertheless, the validity of the analogy remains to be demonstrated. As I have emphasised, the unidirectional character of biological evolutionary or developmental processes is, however, not necessarily paralleled in the world of ideas, which demonstrates an ability and an inclination to appropriate, however critically and selectively, material from the past. The importance of Walter Benjamin's *Geschichtsthesen* lies in their recognition of the anamnetic solidarity of the present with the past (pp. 166–71). A theoretical analysis which suggests that the past cannot be reappropriated is subverted by such historical phenomena, which suggest that the biological model of a unidirectional process of development is inadequate to capture the observable complexities of human intellectual and cultural progress.

In fact, it may be suggested that doctrine is likely to remain a phenomenon of continuing importance within the Christian communities in the foreseeable future. This suggestion is based on the observation that the pressures which I have identified as leading to the genesis of doctrine in the first place may still be discerned within the modern world. Were such pressures absent, it might conceivably be argued that the phenomenon of doctrine was an unecessary intrusion of the past into the present. However, I wish to suggest that the phenomenon of Christian doctrine is sustained, not simply on account of some reverence for the past (although the existence and theological importance of such respect cannot be ignored), but partly through continuing pressures of the type which may be argued to underlie the generation of doctrinal formulations. The substance of our discussion on the nature of doctrine (pp. 35–80) and the role of tradition (pp. 188–93) suggests that doctrine continues to exist because it corresponds to the perceived needs of communities of faith. That the foreseeable future holds a continuing place for doctrine is also suggested by two significant recent trends.

In the first place, the rise of aggressively secular cultures in the west obliges communities of faith to distinguish themselves from the prevailing secular order, unless they are to be absorbed by it. At one level Christian communities differ from the secular order; at another, they differ one from another. Doctrine represents the attempt of such communities to give a public description of their identity-giving beliefs. The assumption that 'church' and 'society' designate substantially the same entity (if viewed from different angles) may have been characteristic of western Europe in the Middle Ages, thus obviating the social necessity of doctrine; this can, however, no longer be maintained without a serious disjunction between theory and observation. A historical contingency relating to medieval western Europe cannot be allowed to become a theologically necessary premise governing Christian communities throughout the world in the modern period. The situation of many Christian communities in the modern western world bears greater similarity to the pre-Constantinian, rather than the medieval European, Christian churches, thus suggesting the continued existence of those social pressures which lead to the generation of new, or which emphasize the importance of existing, doctrinal formulations. A community cannot survive without certain distinctive beliefs, susceptible to public statement, which protect it against degeneration into an amorphous social and ideational entity.[84]

In the second place, the Christian tradition is constrained, both historically and theologically, by its relationship to the history of Jesus of Nazareth. The suggestion (particularly associated with the Enlightenment tradition which advanced the notion of universally valid concepts of rationality) that thought could be purified of historical contingencies such as the history of Jesus of Nazareth led some to argue that Jesus of Nazareth need no longer assume a referential or legitimizing function for Christian communities of discourse. A universally valid mode of reason and thought might therefore replace community- linked and tradition-mediated doctrines. The apparent failure of the Enlightenment to disclose definitively what such modes of thought and reason might be has raised certain pressing questions concerning the credibility of its approach, and led to a creative re-exploration of the role of tradition (see pp. 179–85; 188–93).

In the light of this development, there has been growing sympathy recently for the idea that the Christian tradition orientates itself towards an historical narrative (such as the scripture- and tradition-mediated narrative of Jesus of Nazareth), and thus articulates certain distinctive insights, opens up certain possibilities of existence, and discloses certain patterns of thought which might not otherwise be available. To make such a suggestion involves no special pleading for the Christian tradition in particular; it is to apply to that specific tradition certain observations which relate to traditions in general. Doctrine may thus be regarded as the intellectual self-expression of a living tradition, which recognizes its anamnetic solidarity with Jesus of Nazareth. Christian doctrine does not correspond directly with some universal concepts of divinity or humanity, but represents the perceived significance of Jesus of Nazareth within the community of faith. As such, doctrine must be consonant with other identity-giving functions of that community – such as worship, spirituality and prayer: *lex orandi, lex credendi*.[85] Doctrinal formulations are the product of the lived experience of a community of faith, and are reflected at all levels of its life – in liturgy, prayer, patterns of spirituality, in pastoral practice, and in theological speculation. Their meaning and power can only be appreciated when they are set in this context. A renewed interest in the narrative of Jesus of Nazareth, linked with a growing tendency to question the notion of universal frameworks of rationality, thus points to the continued existence of Christian doctrine in the foreseeable future.

On the cumulative basis of considerations such as those outlined in the present work, I venture to suggest that doctrine is unlikely to be discarded by the Christian communities of faith as outmoded or archaic, but is more likely to be reappropriated as holding the key to the identity and purposes, the goals and aspirations, of those communities in the years which lie ahead. In the end, however, it is living history rather than purely theoretical considerations which will indicate what the future of doctrine might be. Nevertheless, I feel justified in recording the view that the discipline of doctrinal criticism will continue to relate to doctrine as a living reality within the community of faith, rather than as an exhibit from a museum of intellectual history. In that the present work is intended to serve as a prolegomenon to future doctrinal criticism, the present relevance of this point, however controverted, will be evident.

Conclusion

The present work has concentrated upon a cluster of questions relating to Christian doctrine, as a prelude to subsequent engagement with a range of issues relating to the discipline of doctrinal criticism. It will, however, be clear that I am convinced that the embarrassed elimination of large tracts of the Christian doctrinal tradition by those who felt them to pose difficulties to the modern secular world represents an unjustified move in response to a specific set of historical contingencies. Liberal mediation strategies, which attempted to bridge the gap between the community of faith and secular society, appear to have set aside too much in order to gain their slight rewards. I wish to suggest that it is through the critical evaluation and reappropriation of the doctrinal heritage of the Christan tradition that the process of theological reconstruction may proceed. The liberal reformist proposal that hard ideas be made easy or eliminated, itself laudable in its intentions, has proved to have its darker side, surrendering much that now appears vital to the distinctive identity of the Christian religion. An impatience with doctrine now appears to reveal a more fundamental impatience with Christianity itself.

The analysis presented in this study suggests that evangelism is of major future importance for the survival and well-being of the Christian church, in that it is only through individuals coming to stand within the Christian tradition that they will fully understand its values, aspirations – and its doctrines. 'Unless you believe, you will never understand' (Augustine). Outsider perspectives have strictly limited potential in appreciating the 'unsearchable riches of Christ' (Ephesians 3.8), which doctrine attempts to capture and convey. The liberal suggestion that we defend Christianity by making its ideas acceptable to the secular world has been tried, and found wanting; we must now commend the Christian proclamation of judgement and conversion through Christ, with the invitation to stand within the Christian tradition, as an alternative strategy. It is thus evangelism, rather than just apologetics, which commends itself as of strategic importance in the present situation within western culture. For, properly understood, Christian doctrine is not merely a public description of what Christianity is, but represents an invitation to enter a new community and its associated conceptual and experiential world.

It must be conceded that some understanding, however limited, of the values and aspirations of the Christian community must be necessary *outside* that community if conversion *into* the community is to be possible. Some bridge is necessary, by which those outside the community may make the transition to within its bounds through at least a partial glimpse of what commitment might mean. Apologetics, understood as the explanation of Christian ideas to an audience drawn from outside the community of faith, is clearly of continuing importance as part of a broader evangelistic strategy. Nevertheless, it must be suggested that apologetics has traditionally been understood as an attempt to justify the 'rationality' or 'reasonableness' of Christian beliefs on the basis of the classic notion of universally valid patterns of reason and thought. The rise of the historicist and sociological insights discussed in the present study has rendered traditional apologetics highly questionable in its presuppositions and of strictly limited value in its goals. It remains doubtful whether two competing traditions, such as Christianity and Enlightenment rationalism, each with its associated rationalities, can really be said to 'understand' each other, still less to objectively 'evaluate' or 'justify' each other.[86] Apologetics may indeed demonstrate, and perhaps even exploit, a certain degree of overlap between these two competing traditions. Nevertheless, the arguments developed in the present work suggest that it is only by standing within the Christian tradition that the full depth and meaning of its symbols and doctrines can be understood. Evangelism, understood as the deployment of strategies (perhaps including apologetics) by which individuals are brought within the community of faith, would thus seem to combine the merits of epistemological rigour, cultural realism and social pragmatism.

Finally, it may be noted that 'tradition' means something which is handed *over*, as much as handed *down*. It is not that the past has been deposited upon our laps, like some unwanted family heirloom which we would rather do without – it is that we have been given *responsibility* for receiving, evaluating and transmitting the Christologically concentrated heritage of the past to the future. Responsibility for the contextualization and transmission of the kerygma has been transferred from the past to the present. We have been *authorized* to transfer the kerygma from the limiting conditions of the past, and locate it in the historical situation in which we now find ourselves. The doctrinal heritage of the past is thus both a gift and a task, an inheritance and a responsibility. What our forebears in the Christian faith passed down to us must be appropriated, in order that we may wrestle with it within our own situation, before passing it on to those whose day has yet to dawn.[87]

Abbreviations

ARG	*Archiv für Reformationsgeschichte*
CD	*Church Dogmatics*
HeyJ	*Heythrop Journal*
JAAR	*Journal of the American Academy of Religion*
JBL	*Journal of Biblical Literature*
JHI	*Journal of the History of Ideas*
JPh	*Journal of Philosophy*
JR	*Journal of Religion*
JThS	*Journal of Theological Studies*
KuD	*Kerygma und Dogma*
LB	Opera omnia Erasmi Roterodami, ed. J. LeClerc
MPL	Patrologiae cursus completus, series Latina, ed. Migne
MTh	*Modern Theology*
NZSTh	*Neue Zeitschrift für systematische Theologie und Religions-philosophie*
OC	Ioannis Calvini opera omnia quae supersunt
RThAM	*Recherches de théologie ancienne et médiévale*
SJTh	*Scottish Journal of Theology*
STh	*Studia Theologica*
WA	D. M. Luthers Werke: kritische Gesamtausgabe
WABr	D. M. Luthers Werke: Briefwechsel
Z	Huldrych Zwinglis sämtliche Werke (Corpus Reformatorum)
ZKG	*Zeitschrift für Kirchengeschichte*
ZThK	*Zeitschrift für Theologie und Kirche*

Notes

Preface

1 McGrath, *Iustitia Dei*, supplemented by a series of studies detailed in the bibliographies therein.
2 McGrath, *Luther's Theology of the Cross*; idem, *Intellectual Origins of the European Reformation*.
3 Lindbeck, *The Nature of Doctrine*.
4 Foucault, *Language, Counter-Memory, Practice*, 139.
5 On which see Foucault, *The Order of Things*.

Chapter 1 The Genesis of Doctrine

1 For a discussion of the nature and limitations of the Jesus tradition outside the New Testament, see the collection of essays assembled in David Wenham (ed.), *The Jesus Tradition outside the Gospels* (Sheffield, 1984), especially Draper, 'The Jesus Tradition in the Didache'; Harris, 'References to Jesus in Early Classical Authors'. A briefer account may be found in Kee, *Jesus in History*, 42–53.
2 cf. Simon, *General Theory of Authority*; Stout, *Flight from Authority*.
3 An attitude defined by Robin Horton as 'cognitive traditionalism': 'Tradition and Modernity Revisited', 239–41. However, he points out (p. 240) that 'an item of belief is legitimated, *not just* because it is certified as having come down to us from the ancients; but *ultimately* because the beliefs of the ancients have proved their worth down the ages as instruments of explanation, prediction and control.' Skorupski (*Symbol and Theory*, 204) points out that traditionalist thinkers are characterized by their reluctance to reject traditionally handed down ideas, while maintaining an essentially open attitude concerning their own ideas based upon them. It may be noted that the origins of the modern notion that the pastness of an event counts against both its credibility and its authority may be traced back to the middle of the seventeenth century: Hacking, *The Emergence of Probability*.
4 At this stage, no attempt is made to clarify what the New Testament tradition understands by its affirmation concerning the resurrection; I note simply its pervasive occurance at every level of that tradition.
5 Note the interpretation of the 'deposit of faith' entrusted to the church, to be guarded, defended and transmitted (e.g., 1 Timothy 6.20; 2 Timothy 1.12–14; 2.2, 4; 4.3; Titus 1.9; 13), found in Torrance, *The Trinitarian Faith*, 30–1; 257–61.

6 Note the stress within cognitive psychology on the need for humans to attribute meaning to events: see Harvey and Weary, *Perspectives on Attributional Processes*.

7 The term 'authority' is here understood to embrace a complex of functions, as noted by Simon, *General Theory of Authority*, 20–2.

8 See Neusner, et al., *Judaisms and their Messiahs at the Turn of the Christian Era* for documentation of the complexity of this expectation. More generally, see Hahn, *Christologische Hoheitstitel*, 133–225; Vermes, *Jesus the Jew*, 132.

9 See further Cullmann, *Die ersten christliche Glaubensbekenntnisse*; Schlier, 'Die Anfänge der christologischen Credo'.

10 Farrer, *A Rebirth of Images*, 14 'The images [of God] are not through all ages absolutely invariable, and there is no historical study more significant than the study of their transformations. Such a transformation finds expression in the birth of Christianity: it is a visible rebirth of images.'

11 This point has been brought out by Trocmé, *Jésus de Nazareth*, 141–2.

12 See Wilken, *Myth of Christian Beginnings*.

13 E.g., see Mitchell, 'Doctrinal Disagreements'.

14 See McGrath, 'Geschichte, Überlieferung und Erzählung'.

15 See Hays, *Faith of Jesus Christ*, for a careful analysis of the narrative substructure of the theological affirmations of Galatians 3.1–4.11.

16 For the relevance of this narrative to ethical reflection, see McGrath, 'Christian Ethics'.

17 A point stressed by Sykes, *Identity of Christianity*, 11–34. For an excellent account of the diversity within the New Testament, see Dunn, *Unity and Diversity*. Dunn offers a criterion for defining the limits of acceptable diversity – the unity of Jesus the human being with the exalted Christ: *Unity and Diversity*, 378–9.

18 Throughout this work, terms such as 'conceptual framework' or 'framework of conceptualities' are deliberately used loosely, without engaging with the history of the notion in its more precise and limited sense: cf. D'Amico, *Historicism and Knowledge*, 32–51; Davidson, 'On the very idea of a conceptual scheme'; Hacking, *Why does Language matter to Philosophy?*; Rorty, *Consequences of Pragmatism*, 3–18; Stout, *Flight from Authority*, 149–76. For an account of the important differences between Davidson and Wittgenstein, see Kerr, *Theology after Wittgenstein*, 105–9.

19 See Chadwick, *Early Christian Thought and the Classical Tradition*, for judicious illustration. The general theme is subjected to a critical analysis in the fine study of Grillmeier, 'Hellenisierung-Judaisierung des Christentums'.

20 See the seminal study of Pannenberg, 'The Appropriation of the Philosophical Concept of God as a Dogmatic Problem of Early Christian Theology'.

21 However tortuous the path may have been: see François, *Le polythéisme et l'emploi au singulier des mots THEOS, DAIMON*; Burkert, *Greek Religion*, 271–2; 305–37.

22 See Dörrie, 'Was ist "spätantiker Platonismus"?' The tendency to forge Christology into a *Weltanschauung* is evident throughout the history of doctrine: thus for Hegel, Christology functions as the mediation and reconciliation of the transcendent and immanent. See Küng, *The Incarnation of God*, 117–22; 190–242; McGrath, *Making of Modern German Christology*, 32–4.

23 Witness the historically questionable suggestion that 'Christianity came increasingly to be modelled on the Emperor-cult' (Don Cupitt): Hick (ed.), *Myth of God Incarnate*, 139.

24 Grillmeier, 'Hellenisierung-Judaisierung des Christentums'. Cf. Schlier, 'Kerygma und Sophia: Zur neutestamentlichen Grundlegung des Dogmas'.

25 For an excellent discussion of the political and theological dimensions of this controversy see Williams, *Arius: Heresy and Tradition*.

26 Pollard, *Johannine Christology and the Early Church*. For a discussion of a selection of the biblical texts at issue in the controversy between Arius and Athanasius, see Williams, *Arius: Heresy and Tradition*, 107–12.

27 On the *homoousion*, see Ricken, 'Nikaia als Krisis des altchristlichen Platonismus'; Ritter, *Das Konzil von Konstantinopel und sein Symbol*, 270–93.

28 Baum, *Faith and Doctrine*, 121–2.

29 On this general theme, see Simon, *A General Theory of Authority*.

30 Woods, 'Doctrinal Criticism'; Wiles, 'Looking into the Sun'. Woods' paper was published posthumously, the author having regrettably been unable to pursue the significant programme outlined therein.

31 Such a view may still be found in Elert, *Ausgang der altkirchlichen Christologie*, 324–6.

32 e.g. Cyprian, *Ep.* lxxi, 3; lxxiii, 13; lxxiv, 9. The particular dispute involved concerned the question of rebaptism: Willis, *Augustine and the Donatist Controversy*, 146–52. Cf. Woods, 'Doctrinal Criticism', 92: 'Neither logical nor organic continuity determines whether a doctrinal statement or a doctrinal system is true. The criteria of true development must be used together with proper criteria of the truth and adequacy of the tradition which is developing.'

33 Much useful historical material, too detailed to summarize here, may be found in Rahner and Lehmann, 'Kérygme et dogme'; O'Cleirigh, 'Dogma in Origen'.

34 See Beumer, 'Die Regula Fidei Catholicae des Ph. N. Chrisman, O.F.M.'. Chrisman appears to have derived the idea from F. Veronius, S.J. (1575–1649).

35 For an analysis of this phenomenon and its contributing factors, see McGrath, *Intellectual Origins of the European Reformation*, 12–28.

36 Although the reliability of this judgement is open to doubt: see McGrath, *Luther's Theology of the Cross*, 53–63.

37 The associated shifts in meanings of the related concepts of 'faith' and 'heresy' are instructive: Lang, 'Der Bedeutungswandel der Begriffe "fides" und "haeresis"'.

38 See further Deneffe, 'Dogma: Wort und Begriff'; Elze, 'Der Begriff des Dogmas in der Alten Kirche'; Rahner, 'What is a Dogmatic Statement?'; Dulles, 'Hermeneutics of Dogmatic Statements'; Ommen, *Hermeneutic of Dogma*.

39 Deneffe, 'Dogma: Wort und Begriff', 531.

40 See Sauter, 'Dogma – ein eschatologischer Begriff', with particular reference to the use of the term and concept in the writings of Karl Barth. An ingenious, if somewhat over-interpretative, distinction between the two concepts may be found in Jennings, *Beyond Theism*, 177–83; 221–4. Particular attention should be directed to Gerhard Ebeling's influential discussion of the nature of dogma: see, e.g., *Wort Gottes und Tradition*, 128–9; 168. For a response, see

Ommen, *Hermeneutic of Dogma*, 79; 203–8; Rogge, 'Zur Frage katholischer und evangelischer Dogmenhermeneutik'. The question of the Christological grouding of dogma is creatively explored by Williams, 'Incarnation as the Basis of Dogma'.

41 See Lukas Reinhart, *Synopsis theologiae dogmaticae* (1659). The most famous modern work to use this term is, of course, Karl Barth's *Church Dogmatics*. Other terms used in the period of Protestant Orthodoxy include the medieval 'summa' (e.g., Johannes Cocceius, *Summa theologiae ex scripturis repetita* (Amsterdam, 1665)) and 'medulla' (e.g., William Ames, *Medulla theologiae* (Amsterdam, 1628).)

42 Thus Luke 2.1; Acts 17.7; Hebrews 11.23 use the term with the sense 'official decree'; Ephesians 2.15 and Colossians 2.14 with the sense 'Mosaic law'; and Acts 16.4 uses the term in relation to practical conduct.

43 Pelikan, *Historical Theology*, 46–7.

44 See Evans, *Old Arts and New Theology*, for an account of this development.

45 Evans, *Old Arts and New Theology*, 57. Cf. Schleiermacher, *Gelegentliche Gedanken über Universitäten in deutschen Sinn*; Fichte, *Deduzierter Plan einer zu Berlin zu errichtenden höheren Lehranstalt*. This tension is explored by Thiselton, 'Academic Freedom, Religious Tradition and the Morality of Christian Scholarship.'

46 Perhaps I could give a personal example. In the section of my *Iustitia Dei* dealing with the development of the doctrine of justification since the Enlightenment (2.135–91), I followed the convention of concentrating upon the contribution (largely critical, it must be added) of academic theology, and ignored (again, through convention) the role of the doctrine within the life and mission of the church (see my comments, 2.190–1). In that the relevance of this doctrine pertains primarily to the life of the church, I am now convinced that a distorted picture of the relevance of the doctrine in the modern period resulted.

47 For the close relationship between commitment, worship and Christian identity, see Sykes, *Identity of Christianity*, 262–86.

48 Geertz, 'Religion as a Cultural System'.

49 A suggestion to be found in Koehler, *Dogmengeschichte*, and Werner, *Formation of Christian Dogma*.

50 See Lash, *Change in Focus*, 3–18.

51 Both these themes are explored by Pelikan, *Development of Doctrine*, 73–87; 95–119.

52 For the popular petitions demanding that this should be defined as *de fide*, see W. Hentrich and R. W. de Moos, *Petitiones de Assumptione Corporea B. V. Mariae* (2 vols: Vatican City, 1942).

53 Cf. Greenacre, 'Two Aspects of Reception', 49–57. For Karl Rahner's understanding of the notion, see Avis, *Ecumenical Theology*, 66–75.

54 The positive manner in which the decisions of Vatican II are being 'received' by many non-catholics (including the present writer) illustrates this process at work: Tillard, 'Réception de Vatican II'.

55 Although this phrase will seem to some to possess unacceptable Barthian overtones, it reflects much current thinking on the doctrine of the church – e.g., *Anglican-Roman Catholic International Commission: Final Report* (London, 1982), 52 'The confession of Christ as Lord is the heart of the Christian faith.'

Chapter 2   The Nature of Doctrine: A Response to
George Lindbeck

1 Lindbeck, *The Nature of Doctrine*, 15–19.
2 The impact of the book, however, is due to a number of factors: see Michalson, 'The Response to Lindbeck', for an analysis of the issues raised.
3 In this chapter I shall retain Lindbeck's designations for the three main theories of doctrine he identifies, despite their obvious ugliness.
4 Lindbeck, *Nature of Doctrine*, 17.
5 Ibid., 16. However, he acknowledges that 'a theory of religion and doctrine cannot be ecumenically useful unless it is nonecumenically plausible.' (p. 8).
6 E.g., ibid., 129.
7 Ibid., 16.
8 Ibid., 21.
9 E.g., ibid., 16. 'For a propositionalist, if a doctrine is once true, it is always true'.
10 It might also reasonably be pointed out that it pays inadequate attention to what it means to suggest that religious claims are 'cognitive' in the first place: an excellent discussion of this point (published too late to be available to Lindbeck) may be found in Kellenberger, *Cognitivity of Religion*.
11 Lindbeck, *Nature of Doctrine*, 47. But compare the concessions on pp. 80; 105.
12 Gerrish, 'Nature of Doctrine', 87–8.
13 See Parent, 'La notion de dogme au XIIIe siècle'.
14 See Evans, *Alan of Lille*, 64–80, for details.
15 For example, see Bede's careful discussion of various different modes and levels of representation, *tropoi* (such as metaphor, catachresis, metalepsis, anadiplosis and metonymia) and *schememata* (such as anaphora, prolepsis and zeugma). Bede, *de schematibus et tropis*; MPL 90.175A–B.
16 E.g., see Evans, *Alan of Lille*, 33–6. A more recent work which attempts a similar clarification of the word 'God' is Jennings, *Beyond Theism*, especially 59–74.
17 Lindbeck, *Nature of Doctrine*, 65.
18 See ibid., 65, where the same point is made in relation to Shakespeare's *Hamlet*.
19 C. S. Lewis, *Surprised by Joy* (New York, 1955), 17. It is, of course, debatable whether this is the experience Longfellow had intended to convey; this question must, however, lie beyond the present study.
20 On the relation between language and experience, with valuable observations concerning the limitations placed upon the latter, see Phillips, *Death and Immortality*, 4–10; 14–15.
21 The literature on the subject is vast. See Richards, *Philosophy of Rhetoric*; Lakoff and Johnson, *Metaphors we live by*; Cooper, *Metaphor*.
22 E.g., see Ramsey, *Models and Mystery*.
23 E.g., see the classic studies of Mascall, *Existence and Analogy*; Macquarrie, *God-Talk*.
24 Kasper, *Dogma unter dem Wort Gottes*, 128.
25 For the concept, see Burke, *Grammar of Motives*, 503–17; Ricoeur, *Le temps*

raconté, 219–27. For its theological application, see Klemm, 'Toward a Rhetoric of Postmodern Theology'. The role of metaphors in theological language in general, and more specifically in relation to doctrine, has been fruitfully explored by McFague, *Metaphorical Theology*, and Soskice, *Metaphor and Religious Language*. The outcome of such investigations, too nuanced to reproduce here, considerably reduces the force of Lindbeck's polemic against 'cognitive' theories of doctrine.

26 E.g., see Girardin, *Rhétorique et théologique*, 205–73.

27 For what follows see *New Science of Giambattista Vico*, 129–31; White, *Topics of Discourse*, 1–27.

28 White, *Topics of Discourse*, 5; 12.

29 Watts and Williams, *Psychology of Religious Knowing*, 59–74.

30 There are also significant parallels between aesthetic and moral reflection: Newman, 'Aesthetic Sensitizing and Moral Education'.

31 Watts and Williams, *Psychology of Religious Knowing*, 60–2.

32 Ibid., 70–4.

33 Such as those discussed by Dulles, *Models of Revelation*, 36–52.

34 Propounded in *De Revelatione Christiana* (Freiburg, 1930).

35 Lindbeck, *Nature of Doctrine*, 16.

36 Tracy, *Blessed Rage for Order*, 32–4; 97–103. A similar concern for correlating 'common human experience' and faith may be found in Ogden, *Christ without Myth*, and subsequently in his *Reality of God*.

37 Lindbeck, *Nature of Doctrine*, 19–25.

38 Ibid., 23. Cf. Lonergan, *Method in Theology*, 108–9.

39 Lindbeck, *Nature of Doctrine*, 32.

40 Ibid., 23.

41 Ibid., 17.

42 It also raises serious difficulties concerning the public discussion of private experience: cf. Blackburn, 'Private Experience'.

43 E.g., see Spiegler, *Eternal Covenant*, 136–56.

44 See Chadwick, *From Bossuet to Newman*, 1–20.

45 Lonergan, *Philosophy of God and Theology*, 50.

46 Lonergan, for example, is heavily dependent upon the somewhat questionable conclusions (e.g., that the 'higher religions' derive from the same common core experience of transcendence) of Heiler, 'The History of Religion as a Preparation for the Cooperation of Religions'.

47 See von Loewenich, *Luther's Theology of the Cross*; McGrath, *Luther's Theology of the Cross*, 148–75. Luther's ideas are articulated in a more contemporary idiom in McGrath, *The Enigma of the Cross*.

48 See further Ritter, 'Theologie und Erfahrung'.

49 For a penetrating account of the importance of 'conversion', see Fredricksen, 'Paul and Augustine'. Note especially the emphasis on a break or discontinuity with the past.

50 Watts and Williams, *Psychology of Religious Knowing*, 10–23. On the distinction between 'committed' and 'consensual', see Allen and Spilka, 'Committed and Consensual Religion'.

51 Spilka, Hood and Gorsuch, *Psychology of Religion*, 17–28; Watts and Williams, *Psychology of Religious Knowing*, 109–27.

52   Lindbeck, *Nature of Doctrine*, 128.

53   For more reliable characterizations of 'religious experience', see Hay, *Exploring Inner Space*; Godin, *Psychological Dynamics of Religious Experience*; Meissner, *Psychoanalysis and Religious Experience*.

54   Bultmann will serve as an obvious example: see Flückiger, *Existenz und Glaube*.

55   Many 'experiential-expressive' accounts of doctrine would presumably dismiss this anxiety as pointless, given their non-cognitive understanding of the concept of revelation: see Dulles, *Models of Revelation*, 98–114. For a careful analysis of experience as a theological resource, see Lash, *Easter in Ordinary*.

56   Driver, *Patterns of Grace*.

57   Note also Gilkey, *Message and Existence*.

58   For an exploration of this theme, see Kern, 'Atheismus – Christentum – – emanzipierte Gesellschaft'.

59   On the theme of the 'hidden God' in Luther's early theology, see Dillenberger, *God Hidden and Revealed*; Bandt, *Luther's Lehre vom verborgenen Gott*; McGrath, *Luther's Theology of the Cross*, 161–75.

60   A point emphasised by Gerrish, 'Nature of Doctrine', 89–90. Although there are points at which Schleiermacher may appear to echo Lindbeck's characterisation of the 'experiential-expressive' approach (e.g., he clearly asserts the presence of prereflective moments within human religious consciousness), his approach to the relation of doctrine and experience does not fit the 'experiential-expressive' mould defined by Lindbeck.

61   Beisser, *Schleiermachers Lehre von Gott*, 57–68; Offermann, *Einleitung in die Glaubenslehre*, 47–65.

62   Schleiermacher, *The Christian Faith*, 106.

63   Lindbeck, *Nature of Doctrine*, 36–7. Cf. Gerrish, 'Nature of Doctrine', 89–90.

64   See especially Geertz, 'Religion as a Cultural System'.

65   It would seem that Lindbeck's philosophical stances must be related to the long-standing English-language debate concerning 'Wittgensteinian fideism'. Cf. Nielsen, 'Wittgensteinian Fideism' (a term rightly criticized by Kerr, *Theology after Wittgenstein*, 28–31). A full discussion whether, and in what manner, one may 'know' God, particularly in the light of Wittgenstein's contribution to the debate (as stated by Kerr, *Theology after Wittgenstein*, and Penelhum, *God and Scepticism*), must be postponed to a later work. It is one of the many merits of Lindbeck's work to attempt to respond to Wittgenstein, both in the rejection of 'cognitive' models of doctrine and in the affirmation of the value of a 'cultural-linguistic' approach.

66   Lindbeck, *Nature of Doctrine*, 32–41.

67   Ibid., 33.

68   Ibid., 37, drawing on the views of Noam Chomsky and Clifford Geertz.

69   Ibid., 65. A similar approach is adopted by Ian Ramsey in his discussion of the function of the various statements of the Athanasian Creed: Ramsay, *Religious Language*, 174–9.

70   On this point, see the important historical analysis in Nelson, *Fact or Fiction*.

71   For Frei's discussion of the relation of 'fact-likeness' to 'factuality', see Frei, *The Eclipse of Biblical Narrative*, 187. The same theme is dealt with by Frye, *The Great Code*.

72 Lindbeck, *Nature of Doctrine*, 120–2.
73 Ibid., 122.
74 Ibid., 114. Lindbeck argues that an 'extratextual' approach characterises the propositonalist and experiential-expressive approach. For further discussion of this point, see Tracy, 'Lindbeck's New Program for Theology'; Tilley, 'Incommensurability, Intratextuality, and Fideism'.
75 Lindbeck, *Nature of Tradition*, 62.
76 Ibid., 39.
77 Ibid., 39.
78 Schleiermacher, *Brief Outline of the Study of Theology*, 71. A more recent statement of this position may be found in Macquarrie, *Principles of Christian Theology*, 1.
79 Niebuhr, *Schleiermacher on Christ and Religion*, 154–73. Cf. Schleiermacher, *The Christian Faith*, 17–19: 83–93.
80 Hence Barth's rather sharp sugestion that Schleiermacher has no concern for the *truth* of dogmatic statements: Barth, *The Theology of Schleiermacher*, 163.
81 See Phillips, 'Lindbeck's Audience'.
82 Lindbeck, *Nature of Doctrine*, 19.
83 For the argument, see ibid., 92–6.
84 Ibid., 94.
85 For the suggestion that Lindbeck is not merely dependent upon Lonergan at this point, but actually misunderstands him, see Williams, 'Lindbeck's Regulative Christology'.
86 Williams, 'Lindbeck's Regulative Christology', 178.
87 For the case of Nestorius, see Scipioni, *Nestorio e il concilio di Efeso*, 386–92.
88 Williams, 'Trinity and Revelation', 197.
89 McGrath, *Making of Modern German Christology*, 127–85.
90 Lindbeck, *Nature of Doctrine*, 68–9, illustrates this ambiguity.
91 Barfield, *Poetic Diction*, 30.
92 E.g, in his discussion of 'ontological' truth: Lindbeck, *Nature of Doctrine*, 63–7.
93 Suppe, 'Philosophic Understanding of Scientific Theories', 27–36.
94 E.g., see Hempel, 'Empiricist Criteria of Cognitive Significance'.
95 cf. Hanson, *Concept of the Positron*.
96 Suppe, 'Philosophic Understanding of Scientific Theories', 34.
97 Cf. Carnes, *Axiomatics and Dogmatics*, 8.
98 Wittgenstein, *Philosophical Investigations*, 19. We have in mind a cluster of attitudes, practices, beliefs and expectations, shaped by patterns of worship, adoration and prayer. For the history of this *Lebensform*, see Federer, *Liturgie und Glaube*; Wainwright, *Doxology*, 218–50. For its wider theological implications, see Wainwright, *Doxology*; Kavanagh, *On Liturgical Theology*; Taft, 'Liturgy as Theology'; Sauter, 'Das Gebet als Wurzel des Redens von Gott'.
99 Gerrish, 'Nature of Doctrine', 87.
100 Lindbeck, *Nature of Doctrine*, 17.
101 Ibid., 19.
102 I here follow Williams, 'Lindbeck's Regulative Christology'.
103 I should make it clear at this stage that I am not suggesting that history should be the *sole* criterion for judging contemporary doctrinal affirmations.

Chapter 3   The Nature of Doctrine: Four Theses

1   E.g., McGrath, *Making of Modern German Christology*, 55–8. Nevertheless, even this modest historical link between Jesus and Christian doctrine is vulnerable. The point at issue may be illustrated and developed from some remarks of J. L. Austin concerning the term 'Fascism' in his essay 'The Meaning of a Word.' The term 'Fascism' is usually understood to mean forms of polity historically derived from the inspiration of the political ideas and enterprises of Mussolini (in much the same way as Liberal Protestantism apparently conceives the relation of Christianity and Jesus of Nazareth). However, certain political ideas in circulation prior to Mussolini (e.g., those of Charles Maurras and *l'action française*) may legitimately be termed 'Fascist', despite the absence of this pattern of historical causation, in that they conform to the paradigm of Mussolini's movement. Just as the term 'Fascist' cannot thus simply mean '*historically derived* from Mussolini', so the term 'Christian' could refer to persons or ideas historically prior to Jesus. The difficulty thus raised is avoided by our insistence that Christian doctrine is the consequence of reflection within the community of faith *precipitated and controlled by* the history of Jesus of Nazareth.
2   Cf. Rotermund, *Orthodoxie und Pietismus*.
3   See Wainwright, *Doxology*. See also references at n. 19.
4   Luhmann, *Funktion der Religion*, 59–61.
5   Cf. Pannenberg, 'Religion in der säkularen Gesellschaft'; Green, 'Sociology of Dogmatics', for a critical analysis of Luhmann's views. Lindbeck, *Nature of Doctrine*, 74, may echo elements of Luhmann's analysis, especially in his insistence upon the need for operational (or 'operative') doctrines in preserving collective identity.
6   See Watson, *Paul, Judaism and the Gentiles*, 19–22. The interaction of scriptural texts, group organization and historical experience described by Dahl, 'Eschatologie und Geschichte', is of potential importance here.
7   See Meeks, *First Urban Christians*, 84–103, for a discussion of factors conducive to social cohesion in the Pauline communities. More generally, see Olsen, *Process of Social Organization*. Christian's distinction between 'primary' and 'governing' doctrines of religious communities (Christian, *Doctrines of Religious Communities*) shows some promise as a means of refining the social and communal dimensions and function of doctrine.
8   See Meeks, *First Urban Christians*, 150–62, for a discussion of the social function of baptism and the Lord's supper.
9   Markus, 'Problem of Self-Definition', 3.
10 See Meeks, 'Johannine Sectarianism'.
11 On the manner in which the Pauline communities distinguished themselves from society at large, see Meeks, *First Urban Christians*, 84–107.
12 Tertullian, *Apol.*, 42.
13 See Watson, *Paul, Judaism and the Gentiles*, 49–87.
14 Ibid., 178.
15 There is no need to invoke the discredited anachronistic distinction (cf. Hengel, *Judaism and Hellenism*) between Judaism and Hellenism in relation to this point.

16 On this subject, see MacRae, 'Why the Church rejected Gnosticism'; Ménard, 'Normative Self-Definition in Gnosticism'; Vallée, 'Irenaeus' Refutation of the Gnostics', and references therein.

17 Marcus, 'Problem of Self-Definition', 5–7.

18 See Greenslade, 'Heresy and Schism', 5.

19 For the history of this principle until the fifth century see Federer, *Liturgie und Glaube*; Wainwright, *Doxology*, 218–50. For its wider theological implications, see Wainwright, *Doxology*, passim; Kavanagh, *On Liturgical Theology*; Taft, 'Liturgy as Theology'; Sauter, 'Das Gebet als Wurzel des Redens von Gott'. The substance of the principle is often summarized in the Latin tag *lex orandi, lex credendi* (or, more accurately, *legem credendi lex statuat supplicandi*).

20 Armstrong, 'Christianity in Relation to Later Platonism', 79. On the difficulties later Platonism itself faced, see Dillon, 'Self-Definition in Later Platonism'.

21 Meijering, *Orthodoxy and Platonism in Athanasius*.

22 See Williams, *Arius*, 48–81.

23 This is also true, of course, for earlier heretical and schismatic movements: see Frend, 'Heresy and Schism'. Leff, *Heresy in the Later Middle Ages*, is marred by its tendency to treat heresy as a purely religious phenomenon, overlooking its crucial social dimension. A full account of scholarly research into the phenomenon of medieval heresy may be consulted in Berkhout and Russell, *Medieval Heresies*.

24 See McGrath, *Intellectual Origins of the European Reformation*, 9–31.

25 On this, see Wolf, 'Die Rechtfertigungslehre als Mitte und Grenze reformator-sicher Theologie'; McGrath, *Luther's Theology of the Cross*, 7- -26; 95–175; idem, *Iustitia Dei*, 2.3–32, and references therein.

26 Note the affirmation of the Schmalkaldic Articles (1537) on the importance of the doctrine to the beleagured Lutheran community: 'et in hoc articulo sita sunt et consistunt omnia, quae contra papam, diabolum et mundum in vita nostra docemus, testamur et agimus'. *Bekenntnisschriften der evangelisch-Lutherischen Kirche* (Göttingen, 2nd edn, 1952), 416.23–4.

27 On the history of this term, see McGrath, *Iustitia Dei*, 2.193 n.3. On its theological importance, see McGrath, 'The Article by which the Church stands or falls'.

28 For the significance of this development, see McGrath, *Iustitia Dei*, 2.80–1.

29 This is particularly evident in the case of the *decretum de iustificatione*: McGrath, *Iustitia Dei*, 2.63–86.

30 Powicke, *Reformation in England*, 1; 34.

31 For example, see the debates on the doctrine of justification: McGrath, *Iustitia Dei*, 2.98–105.

32 See the important material in Collinson, *Birthpangs of Protestant England*, 1–27. With the rise of a politically and socially significant ecclesial faction within England during the period prior to the Civil War, the Church of England was obliged to define itself, however temporarily, with reference to doctrinal parameters. The coexistence of two ecclesial bodies within the same nation disrupted the social function hitherto assumed by the Church of England, thus precipitating a temporary interest in matters of doctrine. In this respect, the Civil War may indeed be regarded as the last of the European wars of

religion: ibid., 127–55. With the Restoration, the Church of England was able to resume its traditional social function, and its associated (if historically contingent) disinterest in matters of doctrine. The debate continues as to whether the Church of England has any distinctive doctrines. Those who believe it does not include Hodgson, 'Doctrine of the Church'; Neill, *Anglicanism*, 417; Wand, *Anglicanism*, 227. Those who believe it ought to are championed by Sykes, 'Anglican Doctrine of the Church', 157–79.

33 On this, see the magisterial essay of Schilling, 'Die "Zweite Reformation" als Kategorie der Geschichtswissenschaft', and references therein.

34 See Heckel, 'Theologisch-juristische Probleme der reformierten Konfessionalisierung'.

35 Morgan, preface to *Religion of the Incarnation*, xvi.

36 Wright, 'Anglicanism, *Ecclesia Anglicana*, and Anglican', 426–7.

37 Heckel, 'Reichsrecht und "Zweite Reformation"', 37–8.

38 On some of the issues involved, see Staples, 'Towards an Explanation of Ecumenism'.

39 On which see McGrath, *Luther's Theology of the Cross*. The importance of a conversion experience in this respect is emphasized by Fredriksen, 'Paul and Augustine'.

40 It is worth recalling that, until the shift of the political centre of the Reformed church from Zurich to Geneva, via Berne, the Reformed church possessed no thinker who exercised the same influence over its formation as did Luther over the emerging Lutheran church.

41 This is perhaps most evident in the explicit rejection of Luther's 1525 views on the *servum arbitrium* and predestination in the *Formula of Concord*, a criticism widely supported among modern Lutheran writers: see McSorley, *Luther – Right or Wrong?*, 359–66.

42 For a twentieth-century approach on the part of Lutheran and Roman Catholic theologians to the issues which divided them in the sixteenth century, see 'Justification by Faith', *Origins: NC Documentary Service* 13/17 (1983), 277–304.

43 See Bellah, *Habits of the Heart*, for this understanding of religion. For a careful assessment of the significance of the divisiveness of doctrine to the life of the Lutheran churches, see Ebeling, 'Significance of Doctrinal Differences.'

44 E.g., LB 5.45 D; 9.1216 C.

45 Moeller, *Reichstadt und Reformation*, 15–18.

46 Scribner, 'Civic Unity and the Reformation in Erfurt'.

47 This is evident from his views on the interpretation of the scripture, his theology of the church and sacraments, and his political thought. See McGrath, *Reformation Thought*, 112–14; 126–7; 147, and references therein.

48 E.g., McGrath, *Intellectual Origins of the European Reformation*, 49–50. As Ziegler remarks, the Reformation in east Switzerland in general is best regarded as a 'Reformation of life and morals': Ziegler, 'Zur Reformation als Reformation des Lebens und der Sitten'.

49 For comments, see Sykes, *Integrity of Anglicanism*, passim; Sykes, 'Anglican Doctrine of the Church'.

50 A view evaluated, and persuasively found wanting, by Sykes, *Integrity of Anglicanism*, 53–62, especially 60–1.

51 E.g., see Morgan, Preface to *Religion of the Incarnation*.

52 Bec, *Cultura e società a Firenze nell'età della Rinascenza*, 228–44.
53 In part, the appeal of this narrative approach lay in the inevitable imaginative element attending historical reconstruction. For the historico- critical aspects of this appeal to the empathetic imagination at the time of the Renaissance, see Nelson, *Fact or Fiction*. Barth's stress on the need for 'imaginative fantasy' (*CD* III/1, 81; note also the epistemological weight attached to the faculty of imagination, p. 91) has interesting parallels with Coleridge and C. S. Lewis, and the English Romantic tradition in general: cf. Reilly, *Romantic Religion*.
54 Heidegger, *Sein und Zeit*, 387–97.
55 E.g., see McGrath, *Intellectual Origins of the European Reformation*, 38–48.
56 Schmidlin, *Frumm byderb lüt*, 102–24. Similar remarks apply to the highly politicized drama *Das Spiel von den alten und jungen Eidgenossen* (1516): pp. 81–101.
57 See Jones, 'MacIntyre on Narrative'.
58 MacIntyre, *After Virtue*, 223.
59 MacIntyre, *After Virtue*, 222.
60 A theme explored by Harned, *Creed and Personal Identity*; Wilder, *Early Christian Rhetoric*, 63–78.
61 A theme thoroughly and thoughtfully explored by Gaventa, 'Autobiography as Paradigm'.
62 For what follows, see McGrath, 'Christian Ethics', and references therein.
63 For careful discussion of this point, see Harvey, 'Attending to Scripture'.
64 On which see Frei, *Eclipse of Narrative*, a work whose echoes may readily be detected in these paragraphs.
65 For this theme in the theology of Karl Barth, see Ford, 'Barth's Interpretation of the Bible'.
66 E.g., see Harvey, 'Christian Propositions and Christian Stories'; Frei, *Eclipse of Biblical Narrative*.
67 Cottignoli, 'I "Promessi Sposi" nella storia del realismo de sanctisiano', 456–7.
68 Ibid., 458–9.
69 Branca, 'Realismo desanctisiano e tradizione narrativa', especially 9, where narrative is treated *quale storia non solo e non tanto di fatti esistiti o esistenti ma di fatti possibili*.
70 On the relation between Christian ethics and the narrative of Jesus of Nazareth, see McGrath, 'Christian ethics'.
71 The most celebrated exposition of the theory may be found in Aulén, *Christus Victor*. Cf. Gunton, 'Christus Victor Revisited'.
72 Aulén, *Christus Victor*, 4.
73 For which see de Clerck, 'Droits du démon'.
74 McGrath, *Iustitia Dei*, 1.55–62.
75 See Williams, *Arius*, 117–57 and references therein.
76 Williams, *Arius*, 231.
77 This general point has received renewed attention in recent years: Ebeling, 'Die Notwendigkeit des christlichen Gottesdienstes'; Schlink, 'Die Struktur der dogmatischen Aussagen'; Wainwright, *Doxology*.
78 For the significance of Christian worship in the shaping of early Christian doctrine, see Wiles, *Making of Christian Doctrine*, 62–93.

79 See Hays, *Faith of Jesus Christ*, especially 193–246.
80 See the insightful exposition of this theme in Jenson, *The Triune Identity*, 1–56..
81 Lindbeck, *Nature of Doctrine*. 65.
82 Hegel, *Vorlesungen über die Philosophie der Religion*; in *Werke* 11.26. Cf. Clark, *Logic and System*, 57–63.
83 Hart, *Unfinished Man and the Imagination*, 99.
84 Hick, *Myth of God Incarnate*, 3.
85 For biological analogies in relation to doctrinal development, see Blondel, *Letter on Apologetics*, 255–6. There is, however, much to be said for Woods' observation ('Doctrinal Criticism', 91): 'I am not sure that we have yet found any analogy which is very apt as a description of the process of doctrinal development.'
86 E.g., Marshall, 'Incarnational Christology in the New Testament'.
87 For the sociological significance of the RNA/DNA analogy, particularly in relation to the social function of religion, see Luhmann, *Funktion der Religion*, 21.
88 Burkert, *Greek Religion*, 305. For a valuable analysis of the relation of narrative and conceptualities, see Jüngel, *God as the Mystery of the World*, 299–314.
89 See the comprehensive studies of Pieper on Plato and Ritter on Aristotle: Pieper, *Über den Begriff der Tradition*, 20–35; Pieper, *Über die platonischen Mythen*; Ritter, 'Aristoteles und die Vorsokratiker'.
90 An important contribution to this debate is White, *Metahistory*.
91 The Reformation could reasonably be interpreted as an overdue re-examination of the medieval catholic framework of conceptualities in the light of their generative narrative; similarly, the Reformation slogan *ecclesia reformata, ecclesia semper reformanda* could be interpreted as an affirmation of the need to continually correlate the generating narrative and the resulting concepts.
92 See McGrath, *Luther's Theology of the Cross*, 148–81.
93 For Luther's critique of Aristotle, see McGrath, *Luther's Theology of the Cross*, 136–41.
94 For a full analysis, see ibid., 95–181.
95 WA 1.613.23–8.
96 On which see Hamlyn, 'Aristotle's God'.
97 WA 5.176.32–3.
98 For general surveys of 'experience' as a theological category, see Ebeling, 'Die Klage über das Erfahrungsdefizit'; Lange, *Erfahrung und die Glaubenswürdigkeit*; Ritter, 'Theologie und Erfahrung'; Schaeffler, *Fähigkeit zur Erfahrung*.
99 See my critique of Lindbeck's account of the 'experiential-expressive' model of doctrine, pp. 20–6.
100 For a worked example in the case of the doctrine of justification by faith, see McGrath, 'The Article by which the Church stands or falls'.
101 Kerr, *Theology after Wittgenstein*, 162–7. Blackburn's discussion of the 'current coffee sensation' develops this point: 'Private Experience', 203–4.
102 Schleiermacher, *Christian Faith*, 76–8.
103 On the Christological and soteriological points raised, see McGrath, *Making*

of Modern German Christology, 19–26; McGrath, *Iustitia Dei*, 2.154–8, and references therein.

104 For a brief account of the difficulties associated with articulating individual experience, see Blackburn, 'Private Experience'.

105 This is not necessarily to say that *thought* requires language: see L. Weiskranz (ed.), *Thought without Language* (Fyssen Foundation Symposia 2: Oxford, 1988). Rather, it is to suggest that the *articulation and communication* of thought requires language.

106 Woolman, *Journal*, 542.

107 Wordsworth, *The Borders of Vision*, 1–35. The same theme is explored with reference to the idea of 'liminality' by Watson, *Wordsworth's Vital Soul*. These ideas cannot be dismissed simply as outmoded nineteenth-century Romanticism. As Reilly observes (*Romantic Religion*), many seminal ideas of English Romanticism have been appropriated and creatively developed in twentieth-century English religious and literary writings. Thus Owen Barfield and J. R. R. Tolkein exploit Coleridge's doctrine of the creative imagination; while C. S. Lewis, Charles Williams and Tolkein all affirm that 'romantic' experiences (such as *Sehnsucht*) are, or can become, religious experiences.

108 Lewis, 'The Weight of Glory', 98. On the role of the religious imagination at this point, see Reilly, *Romantic Religion*, 98–147.

109 Waugh, *Brideshead Revisited*, 288.

110 Schleiermacher, *The Christian Faith*, 78–83.

111 Gerrish, 'Nature of Doctrine', 92.

112 Lewis, 'Language of Religion', 169. Wittgenstein's cryptic remark to Paul Engelmann (cited Kerr, *Theology after Wittgenstein*, 166), appears to hint at the same point: 'if only you do not try to utter what is unutterable then *nothing* gets lost. But the unutterable will be – unutterably – *contained* in what has been uttered.'

113 Lewis, 'Language of Religion', 167.

114 This has been thoroughly explored in relation to the experience of salvation as given in Jesus by Schillebeeckx, *Christ*, 49–54. For an evaluation, see Dupré, 'Experience and Interpretation'.

115 A point first stressed by Hanson, *Patterns of Discovery*. Cf. Carnes, *Axiomatics and Dogmatics*, 10–15; Hanson, *Perception and Discovery*; Hanson, *Observation and Explanation*.

116 Hanson, *Observation and Explanation*, 131.

117 Ebeling, 'Klage über das Erfahrungsdefizit'.

118 Jüngel, *God as the Mystery of the World*, 32.

119 See McGrath, *Luther's Theology of the Cross*, 148–81.

120 WA 5.279.31.

121 A notion expressed in the concept of *Deus absconditus*: see Bandt, *Luthers Lehre vom verborgenen Gott*; Dillenberger, *God Hidden and Revealed*; Kochler, 'Der *Deus absconditus* in Philosophie und Theologie'.

122 Lucas, 'True', 184. Of interest in this connection is Dummett's philosophical reconstruction of some of the thoughts behind intuitionist mathematics, centering on the concept of bivalence: Dummett, *Truth and Other Enigmas*.

123 Kolakowski, 'Marx and the Classical Definition of Truth'.

124 The subsequent Marxist discussion of the nature of truth, and the criteria to

be employed in the assessment of the validity of theories, is complex: cf. Bhaskar, *Dialectic, Materialism and Human Emancipation.*

125   See Toinet, *Le problème de la verité dogmatique.*

126   For what follows, see Marías, *Reason and Life*, 95–7. For more detailed analysis, see Brunner, *Wahrheit als Begegnung*; Michel, 'Untersuchung über Wahrheit'; von Soden, *Was ist Wahrheit?*; Dodd, *Interpretation of the Fourth Gospel*, 170–8. Note also Dummett, *Truth and Other Enigmas*, 1–24.

127   Heidegger, *Platons Lehre von der Wahrheit*, 32.

128   The celebrated definition of Jean Bodin (1590): McGrath, 'Geschichte, Überlieferung und Erzählung', 234.

129   Danto, *Analytical Philosophy of History*, 111.

130   Cicero, *de oratore* II, xv, 62. Cf. de Fourny, 'Histoire et éloquence d'après Ciceron'.

131   For an analysis, with important criticism of simplistic approaches to this relationship, see Barr, *Semantics of Biblical Language*, 161–205.

132   For the exploration of this theme, see Pannenberg, 'What is truth?'.

133   For recent discussion of the nature of truth, see Puntel, *Wahrheitstheorien in der neueren Philosophie*, where emphasis is placed upon the generation of consensus through the process of communication.

134   See Macquarrie, 'Concept of a Christ-Event'; Macquarrie, 'Tradition, Truth and Christology', 40–2. Paradoxically, those theologians tending to stress the 'Christ-event' (e.g., Bultmann) are those who tend to de-historicize the significance of Jesus of Nazareth.

135   Brunner, *Wahrheit als Begegnung.*

136   For an exhaustive account of the implications of this statement, see de la Potterie, *La verité dans saint Jean.*

137   See Schwarz, 'Lessings "Spinozismus"'.

138   Vass, 'Historical Structure of Christian Truth'.

139   Vass, 'Historical Structure of Christian Truth', 279–80.

140   For an important recent discussion of how the cognitive elements of religious knowing may be analysed, see Kellenberger, *Cognitivity of Religion.*

141   Wisdom, *Paradox and Discovery*, 102.

142   F. W. J. Schelling, *Sämmtliche Werke*, ed. K. F. A. Schelling (Stuttgart, 1856), II/1.52: 'die Sprache selbst sey nur die verblichene Mythologie'. In his celebrated essay 'The Meaning of "Literal"', Owen Barfield points to the metaphorical (i.e., non-literal) roots of many words now understood at the purely 'literal' level. Cf. the oft-cited dictum of Jean Paul, 'every language is a dictionary of faded metaphors (*erblasseter Metaphern*)': *Werke*, ed. N. Miller (Munich, 3rd edn, 1973), 5.184.

143   See Beckmann, *Begriff der Häresie bei Schleiermacher*, 36–62.

144   What follows is based on *The Christian Faith*, 97–101. For a more detailed analysis, see Beckmann, *Begriff der Häresie bei Schleiermacher*, 85–114.

145   Schleiermacher, *The Christian Faith*, 98.

146   Cf. McGrath, 'Article by which the Church stands or falls.'

147   Kierkegaard, *Unscientific Postscript*, 182. The entire section on 'truth is subjectivity' (169–224) merits close attention. Kierkegaard's emphasis upon the importance of the statement of the Fourth Gospel, to the effect that Jesus *is* the truth, is significant: Malantschuk, *Kierkegaard's Thought*, 95–101. Note

also Gadamer's concept of 'understanding as participation': Warnke, *Gadamer*, 64–72.

148 See Gouwens, 'Kierkegaard's Understanding of Doctrine'.

149 This response can be articulated at both the moral and spiritual levels, treating doctrinal affirmations as 'performative' (in the sense popularized by Austin, 'Performative Utterances'), pointing to a mode of existence which corresponds or conforms to the understanding of God being affirmed. I take it that this is what Lindbeck is attempting to convey in his suggestion that *'Christus est Dominus'* is false when 'used to authorize cleaving the skull of an infidel' (Lindbeck, *Nature of Doctrine*, 64).

150 Kierkegaard, *Unscientific Postscript*, 339. Kierkegaard's attitude to propositions in general is of importance in understanding his specific hostility to purely propositional conceptions of doctrine: cf. Holmer, 'Kierkegaard and Religious Propositions'. Kierkegaard elaborates the 'existential contradiction' involved as 'the problem of an eternal happiness decided in time by a relationship to something historical': *Unscientific Postscript*, 340.

151 For the argument, see Kellenberger, *Religious Discovery, Faith and Knowledge*.

152 Temple, 'Theology Today', 330.

153 Kierkegaard, *Unscientific Postscript*, 332.

154 Kellenberger, *Cognitivity of Religion*. Kellenberger argues that 'discovery perspectives' overcome at least some of the traditional difficulties associated with rationalist and fideist approaches to religious cognition.

Chapter 4 On Being Condemned to History

1 See Hacking, *Why does Language matter to Philosophy?* Hamann's criticism of Kant is of particular relevance to this subject, particularly in relation to the non-historical notion of 'eternal truth': Hempelmann, 'Hamanns Kontroverse mit Kant über Sprache und Vernunft'.

2 *Kant's Political Writings*, 54. For Gadamer's critique of this position, see *Truth and Method*, 241–5.

3 Note the attitude of Thomas Jefferson, as described in Boorstin, *Lost World of Thomas Jefferson*, 225–6: 'The Jeffersonian was not confined by any particular tradition. He had sought to reform the Christian tradition, he had disavowed the humanist tradition, and he had set himself outside the English tradition. The past, through which other men had discovered human possibilities, was for him corrupt and dead.'

4 Emerson, 'Phi Beta Kappa Address'.

5 Murdoch, *The Sovereignty of the Good*, 80.

6 His most recent collection – *Politics, Philosophy and Culture* – brings out some of these themes, particularly the relation between personal identity, knowledge and power.

7 E.g., see Cole et. al., *Cultural Context of Learning*; Douglas, *Implicit Meaning*. On the sociological dimensions of 'common sense knowledge', see Berger and Luckmann, *Social Construction of Reality*, 33–42. In the remainder of this chapter, I shall take social anthropology to be included in the term 'sociology'.

8 Of particular importance here is the concept of 'cognitive relativism', as

developed by Steven Lukes, 'Relativism: Cognitive and Moral'. See further Trigg, *Reason and Commitment*.

9   This point has been noted by Wiles, *Making of Christian Doctrine*, 158–9. The fathers, Wiles argues, commited what we now recognize to be errors of reasoning which were perfectly understandable, given their cultural and philosophical milieu. What was self-evident to them is now regarded as erroneous. A similar point is made by Anthony Kenny in his treatment of Thomas Aquinas' arguments for the existence of God: Kenny, *The Five Ways*. What appears to us as logical error was accepted wisdom in the thirteenth century.

10   A point stressed by Stark, *Sociology of Knowledge*, 13–14. Once more, Hamann's critique of Kant's understanding of the relation of language and reason should be noted: Hempelmann, 'Hamanns Kontroverse mit Kant'.

11   For a classic presentation of several dimensions of this problem, see Lowenthal, *The Past is a Foreign Country*.

12   See Lukes, 'Some Problems about Rationality'. A radical statement of this thesis may be found in Feyerabend, *Science in a Free Society*, 65–70. Nevertheless, full attention must be paid to Davidson's important argument to the effect that the notion of totally incommensurate conceptual frameworks is radically incoherent: Davidson, 'On the Very Idea of a Conceptual Scheme'.

13   In other words, truth is understood to be intratheoretic, not merely reflecting, but actively constituted by the structure of the prevailing cultural framework. Cf. Kuhn, 'Reflections on my Critics', especially 259–66.

14   Pascal, *Pensées*, Papiers classés III 60 (294); 51.

15   See Sykes, 'Ernst Troeltsch and Christianity's Essence'; idem, *Identity of Christianity*, 148–73.

16   See Winch, 'Understanding a Primitive Society'. For its theological dimension, see Nineham, *Use and Abuse of the Bible*. Nineham, unfortunately, appears to confuse two senses of the term 'relativism': the need to consider a statement in its original context; and the suggestion that a given statement is true only in a specific context. See Coakley, 'Theology and Cultural Relativism'. For a more positive, if still critical, assessment of Nineham, see Barton, 'Reflections on Cultural Relativism'.

17   A difficulty must be noted with the concept of 'historicism' itself, which is rarely defined with any precision: see Nabrings, 'Historismus als Paralyse der Geschichte', 157. More generally, see D'Amico, *Historicism and Knowledge*. Although I have some reservations about the characterisation of historicism in Stout, *Flight from Authority*, 4–8, this seems to me to express much of what is of genuine significance in relation to the notion.

18   Russell, *Principles of Mathematics*, Appendix B.

19   Richardson, *History Sacred and Profane*, 90–9.

20   Troeltsch, 'Geschichte und Metaphysik', 68. Note also the phrase 'a latent theology of historicism' (p. 69).

21   The clearest statement of this argument remains Trigg, *Reason and Commitment*. One of the finest, if ultimately unconvincing, responses to this criticism, with specific reference to the sociology of science, may be found in Hesse, *Revolutions and Reconstructions in the Philosophy of Science*.

22   For exploration of a range of issues raised by historicism, see Faber,

'Ausprägungen des Historismus'; Nabrings, 'Historismus als Paralyse der Geschichte'.

23 A points stressed by Stout, *Flight from Authority*, 5–7.

24 Cumming, *Human Nature and History*.

25 Hick (ed.), *The Myth of God Incarnate*.

26 For a selection of quotations illustrating this conviction, see Coakley, 'Theology and Cultural Relativism', 223–4.

27 J. L. Houlden, in *The Myth of God Incarnate*, 125.

28 Thus Luther strikes those who read him as a very medieval person – but this does not alter the fact that he was able to introduce a new paradigm, opening the way to a more complete break with the medieval outlook. It is quite possible that what individuals such as Luther or Marx 'left unchallenged in the presuppositions of their times was far, far more than anything they challenged or changed' (Nineham, *Use and Abuse of the Bible*, 13); nevertheless, the *cumulative force* of many such individuals is to effect a change in the prevailing cultural paradigm.

29 Nineham, however, appears to vacillate on the question of whether there may be said to be 'monolithic cultural units': *Use and Abuse of the Bible*, 28, 30.

30 I shall pursue this question further in chapter 5. The basic theme, however, may be studied from Weiss, *Renaissance Discovery of Classical Antiquity*.

31 Cf. Evans-Pritchard, *Witchcraft, Oracles and Magic among the Azande*, based on research carried out during this period.

32 E.g., Danto, 'The Problem of Other Periods'.

33 Oexle, 'Geschichtswissenschaft im Zeichen des Historismus'.

34 Walsh, *Introduction to Philosophy of History*, 68. Cf. 33–4. Precisely this dismissive view appears to underlie the contribution of Leslie Houlden to *The Myth of God Incarnate*, 132: 'on what basis may the words of one age be carried into the speech of another?'

35 E.g, see Danto, 'Historical Language and Historical Reality'; Hanson and Martin, 'The Problem of Other Cultures'. A more detailed analysis of the problem may be found in Hanson, *Meaning in Culture*.

36 *Myth of God Incarnate*, 23; 4.

37 See the destructive criticism of Berger, *Rumour of Angels*. Note especially the *bon mot* (p. 62): 'while other analytic disciplines free us from the dead weight of the past, sociology frees us from the tyranny of the present.'

38 Kennedy, *Destutt de Tracy and the Origins of Ideology*.

39 On which see Lash, *Matter of Hope*, 125–34.

40 Topitsch, *Vom Ursprung und Ende der Metaphysik*. See also Geiger, *Ideologie und Wharheit*; Kelsen, *Aufsätze zur Ideologiekritik*.

41 In the case of biblical literature, the following may be noted: Shalit, 'A Clash of Ideologies'; Miller, 'Faith and Ideology in the Old Testament'; Gager, *Kingdom and Community*; Gottwald, *Tribes of Yahweh*; Elliott, *Home for the Homeless*. Of particular interest is the work of Gerd Theissen, particularly his *Urchristliche Wundergeschichten*; *Sociology of Early Palestinian Christianity*; *Social Setting of Pauline Christianity*. For a critique, see Boers, 'Sisyphus and His Rock'; Achtemeier, 'An Imperfect Union'.

42 E.g., see McGrath, *Making of Modern German Christology*, 13–15.

43 For a balanced assessment of this point, see Stout, *Flight from Authority*,

149–76.

44 See Lash, *Matter of Hope*, 112–24; Plekhanov, *Fundamental Problems of Marxism*, 70; Williams, 'Base and Superstructure in Marxist Cultural Theory'. Kautsky's highly idiosyncratic views on the origins of Christianity (reflecting the stance adopted in his essay 'Das Verhältnis von Unterbau und Überbau'), are best studied from *Der Ursprung des Christentums* (1921): see Keck, 'On the Ethos of Early Christians'. For a useful summary of Marxist–Leninist attitudes on the question, see Stasiewski, 'Ursprung und Entfaltung des Christentums in sowjetischer Sicht'.

45 The difficulty raised by this point was felt by Max Scheler, for whom sociology was essentially *ancilla philosophiae*. Social factors determined the presence, but not the nature, of ideas. In other words, an ideational core exists, independent of social factors. Cf. Berger and Luckmann, *Social Construction of Reality*, 19–21.

46 Lukács, *Geschichte und Klassenbewusstsein*, remains one of the finest statements of this belief.

47 E.g., Steinmetz, *Deutschland von 1476 bis 1648*, 90, suggests that Luther's religious ideas are simply the theological expression of an economic and political struggle. For a detailed analysis of the Marxist interpretation of the Reformation, see Dickens and Tonkin, *Reformation in Historical Thought*, 234–63.

48 Thus Swanson, *The Birth of the Gods*, is concerned with articulating a consciously Durkheimian response to the question of how individuals came to believe in the supernatural.

49 The classic study remains Berger and Luckmann, *The Social Construction of Reality*. See also Mannheim, *Sociology of Culture*. It should be noted that mathematics and natural sciences are generally exempted, wholly or partially, from this influence.

50 The gulf separating Greek habits of thought from those of their predecessors in the ancient near east has been brought out by Frankfort et al., *Before Philosophy*, 237–63; cf. Burkett, *Greek Religion*, 305–37.

51 A point emphasized by Martin, 'Sociology and Theology', 36.

52 This tension may be traced back to Marx himself, in that the epistemological weight he attaches to the concept of 'essence' appears to be vitiated by social subjectivism: Kain, 'History, Knowledge and Essence in the Early Marx'.

53 For what follows, see MacIntyre, 'Epistemological Crises, Dramatic Narrative and the Philosophy of Science'; MacIntyre, *Whose Justice? Which Rationality?*, 390; Stout, *Flight from Authority*, 4–8; 149–76; 256–72, and references therein.

54 MacIntyre, *Whose Justice? Which Rationality*, 389–403, especially 390–1.

55 See Lindbeck, *Nature of Doctrine*, 47.

56 Cf. Brunner's criticism of Ritschl on this point: Scheld, *Die Christologie Emil Brunners*, 105–11.

57 See Scroggs, 'The Sociological Interpretation of the New Testament'.

58 e.g, see Curtis and Petras (eds.), *The Sociology of Knowledge*.

59 Berger, *Rumour of Angels*, 57 (emphasis in original).

60 Cf. Wisan, 'Galileo and the Emergence of a New Scientific Style'; Rorty, *Philosophy and the Mirror of Nature*, 328–31, suggests that both approaches must be regarded as equally 'rational', given his rejection of the rational

foundations of knowledge.

61 Hacking, 'Spekulation, Berechnung und die Erschaffung von Phänomen'.

62 A comparison noted by Dawkins, *The Blind Watchmaker*.

63 The idea of 'perspectivism' – that apparently contradictory statements relate to different perspectives of reality – should be noted here: Coakley, 'Theology and Cultural Relativism', 229.

64 This point has been discussed in two papers by Hamnett: 'Sociology of Religion and Sociology of Error'; 'A Mistake about Error'. One of the many curious features of the writings of Gerd Theissen is that his vigorous rejection of any 'recourse to privileged knowledge' on the part of the theologian (e.g, *On Having a Critical Faith*, 10–11) is linked with what gives every indication of being an *uncritical* acceptance of such privileged observer status for contemporary sociology.

65 Habermas, *Knowledge and Human Interests*; Habermas, *Legitimation Crisis*; see further Bottomore, *Frankfurt School*; McCarthy, *Critical Theory of Jürgen Habermas*.

66 Fortes, *Oedipus and Job in West African Religion*, 66–8. The same point is made by Malinowski in his study of the Trobiander: *The Sexual Life of Savages in North-Western Melanesia*, 425–9. Such approaches have rightly been criticized as Eurocentric: Wiredu, *Philosophy and an African Culture*. Note also the view of Fenn, 'The Sociology of Religion: A Critical Survey', 123 'The functionalist synthesis in the sociology of religion has disappeared . . . Functionalism provided a privileged methodological stance from which the sociologist could interpret and transcend the accounts of groups and individuals.'

67 E.g., see Wilson, *Religious Sects: A Sociological Study*. His older study exemplifies the genre: *Sects and Society*.

68 Malcolm Bradbury, *The History Man* (London, 1977), 20.

69 For an attempt to analyse the emergence of Christianity on the basis of the model of the religious sect, see Scroggs, 'The Earliest Christian Communities as Sectarian Movements'. The use of the word 'sect' to refer to any movement prior to the development of a sacerdotal and sacramental systems (a process of institutionalization not realized until the Gregorian reforms of the eleventh century) is, strictly speaking, unhistorical. It is reasonable to point to 'family resemblances' between sixteenth-century sectarian movements, and the early Christian communities as revealed by recent scholarship (although the metaphor of 'family resemblance' is stretched somewhat on account of the significant time-span involved in the comparison).

70 See the two important recent discussions of Sperber, 'Is Symbolic Thought Prerational?'; Sperber, 'Apparently Irrational Beliefs'.

71 See, for example, Burrow, *Evolution and Society*.

72 Timpanaro, *The Freudian Slip*, 168. Cf. M. Mulkay and G. N. Gilbert, 'Accounting for Error', *Sociology* 16 (1982), 165: 'Correct belief is treated as the normal state of affairs ... and as requiring no special explanation.'

73 A classic statement of this so-called 'arationality' axiom is found in Laudan, *Progress and Its Problems*, 203: 'whenever a belief can be explained by adequate reasons, there is no need for, and little promise in, seeking out an alternative explanation in terms of social causes.'

74 Evans-Pritchard, *Theories of Primitive Religion*, 15.

75 Evans-Pritchard, 'Religion and the Anthropologists', 205.
76 Prickett, *Words and The Word*, 218. See further Ferreira, *Scepticism and Reasonable Doubt*. For the 'crisis of knowing' in the earlier modern period, see Macintyre, 'Epistemological Crises'; Shapiro, *Probability and Certainty*.
77 See Radcliffe, 'Relativising the Relativisers'.
78 Winch, *Idea of a Social Science*, passim; Taylor, 'Interpretation and the Sciences of Man'.
79 Giddens, *New Rules of Sociological Method*, 158.
80 See Ayer, *Language, Truth and Logic*; Ayer, *Logical Positivism*; Braithwaite, *Empiricist's View of the Nature of Religious Belief*; Ferré, *Language, Logic and God*.
81 Gellner, *Words and Things*, 79. This is not, it may be added, the position of Wittgenstein.
82 See further Kolakowski, *Positivist Philosophy*; cf. Stockman, *Antipositivist Theories of the Sciences*.
83 It is not my purpose here to pursue the consequences of logical positivism. One example of its relevance concerns the concept of 'meaning' itself, given impetus by the dictum of Moritz Schlick, 'the meaning of a sentence is its method of verification': Schlick, 'Meaning and Verification', *The Philosophical Review* 46 (1936), 261. A more sensitive analysis would suggest that the semantic interpretation and epistemic assessment of a sentence depend upon the other sentences which it 'consorts with': Glymour, *Theory and Evidence*, 145–55.
84 Steiner, *After Babel*.
85 E.g., Steiner, *After Babel*, 136 'The meaning of a word or sentence uttered in the past is no single event or sharply defined network of events. It is a recreative selection made according to hunches or principles which are more or less informed, more or less astute and comprehensive. The illocutionary force of any past statement is diffused in a complex pragmatic field which surrounds the lexical core.'
86 This point is particularly significant in relation to Christian theology, (including those theologies regarded by Lindbeck as 'cognitive-propositionalist') which has always emphasized the imperfection and the provisionality of its utterances concerning God. It is not merely the apophatic tradition which refuses to speak of God in terms paralleling those of logic or the natural sciences!
87 See Ebeling, 'Significance of the Critical Historical Method', 26–7. This essay is a masterly consideration of the problem under consideration, but should be supplemented by Stout, *Flight from Authority*, 149–76; 256–72.
88 This question is addressed, on the basis of a linguistic approach to understanding, by Gadamer, *Truth and Method*, 345–447. Gadamer suggests that the relativistic thesis fails on account of its implicit assumption of a determinate concept of meaning – 'meaning in itself' – whereas one's specific historical situation ought to be viewed as the horizon or perspective from which understanding first becomes possible. Cf. Warnke, *Gadamer*, 81–2.
89 Cf. Campbell, *Towards a Sociology of Irreligion*, 8–9.
90 Barnes and Bloor, 'Relativism, Rationalism and the Sociology of Knowledge', 23.
91 See Laeuchli, 'Das "Vierte Jahrhundert" in Karl Barths Prolegomena'. Similar

suggestions of a more rhetorical character, lacking serious historical and theological substantiation, are associated with Don Cupitt: Hick (ed.), *Myth of God Incarnate*, 139.

92 Elster, 'Belief, Bias and Ideology', 143.

Chapter 5 The Authority of the Past in Christian Thought

1 Davis, *Problem of Slavery*, 14. We have used this concept of ideology on account of its neutral and balanced stance: it should not be confused with the Marxian concept of false consciousness or the dominant ideas of the dominant class(es), or the Mannheimian notion of unrealized situationally transcendent ideas. The term 'ideology' is, of course, encountered in a wide variety of senses, often with negative connotations – e.g., see Geiger, *Ideologie und Wahrheit*; Bell, *End of Ideology*. Thompson refines and reformulates the concept of ideology to indicate the manner in which meaning or signification 'serves to sustain relations of domination': Thompson, *Studies in the Theory of Ideology*, 131–2.

2 Kelley, *Beginning of Ideology*, 4.

3 Spitz, *Renaissance and Reformation Movements*. For the difficulties this creates in relation to historical periodization, see Oberman, 'Reformation: Epoche oder Episode?'.

4 E.g., Antal, *Florentine Painting and its Social Background*.

5 Weisinger, 'English Origins of the Sociological Interpretation of the Renaissance'.

6 Lopez, 'Quattrocento genovese'. But see Cipolla, 'Economic Depression of the Renaissance?'.

7 Burke, *Renaissance Sense of the Past*, 1–6.

8 A classic study of various time scales may be found in Braudel, *Mediterranean World in the Age of Philip II*. Braudel draws a distinction between short-term change, linked with specific events, and of which contemporaries were conscious; and long-term change, almost impossible to notice at the time, but perceptible with historical hindsight. It is also possible that the absence of any notion of inductive evidence (i.e., inferring one thing from another) in the early Renaissance contributed to this lack of historical awareness: cf. Hacking, *Emergence of Probability*, 31–8.

9 A point stressed by Bloch, *Land and Work in Medieval Europe*.

10 Terms such as 'Italy', 'Germany' and 'Switzerland' do not have the same referent in the sixteenth and twentieth centuries. Following general practice, the terms are here used in a geographical, rather than political, sense.

11 Cf. Cipolla, *Clocks and Culture*.

12 Francastel, 'Valeurs socio-psychologiques et de l'espace-temps figuratif de la Renaissance'; Francastel, *L'ordre visuel du quattrocento*.

13 On which see further Struever, *History in the Renaissance*.

14 Salutati, *Epistolario*, 2.45.

15 Weiss, *Renaissance Discovery of Classical Antiquity*, 133.

16 Salutati, *Epistolario*, 1.326.

17 ' . . . mansit tamen in proximis successoribus similitudo quedam et aliquale

vestigium antiquitatis': *Epistolario*, 3.80.

18 See Brucker, *Civic World of Early Renaissance Florence*; Gilbert, 'Florentine Political Assumptions'; Goldthwaite, *Building of Renaissance Florence*; Martines, *Social World of the Florentine Humanists*; Plaisance, 'Culture et politique à Florence de 1542 à 1551'; Stephens, *The Fall of the Florentine Republic, 1512–1530*.

19 *Purgatorio* canto vi, lines 149–51.

20 See Baron, *Crisis of the Early Italian Renaissance*.

21 Cf. Seigel, '"Civic Humanism" or Ciceronian Rhetoric?'; McGrath, *Intellectual Origins of the European Reformation*, 32–8.

22 In fact, of course, the invasion stimulated the development of humanism in France, consolidating a process begun in Petrarch's Avignonese period: Simone, 'Il contributo degli umanisti veneti al prima sviluppo dell'umanesimo francesce.'

23 Bruno, 'Oratio in funere Nannis Strozzae', *Stephani Baluzii Miscellanae* (Lucca, 1764), 4.4.

24 Cf. Burke, *Italian Renaissance*, 28–39.

25 *Rerum Familiarum libri* VI.2.

26 Cf. Schmitt, 'Zur Wiederbelebung der Antike im Trecento'.

27 A masterly account of this development may be found in Weiss, *Renaissance Rediscovery of Antiquity*.

28 Ibid., 111–12.

29 An account of this discovery may be found in Biblioteca Laurenziana, MS Ashburnham 1657, fol. 107v–109r.

30 Newald, *Nachleben des antiken Geistes*, 2–4.

31 E.g., see Butler, *Tyranny of Greece over Germany*; Hatfield, *Aesthetic Paganism in German Literature*.

32 Marti, 'De Sanctis e il realismo dantesco'; Bonara, 'L'interpretazione del Petrarca e la poetica del realismo in De Sanctis'; Tateo, 'Il realismo critico desanctisiano e gli studi rinascimentali'.

33 For such debates, see Fumaroli, *Age de l'éloquence*, 91–2; Greene, *Light in Troy*.

34 For a brief summary, see Gray, 'Pursuit of Eloquence'. For a more general analysis, see McGrath, *Intellectual Origins of the European Reformation*, 32–43.

35 Hay, 'Flavio Biondo and the Middle Ages'.

36 It is thus significant that European writers of the Renaissance period north of Italy did not think of themselves as 'medieval': cf. Voss, *Das Mittelalter im historischen Denken Frankreichs*; Smalley, *English Friars and Antiquity*. The specific term *medium aevum* is first encountered in du Cange's *Glossarium* (Paris, 1678).

37 Bertola, 'La *Glossa Ordinaria* biblica ed i suoi problemi'; Smalley, 'The Problem of the *Glossa Ordinaria*'; Smalley, 'La *Glossa Ordinaria*, quelques prédécesseurs d'Anselme de Laon'; Smalley, 'Les commentaires bibliques de l'époque romane'.

38 The celebrated tension between the *mos gallicus* and *mos italicus* illustrates this tendency within late medieval legal circles: Kisch, *Humanismus und Jurisprudenz*, 9–76.

39 Cf. Struever, *History in the Renaissance*; Kelley, *Foundations of Modern Historical Scholarship*.

40 Salutati, *de laboribus Herculis*, I, x, 10.
41 Von Leyden, 'Antiquity and Authority: A Paradox in the Renaissance Theory of History'. Note especially the attitude of Vives, (p. 490), who tends to treat antiquity as a synonym for 'truth'.
42 Trinkaus, *In Whose Image and Likeness*, 689–721.
43 Cf. Newald, *Nachleben des antiken Geistes*, 39; 408–24.
44 On which see Burke, *Italian Renaissance*, 162–74.
45 See Bainton, *Erasmus of Christendom*, 248–52.
46 Oberman, *Werden und Wertung der Reformation*, 93–5.
47 For this understanding of 'classic', see Kermode, *The Classic*, 21.
48 On which see Burke, *Italian Renaissance*, 143–61.
49 McGrath, *Intellectual Origins of the European Reformation*, 122–39.
50 See Chomorat, 'Les *Annotations* de Valla'; Bentley, 'Erasmus' *Annotationes in Novum Testamentum*'.
51 It is interesting to note the extent to which this attitude was shared by most Italian bishops of the early sixteenth century, who found it virtually impossible to understand why Luther was making so much fuss about such an irrelevance as doctrine: cf. Alberigo, *I vescovi italiani*, 388–9.
52 See Dickens and Tonkin, *Reformation in Historical Thought*, 179–321.
53 For example, by suggesting that the German Reformation is the ideological expression of the class conflict evident in the Peasants' War, the common theme of the (Marxist) collection of essays in Steinmetz, *Der deutsche Bauernkrieg*, which may be compared with the more perceptive and critical collection in Scribner and Benecke, *The German Peasant War, 1525*.
54 Laube, 'Radicalism as a Research Problem'.
55 Fraenkel, *Testimonia Patrum*, 77–82.
56 E.g., see McGrath, *Intellectual Origins of the European Reformation*.
57 Cf. Locher, 'Von Bern nach Genf'.
58 See Bonorand, 'Die Bedeutung der Universität Wien für Humanismus und Reformation'; Bonorand, *Aus Vadians Freundes- und Schülerkreis in Wien*. See further Ankwick-Kleehoven, *Der Wiener Humanist Johannes Cuspinian*.
59 Farner, *Huldrych Zwingli*, 2.114–24.
60 Z 4.870.8–871.15. A similar strategy is associated with Origen and Augustine, possibly influencing Zwingli at this point.
61 See Goeters, 'Zwinglis Werdegang als Erasmianer'.
62 McGrath, *Iustitia Dei*, 2.32–3.
63 Goeters, 'Zwinglis Werdegang als Erasmianer'; Stauffer, 'Einfluß und Kritik des Humanismus in Zwinglis "Commentarius de vera et falsa religione"'.
64 Z 1.236–7; 247.5–23; 2.132–5.
65 Ziegler, 'Reformation des Lebens und der Sitten'.
66 This position, characteristic of Erasmus, is also associated with Bucer: cf. McGrath, *Intellectual Origins of the European Reformation*, 154–72, and references therein. This strong moralism also goes some way towards accounting for Zwingli's disinterest in the doctrine of justification by faith alone, which could be (and, it may be added, generally was) construed as anti-moralist.
67 See Neusner, *Die reformatorische Wende bei Zwingli*, 38–74.
68 McGrath, *Luther's Theology of the Cross*, 27–53.

69 WABr 1.153.3–154.1.
70 Cf. Grossmann, *Humanism in Wittenberg 1485–1517*.
71 For Luther's list of the alterations, see WABr 1.155.41–5.
72 WABr 1.99.8–13.
73 de Vooght, *Les sources de la doctrine chrétienne*; Schüssler, *Der Primät der Heiligen Schrift*.
74 Moeller, 'Die deutschen Humanisten', 53–4.
75 WATr 2.439.25 (no. 2383).
76 WADB 8.12.5. The reference seems to be to scripture in general, rather than the Old Testament in particular.
77 WADB 7.385.25–30. The German verb 'treiben' (here translated as 'inculcate') has various shades of meaning, including 'impel' and 'propel'.
78 On this, see Ebeling, 'Die Anfänge von Luthers Hermeneutik'; McGrath, *Luther's Theology of the Cross*, 76–81.
79 McGrath, *Intellectual Origins of the European Reformation*, 153–4; 160–2; 171.
80 E.g., WA 3.211.23–5. For other occurances of such images in the *Dictata*, see WA 3.131.15–16; 132.21–3; 212.27–35; 254.24–32.
81 WA 55 II.105.6–9.
82 McGrath, *Intellectual Origins of the European Reformation*, 154–8. Much the same point underlies the celebrated distinction between *Historie* and *Geschichte* in more recent German theology: cf. McGrath, *Making of Modern German Christology*, 77–80.
83 WA 40 I.78.16.
84 Like all the magisterial reformers, Luther allows a natural knowledge of God – but this is in no way compromises his Christological concentration at this point. See McGrath, *Luther's Theology of the Cross*, 161–4.
85 WA 40 II.328.17–18. Commenting on this passage, Wolf writes: 'It is not a metaphysical being, but an concrete historical event – God's saving action towards sinners – which is the object of theology': Wolf, 'Rechtfertigungslehre', 12.
86 A Christological mode of exegesis of the Old Testament is also indicated.
87 Friedensburg, *Geschichte der Universität Wittenberg*, 154.
88 Oberman, *Werden und Wertung der Reformation*, 82–140.
89 E.g., McGrath, *Intellectual Origins of the European Reformation*, 183.
90 For a full discussion, see Peters, *Glaube und Werk*.
91 Melanchthon, *Loci Communes* (1521), praefatio. This reference was dropped in later editions of the work (such as that of 1533), as Melanchthon came under increasing pressure (based largely on educational considerations) to extend his systematic theology to include such matters as the incarnation and the Trinity. The fact remains, however, that Melanchthon's initial concerns were thoroughly soteriological.
92 Warfield, *Calvin and Augustine*, 322.
93 It may also be noted that the same set of criteria are used in the critical evaluation of other fathers, as the rise of the new literary genre of Lutheran patrologies makes clear: Fraenkel, *Testimonia Patrum*, 283–306. Each father is assessed in terms of his theological reliability, using explicitly theological criteria (which would have horrified Erasmus) reflecting the concerns of the Wittenberg reformers.

94   See the perceptive discussion of Fraenkel, *Testimonia Patrum*, 70–96.
95   See Meijering, *Melanchthon and Patristic Thought*, for an excellent analysis.
96   McGrath, *Iustitia Dei*, vol. 2, pp. 11–19; 23–5.
97   Brunner, *Vom Werk des heiligen Geistes*, 38; Kolfhaus, *Christusgemeinschaft bei Johannes Calvin*, 11–23; Krusche, *Das Wirken des heiligen Geistes bei Calvin*, 266.
98   Kolfhaus, *Christusgemeinschaft*, 36.
99   E.g., OC 47.64; 321–2; 354; 50.205; 51.183.
100 On account of the presuppositions of his age, Calvin has little to say on the problem of how belief in scripture and faith in Christ were related: Dowey, *Knowledge of God in Calvin's Theology*, 161–4. In his lucid study, Rist suggests that Calvin's conjunction of Word and Spirit may be the key to such riddles: 'Méthode théologique de Calvin', 24.
101 While there are obvious shortcomings in the parallel, it will be clear that there are certain striking similarities between the general thrust of the approaches of both Luther and Calvin to the history of Jesus of Nazareth, and that of Bultmann. The history of Jesus, when properly interpreted, is treated as possessing existential significance, capable of being mediated through word and proclamation to ages other than its own. The *kerygma* discloses both the possibility and the shape of the new existence, which is grounded in and illustrated by the history of Jesus of Nazareth.
102 Cf. Rist, 'Méthode théologique de Calvin', 24. The appeal to the Holy Spirit as a hermeneutical surety serves to distinguish Reformation hermeneutics from those of the later Renaissance, which tended to rely solely upon philological, textual and literary tools.
103 For a full analysis, see McGrath, *Intellectual Origins of the European Reformation*, 140–51.
104 It is this point which causes such difficulties for Luther's ecclesiology. Luther concedes that the medieval church did indeed transmit and propagate the *kerygma*, in word and sacrament. This would seem to suggest that it is indeed the 'true church', to which Luther is obliged to make the (unsatisfactory) response, that it merely retains the outward appearance of such a church.
105 The introduction of this fiction dates from 1788, in the course of Lessing's attempt to discredit the Lutheran writer Melchior Goeze: Bornkamm, *Luther im Spiegel der deutschen Geistesgeschichte*, 14–15; 199–202.
106 There are obvious parallels here with Karl Barth's concept of 'the Word of God in its three-fold form'.
107 The suggestion that it could was particularly associated with the Radical Reformation.
108 Cf. Lohff, 'Limits of Doctrinal Pluralism'.
109 Stayer, 'Christianity in One City', 117 n.1.
110 Laube, 'Radicalism as a Research Problem', 20, with documentation.
111 A point stressed by Laube, 'Radicalism as a Research Problem', 13.
112 Van Dülmen, *Reform als Revolution*.
113 The case for accepting the influence of Taborite eschatology upon Müntzer seems convincing: Schwarz, *Die apokalyptische Theologie Thomas Müntzers*.
114 For the Enlightenment in general, see Porter and Teich, *Enlightenment in National Context*; Yolton et al., *Blackwell Companion to the Enlightenment*. On

its ecclesiastical dimension, see Cragg, *Church and the Age of Reason*. The phenomenon of the 'flight from authority' in the areas of philosophy, theology and ethics has been fully documented and analysed by Stout, *Flight from Authority*.

115   For some of the political currents, see Valjavec, *Entstehung der politischen Strömungen*.

116   And subsequently those of Romanticism. Brunschwig, for example, seems to suggest that the genesis of a Romantic ideology in the 1790s may be dismissed as an irrational reaction to social frustration: *La crise de l'état prussien*.

117   Davis, *Problem of Slavery*, 14. See the earlier discussion, p. 89.

118   E.g., see Gerth, *Die sozialgeschichtliche Lage der bürgerlichen Intelligenz*, 80–95.

119   Cf. McGrath, *Iustitia Dei*, vol. 2, 136–47.

120   On the intellectual side of the Enlightenment, see Hazard, *La pensée européenne au XVIIIe siècle*. On its more theological aspects, see McGrath, 'Reformation to Enlightenment', 206–29.

121   Walker, *German Home Towns*, 119–33, especially 129; Krieger, *German Idea of Freedom*, 8.

122   Cf. Gerth, *Die sozialgeschichtliche Lage der bürgerlichen Intelligenz*.

123   Bertaux, *Hölderlin und die französische Revolution*, is helpful in evoking a sense of historical empathy at this point.

124   Shelton, *Young Hölderlin*, 107–18; Samuel, *Friedrich von Hartenberg*, 64–89; Behler, *Friedrich Schlegel*, 20–9; Haym, *Rudolf von Humboldt*, 32–66.

125   See Epstein, *Genesis of German Conservatism*, 41–4; 52–3.

126   Schlingensiepen-Pogge, *Sozialethos der lutherischen Aufklärungstheologie*.

127   E.g., see Hasselhorn, *Der altwürttembergische Pfarrstand im 18. Jahrhundert*.

128   Gramsci, *The Modern Prince*, 118–20.

129   See Toews, *Hegelianism*, 72–5.

130   A similar pattern emerges for the early nineteenth century: Ayconberry and Droz, 'Structures sociales et courants idéologiques dans l'Allemagne prérévolutionaire'.

131   Usefully illustrated in the case of Württemberg by Lehmann, *Pietismus und weltliche Ordnung*.

132   The comparison with England is instructive: Dyson, 'Theological Legacies of the Enlightenment'. In France – where no equivalent of Pietism developed – religion was easily marginalized as an irrelevance.

133   Loofs, *Leitfaden*, 1.

134   Steinbart, *Glückseligkeitslehre*, 87–9; 146–9. Cf. McGrath, *Iustitia Dei*, 2.146–7.

135   See Reventloh, *The Authority of the Bible and the Rise of the Modern World*, 289–308. Schweitzer, *Quest of the Historical Jesus*, begins his analysis of the discussion a century later.

136   See Pelikan, *Jesus through the Centuries*, 182–93.

137   For a useful discussion of Lessing's use of the metaphor of 'binding' in relation to the human response to a religious message, see Michalson, 'Faith and History', 283–7.

138   Lessing, 'Über den Beweis des Geistes und der Kraft', in *Werke*, 8.8. Cf. Michalson, 'Faith and History'; Michalson, *Lessing's 'Ugly Ditch'*.

139   Lessing, 'Über den Beweis des Geistes und der Kraft'; *Werke* 8.14.

140 Schwarz, 'Lessings "Spinozismus"'. Cf. Hermann, 'Lessings religionsphiloso-phischer und theologischer Problematik'.
141 Reimarus, 'Von Verschreiung der Vernunft auf den Kanzeln', in Lessing, *Werke*, 7.673–85.
142 A virtual neglect of this crucial point reduces the value of Harvey, *Historian and the Believer*, which otherwise offers an excellent introduction to the problems attending the specific issue of historical knowledge on account of its temporal distance.
143 Reimarus, 'Verschreiung der Vernunft', 689.
144 Lessing, 'Über den Beweis des Geistes und der Kraft', 11–12.
145 Ibid., 11.
146 The proper use of the 'principle of analogy' as a historical tool underlies the different position of Troeltsch and Pannenberg on the historicity of the resurrection: cf. McGrath, *Making of Modern German Christology*, 81–5; 170–2; Michalson, 'Pannenberg on the Resurrection and Historical Method'.
147 Lessing, 'Über den Beweis des Geistes und der Kraft', 15.
148 Fackenheim, 'Kant and Radical Evil'. For the rejection of this notion in more recent modern theologies, see Scheld, *Die Christologie Emil Brunners*, 117–22.
149 Useful surveys of the whole field may be found in Steck, 'Dogma und Dogmengeschichte'; Kantzenbach, *Evangelium und Dogma*; Lohse, 'Was verstehen wir unter Dogmengeschichte'; Lohse, 'Theorien der Dogmengesch-ichte'; Neufeld, 'Liberale Dogmengeschichtserforschung'; Flückiger, *Der Ursprung des christlichen Dogmas*.
150 Kantzenbach, *Evangelium und Dogma*, 81–91. His very brief statements on the question are summarized by Kantzenbach on pp. 82–4.
151 Ibid., 98–101.
152 Cf. ibid., 61–114.
153 Ibid., 114–30.
154 Cf. the different approaches and evaluations in Hodgson, *Formation of Historical Theology*, and Geiger, *Spekulation und Kritik*.
155 Cf. *Lehrbuch der christlichen Dogmengeschichte*, 59.
156 Harnack, *Dogmengeschichte*, 3rd edn, 1.69–70.
157 Ibid., 1.15–16.
158 For an analysis, see Meijering, *Theologische Urteile über die Dogmengeschichte*, 87–101.
159 Schmitz, *Frühkatholizismus bei Adolf von Harnack*, 51.
160 Meijering, *Theologische Urteile über die Dogmengeschichte*, 12–24; 34–59.
161 E.g., Harnack, *Dogmengeschichte*[3], 1.14; 79.
162 Harnack, *Wesen des Christentums*, 92.
163 Meijering, *Hellenisierung des Christentums*, 19–48.
164 Ibid., 99–102, for an analysis of the main passages.
165 More generally, see Schmitz, *Frühkatholizismus bei Adolf von Harnack*, 50–93.
166 Meijering, *Der 'ganze' und der 'wahre' Luther*, 17, for a summary of the main points for which Harnack praises Luther.
167 Cited Neufeld, *Adolf von Harnack*, 109.
168 Particular criticism has been directed against the prioritization of the 'Hellenization' theme, along with the lack of clarity attending the concept: see Grillmeier, 'Hellenisierung-Judaizierung des Christentums'. For more

general assessments, see Lohse, 'Theorien der Dogmengeschichte'; Neufeld, 'Liberale Dogmengeschichtserforschung'. For a critical assessment of more recent works, see Flückiger, *Der Ursprung des christlichen Dogmas* (this last-mentioned concentrating upon Schweitzer and Werner). The three volumes of the *Handbuch der Dogmen- und Theologiegeschichte* (ed. Andresen) include some important criticisms of Harnack and Loofs, while demonstrating a curious reticence to engage with the question of what 'dogma' might actually designate.

169 For Ritschl's Kantianism (which predisposes him towards antimetaphysical attitudes in his *dogmengeschichlich* studies) see Wrzecionko, *Die philosophische Wurzeln der Theologie Albrecht Ritschls*.

170 Harnack, *Das Wesen des Christentums*, 126–8; 144–6.

171 Bévenot, 'Primacy and Development', 407.

172 Cf. Edwards, 'Pagan Doctrine of the Absoluteness of God'; Pollard, 'Impassibility of God'.

173 E.g., Surin, 'Impassibility of God and the Problem of Evil'.

174 McGrath, *Luther's Theology of the Cross*, 161–75.

175 McGrath, '"The Righteousness of God" from Augustine to Luther'; McGrath, *Iustitia Dei* 1.4–16; 51–70; McGrath, *Luther's Theology of the Cross*, 93–147.

176 MacIntyre, *Religious Significance of Atheism*, 14.

177 On which, see Kerr, *Theology after Wittgenstein*.

178 Mariology is an area of doctrinal difference which seems particularly vulnerable in this respect: cf. Johnson, 'Marian Devotion in the Western Church'.

179 MacIntyre, *Whose Justice? Which Rationality?*, 5.

180 Monzel, *Phänomenologische und religionssoziologische Untersuchungen über den Traditionalismus*, 41–6. Four senses of 'traditionalism' are distinguished: 13–14.

181 E.g., Thiselton, 'Academic Freedom, Religious Tradition, and the Morality of Christian Scholarship'. It seems to us that Thiselton perhaps fails to appreciate the importance of *institutional* autonomy in his understanding of 'academic freedom', a concept which may be usefully explored from the history of the German academic community in the period 1890–1933: Ringer, *Decline of the German Mandarins*.

182 Rosenkranz, *Das Zentrum der Spekulation*.

183 Massey, 'Literature of Young Germany'.

184 Riehl, *Die bürgerliche Gesellschaft*, esp. 299.

185 Conrad, *German Universities*, 71. Lawyers – the next most numerous class of graduates – accounted for three in every ten. By the end of the decade, however, the number of theological graduates began to decline (p. 74).

186 Ibid., 88.

187 Dieterici, *Geschichtliche und statistiche Nachrichten*, 117.

188 E.g., see Busch, *Geschichte der Privatdozenten*, 46–7.

189 Barnes and Bloor, 'Relativism, Rationalism and the Sociology of Knowledge', 23.

190 Once more, Elster's cautionary *dictum* should be borne in mind (Elster, 'Belief, Bias and Ideology', 143): 'there is no reason to suppose that beliefs that serve certain interests are also to be explained by those interests.' The social factors here identified point to a predisposition towards plausibility in

the case of both conservative and progressive views; neither view, however, may be said to be *generated* by these social factors on the basis of the evidence available.

191 On this theme, see Berger and Luckmann, *Social Construction of Reality*.

192 Blanke et al., 'German Tradition of *Historik*, 1750–1900'.

193 Rorty, *Consequences of Pragmatism*, 60–71.

194 Goldstein, 'Foucault among the Sociologists'.

195 A development charted, analysed and evaluated by Morgan, *Biblical Interpretation*.

196 E.g., Hirsch, *Geschichte der neuern evangelischen Theologie*; Blumenberg, *Legitimät der Neuzeit*.

197 Such as that I myself followed in writing *The Making of Modern German Christology*, and the section of *Iustitia Dei* dealing with the modern period.

198 Recent developments within the field of social history – such as those documented by Charles Tilly, 'Vecchio e nuovo nella storia sociale' – reinforce, rather than weaken, this argument.

199 One of the criticisms directed against Lindbeck's *Nature of Doctrine* by its 'experiential-expressive' opponents: see David Ford's review of Lindbeck's book in *Journal of Theological Studies* 37 (1986), 277–82; 281.

200 The term 'conservative' possesses depths of meaning usually overlooked in theological discussion of a more overtly polemical nature. Cf. Mannheim, 'Das konservative Denken'; Thielicke, *Der evangelische Glaube*, 1.20–2.

201 MacIntyre, *Whose Justice? Which Rationality?*, 346.

202 Ibid., 326–48. 203 Ibid., 345.

204 Ibid., 344.

205 Davidson's arguments for the incoherence of the notion of radically incommensurable conceptual frameworks should be noted here: Davidson, 'On the Very Idea of a Conceptual Scheme'. According to Davidson, conceptual schemes are, at least to some extent, commensurate.

206 For a nuanced exposition, see Cohen, *Marx's Theory of History*.

207 See Shaw, *Marx's Theory of History*. It must be stressed that historical materialism makes no claims to explain the fine details of history, nor can it be said to constitute a form of historical determinism.

208 Cf. Ramsden, *The 1898 Movement*.

209 Walgrave, *Unfolding Revelation*, 31.

210 For a penetrating analysis, see Lenhardt, 'Anamnetic Solidarity'.

211 For the text of the *Theses*, see Benjamin, *Gesammelte Schriften* 2.691–704. There are 18 theses, with two appended as 'A' and 'B'. For modern studies, see Greffrath, *Metaphorischer Materialismus*; Habermas, 'Exkurs zu Benjamins Geschichtsphilosophischen Thesen'; Neuhaus, *Transzendentale Erfahrung als Geschichtsverlust?*, 277–333; Zons, 'Walter Benjamins "Thesen über den Begriff der Geschichte"'.

212 For comment, see Habermas, 'Exkurs', 20–1.

213 E.g., see Greffrath, *Metaphorischer Materialismus*, 65–71.

214 Habermas, 'Exkurs', 23–4.

215 For the distinction, see McGrath, *Making of Modern German Christology*, 76–8.

216 It is interesting to note that Benjamin suggests that Marx's approach to history, especially the outcome of the class struggle, is essentially the

secularization of messianic expectations: *Werke* 3.1231.

217 For the imagery, see Scholem, 'Walter Benjamin und sein Engel'.

218 Benjamin uses the following lines from Gerhard Scholem's 'Gruß vom Angelus' as a motto for Thesis 9: 'Mein Flügel ist zum Schwung bereit/*ich kehrte gern zurück*' (emphasis Benjamin's).

Chapter 6 Tradition: Access to the Identity-Giving Past

1 See the seminal analysis by Ebeling, *Wort Gottes und Tradition*, 25–6; 99; 142, in which he argues that the subject matter of tradition is Christologically concentrated to the point at which the entire gospel may be summarised in a name – Jesus of Nazareth. A related line of argument may be found in Macquarrie, 'Tradition, Truth and Christology'.

2 E.g., see MacIntyre, *After Virtue*; Root, 'Narrative Structure of Soteriology'; Jones, 'Narrative, Community and the Moral Life'; Macquarrie, 'Tradition, Truth and Christology'.

3 Scott Holland, 'Faith', 46. Cf. Morgan, 'Faith', which analyses and extends Scott Holland's discussion.

4 But see the important discussion of Geiselmann, 'Trient über das Verhältnis der Heiligen Schrift und der nicht geschriebenen Traditionen'.

5 E.g., see van Leer, *Tradition and Scripture in the Early Church*; van den Brink, 'Traditio im theologische Sinne'; Cullmann, 'Scripture and Tradition'.

6 E.g., de Vooght, *Les sources de la doctrine chrétienne*; Schüssler, *Der Primät der Heiligen Schrift*; McGrath, *Intellectual Origins of the European Tradition*, 140–51.

7 Cf. Lengsfeld, *Überlieferung: Tradition und Schrift* for an excellent analysis. For a more recent discussion, see Brosseder, 'Überlieferung'.

8 For one line of argument, see Kaspar, 'Tradition als theologisches Erkenntnisprinzip'.

9 See Dulles, *Models of Revelation*, for a discussion. Note especially the argument (p. 13): 'The Jewish and Christian view of God, the world and human life is inseparably entwined with the conviction that God is free and personal, that he acts on behalf of those whom he loves, and that his action includes, already within history, a partial disclosure of his nature, attributes, attitudes and intentions. The acceptance of revelation, therefore, is of fundamental importance to the Christian faith.'

10 The view of Lessing: McGrath, *Making of Modern German Christology*, 11–13; Michalson, 'Faith and History'.

11 On which see further Schwarz, 'Lessings "Spinozismus"'.

12 Shaw, *Marx's Theory of History*.

13 Downing, *Has Christianity a Revelation?*; Barr, 'Revelation through History'; idem, *Old and New in Interpretation*, 65–102.

14 Pannenberg, 'Revelation in Early Christianity'.

15 McGrath, *Iustitia Dei*, vol. 1, 23–36; 71–4.

16 Hart, *Unfinished Man and the Imagination*, 83–105.

17 Jaspers, *Philosophical Faith*, 145.

18 It is important to notice how New Testament uses the same Greek verb (*paradidonai*) to refer to both the Father's 'handing over' of the Son, and also

the community's 'handing down' of the tradition thus generated: see Barth, *CD* II/2, 484; Popkes, *Christus Traditus*. For Moltmann's use of this theme, as developed by Popkes, see McGrath, *Making of Modern German Christology*, 188–91. The full significance of the New Testament theme of *Christus traditus* is often overlooked by English language theologians, in that the theme of 'betrayal' tends to overshadow the theologically more significant motif of 'handing over'.

19 Macquarrie, 'Tradition, Truth and Christology', 40–2.

20 Brunner, *Wahrheit als Begegnung*.

21 For an exhaustive account of the implications of this statement, see de la Potterie, *La verité dans saint Jean*.

22 An important (and controversial) discussion of this theme is to be found in Gottwald, *Tribes of Yahweh*.

23 Cf. McGrath, *Iustitia Dei*, 1.67–70.

24 See Rawls, *Theory of Justice*, 5.

25 Battles, 'God was Accomodating Himself to Human Capacity'.

26 See McGrath, *Making of Modern German Christology*, 112–13.

27 Ricoeur, 'Ethics and Culture', 157.

28 'C'est ça ma tradition, je n'en ai pas d'autre. Ni la tradition orientale, ni la tradition juive. Elles me manquent par mon historicité.' As reported in *Le Nouvel Observateur*, 10 March 1980, 93.

29 The reader who is surprised by the inclusion of this third category of thinkers is invited to reflect upon Ziman, *Public Knowledge*.

30 Individualism is a characteristic feature of both the rationalism of Descartes and the empiricism of Locke. Schouls persuasively suggests that this reflects shared methodological presuppositions: Schouls, *Imposition of Method*, 5–25. Berkeley's idea of God as guarantor of reality and Hume's scepticism concerning evidence even for the existence of the external world may be regarded as the direct outcome of the individualism of the empiricist tradition. Cf. Bennett, *Locke, Berkeley, Hume*, 165–98; 313–53.

31 E.g., Gurvitch, *Social Frameworks of Knowledge*. Cf. the discussion in chap. 4.

32 Kolakowski, 'Anspruch auf die selbstverschuldete Unmündigkeit', 1.

33 Bowker, 'Religions as Systems'. For the same process in the tradition of the natural sciences, see Barnes, *Scientific Knowledge and Sociological Theory*, 66–7.

34 The term 'tradition' is used loosely at this stage, fully recognizing that 'a range of traditions' might be a more appropriate designation of the empirical situation.

35 See McGrath, 'Christian Ethics'.

36 A point stressed by Sykes, *Identity of Christianity*, 276–86, following Wainwright, *Doxology*.

37 See McGrath, 'Geschichte, Überlieferung und Erzählung'.

38 Cf. Torrance, *Theological Science*, 9–11; Carnes, *Axiomatics and Dogmatics*, 10–16; 51–3.

39 Stout, *Flight from Authority*, 2–3.

40 See further Aner, *Theologie der Lessingszeit*; Cassirer, *Philosophy of the Enlightenment*; Hazard, *La pensée européenne*; McGrath, 'Reformation to Enlightenment', 199–229; Wolff, *Weltanschauung der deutschen Aufklärung*.

41 Polanyi, *Personal Knowledge*, 269. For a summary of various anti- authoritarian

stances in the modern period, see Simon, *General Theory of Authority*, 13–20; 157–61. For a contemporary statement of the rhetoric of total ethical and spiritual autonomy, see Cupitt, *Taking Leave of God*.

42   e.g. Cupitt, *Taking Leave of God*, 9 'Modern people ... want to live their own lives, which means making their own rules, steering a course through life of one's own choice.' Cf. Williams, 'Religious Realism', 5–7.

43   Thus Cupitt's quest for individual moral and spiritual autonomy apparently takes place outside history and society, somewhat reducing its potential relevance.

44   E.g., see Berger and Luckmann, *Social Construction of Reality*; Barnes, *Interests and the Growth of Knowledge*.

45   Stout, *Flight from Authority*, 3.

46   Gadamer, *Truth and Method*, 239–40. Gadamer himself may be regarded as developing Heidegger's projective conceptual *Vorgriff* into the concept of 'horizon'. Cf. Bleicher, *Contemporary Hermeneutics*, 111–13.

47   Gadamer, *Truth and Method*, 271. A similar point was made by Bukharin in 1931, criticizing Wittgenstein's *Tractatus Logico-Philosophicus* (1921) as failing to deal with the *real* subject – 'social and historical man'. Bukharin, 'Theory and Practice', 1–7. (Bukharin was liquidated during the Stalinist purges of 1938).

48   Gadamer, *Truth and Method*, 239.

49   German readers of this work might care to note that the English word 'scientific' in this context should be understood as *naturwissenschaftlich*, rather than *wissenschaftlich*.

50   For a discussion, see Thomson, *Tradition and Authority in Science*, 1–35.

51   For critical assessment of Kuhn's concept of 'paradigm', see Mastermann, 'Nature of a Paradigm'.

52   See Kuhn, *Structure of Scientific Revolutions*. It may be noted, however, that Toulmin prefers the biological metaphor of 'evolution' rather than the political metaphor of 'revolution' in relation to scientific development: Toulmin, *Human Understanding*.

53   Bradley, 'Gadamer's "Truth and Method"', is a useful introduction at this point.

54   For what follows, see Warnke, *Gadamer*, 75–7. A more detailed analysis of Gadamer's approach to tradition, authority and reason may be found in Thiselton, *Two Horizons*, 293–326. For important parallels between Newman and Gadamer, see Louth, 'Nature of Theological Understanding'.

55   Gadamer, *Truth and Method*, 235–53.

56   See McGrath, 'Reformation to Enlightenment', 199–203.

57   Jüngel, *God as the Mystery of the World*, 13.

58   A theme creatively explored by Williams, 'Trinity and Revelation'.

59   E.g., Meeks, 'The Stranger from Heaven in Johannine Sectarianism'; Elliott, *A Home for the Homeless*.

60   Furlong, *Study in Memory*, 6.

61   Reiff and Scheerer, *Memory and Hypnotic Age Regression*, 25.

62   Tulving, *Elements of Episodic Memory*, 17–120.

63   Bower and Clark, 'Narrative Stories as Mediators for Serial Learning'.

64   Gruneberg, 'Memory Processes Unique to Humans', 253–9.

65 See Rundus, 'Analysis of Rehearsal Processes in Free Recall'.

66 See McGrath, 'Geschichte, Überlieferung und Erzählung'; Wainwright, *Doxology*.

67 E.g., see de Sanctis' *Lezioni zurighesi sul Petrarca* and *Lezioni e saggi sul Dante*. Cf. Marti, 'De Sanctis e il realismo dantesco'; Bonara, 'L'interpretazione del Petrarca e la poetica del realismo in De Sanctis'; Tateo, 'Il realismo critico desanctisiano e gli studi rinascimentali'. More generally, see Biscione, *Neo-umanesimo e Rinascimento*; Landucci, *Cultura e ideologia in Francesco De Sanctis*; Mirri, *Francesco De Sanctis politico e storico della civiltà moderna*.

68 A point stressed by Butler, *Tyranny of Greece over Germany*; Hatfield, *Aesthetic Paganism in German Literature*.

69 Cf. MacIntyre, *After Virtue*, 220–1; Jones, 'MacIntyre on Narrative'.

70 Cf. MacIntyre, 'Epistemological Crises'.

71 McGrath, *Reformation Thought*, 122–5.

72 This does not imply the Enlightenment notion of 'exemplarism' or 'imitation', but rather a process of being conformed to Christ through faith: McGrath, 'Christian Ethics'.

73 MacIntyre, *After Virtue*, 461.

74 This question is too vast to be explored fully here. For the recent and influential view that it is the apocalyptic framework of rationality that serves to identify Jesus, see Pannenberg, *Jesus – God and Man*. Other views are documented in McGrath, *Making of Modern German Christology*.

75 MacIntyre, *Whose Justice? Which Rationality?*, 6.

76 This suggestion opens up potentially important functionalist ways of defining 'faith' – for example, as adherence to a community and its specific way of thinking.

77 E.g., see Dewart, *Future of Belief*, 50–1. For a response, see Lonergan, 'Dehellenization of Dogma'.

78 This is not true in the case of F. C. Baur. Here, the Hegelian model which appears to undergird the phenomenon of doctrinal development concerns the recognition that Christian doctrines (such as the incarnation) are essentially religious representations (*Vorstellungen*) of pure concepts (*Begriffe*). The development of doctrine may thus be linked with the shift towards more conceptual modes of thought. Cf. Rosen, *Hegel's Dialectic*, 55–121.

79 E.g., Rashdall, *Idea of Atonement*. For the implications that the theory of evolution appeared to have for the development of doctrine in the final decade of the nineteenth century, see Illingworth, 'Incarnation in Relation to Development', 181–2. For documentation and bibliographies, see Moore, 'Evolution of Protestant Liberals'; Peacocke, 'Biological Evolution and Christian Theology'.

80 At one level, this might take the form of transposing dogmatic to moral statements: for illustration and critique of this development in the early twentieth century, see Forsyth, *Cruciality of the Cross*, esp. 175–218; Forsyth, *Person and Place of Jesus Christ*, 213–57.

81 Piaget, *Child's Construction of Reality*.

82 E.g., the views of L. Kohlberg, summarized by Duska and Whelan, *Moral Development*.

83 To date, the only work I have come across to draw upon Piaget in an

informed manner is Fowler, *Stages of Faith*, which does not touch on the issues we have in mind.

84 A point stressed by Lindbeck, *Nature of Doctrine*, 74.

85 On worship, see Kavanagh, *On Liturgical Theology*; Taft, 'Liturgy as Theology'; Wainwright, *Doxology*; on prayer, see Sauter, 'Das Gebet als Wurzeln des Redens von Gott'; and references therein.

86 Cf. Tilley, 'Incommensurability, Intratextuality, and Fideism'.

87 Cf. Goethe, *Faustus* 1. Theil, 'Nacht', 682–3. 'Was du ererbt von deinen Vätern hast/Erwirb es, um es zu besitzen.'

Bibliography

Achtemeier, P. J., 'An Imperfect Union: Reflections on Gerd Theissen, *Urchristliche Wundergeschichten*', *Semeia* 11 (1978), 49–68.

Alberigo, G., *I vescovi italiani al concilio di Trento* (Florence, 1959).

Allen, R. O., and Spilka, B., 'Committed and Consensual Religion', *Journal for the Scientific Study of Religion* 6 (1967), 191–206.

D'Amico, R., *Historicism and Knowledge* (New York, 1989).

Andresen, C. (ed.), *Handbuch der Dogmen- und Theologiegeschichte* (3 vols: Göttingen, 1980–4).

Aner, K., *Die Theologie der Lessingszeit* (Halle, 1929).

Ankwick-Kleehoven, H., *Der Wiener Humanist Johannes Cuspinian, Gelehrter und Diplomat zur Zeit Kaiser Maximilians* (Graz, 1959).

Antal, F., *Florentine Painting and its Social Background* (London, 1947).

Armstrong, A. H., 'The Self-Definition of Christianity in Relation to Platonism', in E. P. Sanders (ed.), *Jewish and Christian Self-Definition* (3 vols: London, 1980–2), 1.74–99.

Aulén, G., *Christus Victor: An Historical Study of the Three Main Types of the Idea of Atonement* (London, 1931).

Austin, J. L., 'The Meaning of a Word', in *Philosophical Papers*, (Oxford, 2nd edn, 1970), 23–43.

———, 'Performative Utterances', in *Philosophical Papers*, 232–52.

Avis, P. D. L., *Ecumenical Theology and the Elusiveness of Doctrine* (London, 1986).

Ayconberry, P. and Droz, J., 'Structures sociales et courants idéologiques dans l'Allemagne prérévolutionaire, 1835–1847', *Annali Feltrinelli* 6 (1963), 164–236.

Ayer, A. J., *Language, Truth and Logic* (London, 1936).

———, *Logical Positivism* (London, 1959).

Bainton, R. H., *Erasmus of Christendom* (London, 1969).

Bandt, H., *Luthers Lehre vom verborgenen Gott* (Berlin, 1958).

Barfield, O., *Poetic Diction* (London, new edn, 1952).

———, 'The Meaning of "Literal"', in *The Rediscovery of Meaning* (Middletown, Conn., 1977), 32–43.

Barnes, B., *Interests and the Growth of Knowledge* (London, 1977).

———, *Scientific Knowledge and Sociological Theory* (London, 1980).

———, and Bloor, D., 'Relativism, Rationalism and the Sociology of Knowledge', in M. Hollis and S. Lukes (eds), *Rationality and Relativism* (Oxford, 1985), 21–47.

Baron, H., *The Crisis of the Early Italian Renaissance* (Princeton, rev. edn, 1966).

Barr, J., *Semantics of Biblical Language* (Oxford, 1961).

———, 'Revelation through History in the Old Testament and in Modern Theology', *Interpretation* 17 (1963), 193–205.

——, *Old and New in Interpretation* (London, 1966).

Barth, K., *Church Dogmatics* (13 vols: Edinburgh, 1956–75).

——, *The Theology of Schleiermacher* (Edinburgh, 1982).

Barton, J., 'Reflections on Cultural Relativism', *Theology* 82 (1979), 103–9; 191–9.

Battles, F. L., 'God was Accommodating Himself to Human Capacities', *Interpretation* 31 (1977), 19–38.

Baum, G., *Faith and Doctrine: A Contemporary View* (New York, 1969).

Baur, F. C., *Die christliche Lehre von der Versöhnung in ihrer geschichtlichen Entwicklung* (Tübingen, 1838).

——, *Lehrbuch der christlichen Dogmengeschichte* (Tübingen, 3rd edn, 1867).

Bec, C., *Cultura e società a Firenze nell'età della Rinascenza* (Rome, 1981).

Beckmann, K.-M., *Der Begriff der Häresie bei Schleiermacher* (Munich, 1959).

Behler, E., *Friedrich Schlegel* (Hamburg, 1966).

Beisser, F., *Schleiermachers Lehre von Gott* (Göttingen, 1970).

Bell, D., *The End of Ideology* (New York, 1960).

Bellah, R., *Habits of the Heart: Individualism and Commitment in American Life* (Berkeley, 1985).

Benjamin, W., *Gesammelte Schriften* (3 vols: 1972–80).

Bennett, J., *Locke, Berkeley, Hume: Central Themes* (Oxford, 1977).

Bentley, J. H., 'Erasmus' *Annotationes in Novum Testamentum* and the Textual Criticism of the Gospels', *ARG* 67 (1976), 33–53.

Berger, P., *A Rumour of Angels: Modern Society and the Rediscovery of the Supernatural* (Harmondsworth, 1970).

——, and Luckmann, T., *The Social Construction of Reality: A Treatise in the Sociology of Knowledge* (Harmondsworth, 1984).

Berkhout, C. T., and Russell, J. B., *Medieval Heresies: A Bibliography 1960–1979* (Toronto, 1981).

Bertaux, P. *Hölderlin und die franzözische Revolution* (Frankfurt, 1969).

Bertola, E., 'La *Glossa Ordinaria* biblica ed i suoi problemi', *RThAM* 45 (1978), 34–78.

Beumer, J., 'Die Regula Fidei Catholicae des Ph. N. Chrisman, O.F.M. und ihre Kritik durch J. Kleutgen, S.J.', *Franziskanische Studien* 46 (1964), 321–34.

Bévenot, M., 'Primacy and Development', *HeyJ* 9 (1968), 400–13.

Bhaskar, R., *Dialectic, Materialism and Human Emancipation* (London, 1983).

Biscione, M., *Neo-umanesimo e Rinascimento* (Rome, 1962).

Blackburn, S., 'How to refer to Private Experience', *Proceedings of the Aristotelian Society* 75 (1974), 201–14.

Blanke, H. W., Fleischer, D., and Rusen, J., 'Theory of History in Historical Lectures: The German Tradition of *Historik*, 1750–1900', *History and Theory* 23 (1984), 331–56.

Bleicher, J., *Contemporary Hermeneutics: Hermeneutics as Method, Philosophy and Critique* (London, 1980).

Bloch, M., *Land and Work in Medieval Europe* (London, 1967).

Blondel, H., *Letter on Apologetics and History and Dogma* (London, 1964).

Blumenberg, H., *Die Legitimät der Neuzeit* (Frankfurt, 1966).

Boers, H., 'Sisyphus and His Rock: Concerning Gerd Theissen, *Urchristliche Wundergeschichten*', *Semeia* 11 (1978), 1–48.

Bonara, E., 'L'interpretazione del Petrarca e la poetica del realismo in De Sanctis', in G. Cuomo (ed.), *De Sanctis e il realismo* (2 vols: Naples, 1978), 1.377–98.

Bonorand, C., 'Die Bedeutung der Universität Wien für Humanismus und Reformation, insbesondere in der Ostschweiz', *Zwingliana* 12 (1964–8), 162–80.

———, *Aus Vadians Freundes- und Schülerkreis in Wien* (St Gallen, 1965).

Boorstin, D. J., *The Lost World of Thomas Jefferson* (Boston, 1960).

Bornkamm, H., *Luther im Spiegel der deutschen Geschichte* (Heidelberg, 1955).

Bottomore, T. B., *The Frankfurt School* (London, 1984).

Bower, G. H. and Clark, M. C., 'Narrative Stories as Mediators for Serial Learning', *Psychonomic Science* 14 (1969), 181–2.

Bowker, J., 'Religions as Systems', in *Believing in the Church* (London, 1981), 159–89.

Bradley, J., 'Gadamer's "Truth and Method"', *HeyJ* 18 (1977), 420–35.

Braithwaite, R. B., *An Empiricist's View of the Nature of Religious Belief* (Cambridge, 1955).

Branca, V., 'Realismo desanctisiano e tradizione narrativa', in G. Cuomo (ed.), *De Sanctis e il realismo* (2 vols: Naples, 1978), 1.1–19.

Braudel, F., *The Mediterranean and the Mediterranean World in the Age of Philip II* (2 vols: London, 1972–3).

van den Brink, J. N. B., 'Traditio im theologische Sinne', *Vigiliae Christianae* 13 (1959), 65–86.

Brosseder, J., 'Überlieferung – ihre Bedeutung im Sachzusammenhang von "Schrift und Tradition"', in K. Kertelge (ed.), *Die Autorität der Schrift im ökumenischen Gesprach* (Frankfurt, 1985), 53–63.

Brucker, G., *The Civic World of Early Renaissance Florence* (Princeton, 1977).

Brunner, E., *Wahrheit als Begegnung: Sechs Vorlesungen über das christliche Wahrheitsverständnis* (Zurich, 2nd edn, 1963).

Brunner, P., *Vom Werk des heiligen Geistes* (Tübingen, 1935).

Brunschwig, H., *La crise de l'état prussien à la fin du XVIIIe siècle et la genèse de la mentalité romantique* (Paris, 1947).

Bukharin, N. I., 'Theory and Practice from the Standpoint of Dialectical Materialism', in *Science at the Cross-Roads* (London, 1931), 1–23.

Burke, K., *Grammar of Motives* (Berkeley, 1962).

Burke, P., *The Renaissance Sense of the Past* (London, 1969).

———, *The Italian Renaissance: Culture and Society in Italy* (Oxford, rev. edn, 1987).

Burkert, W., *Greek Religion: Archaic and Classical* (Cambridge, Mass., 1985).

Burrow, J. W., *Evolution and Society* (Cambridge, 1966).

Busch, A., *Die Geschichte der Privatdozenten: eine soziologische studie zur grossbetrieblichen Entwicklung der deutschen Universitäten* (Stuttgart, 1959).

Butler, E. M., *The Tyranny of Greece over Germany* (Cambridge, 1935).

Campbell, C., *Towards a Sociology of Irreligion* (London, 1971).

Carnes, J. R., *Axiomatics and Dogmatics* (Belfast, 1982).

Cassirer, E., *Philosophy of the Enlightenment* (Boston, 1951).

Chadwick, H., *Early Christian Thought and the Classical Tradition* (Oxford, 1966).

Chadwick, O., *From Bossuet to Newman: The Idea of Doctrinal Development* (Cambridge, 1957).

Chomorat, J., 'Les *Annotations* de Valla, celles d'Erasme et la grammaire', in O. Fatio and P. Fraenkel (eds), *Etudes de l'exégèse au XVIᶜ siècle* (Geneva, 1978), 202–28.

Christian, W. A., *Doctrines of Religious Communities* (New Haven/London, 1987).

Cipolla, C.-M., 'Economic Depression of the Renaissance?', *Journal of Economic History* 16 (1964), 519–24.

——, *Clocks and Culture* (London, 1967).

Clark, M., *Logic and System: A Study of the Transition from Vorstellung to Thought in the Philosophy of Hegel* (The Hague, 1970).

Clerck, D. E. de, 'Droits du démon et nécessité de la rédemption', *RThAM* 14 (1947), 32–64.

Coakley, S., 'Theology and Cultural Relativism: What is the Problem?', *NZSTh* 21 (1979), 223–43.

Cohen, G. A., *Karl Marx's Theory of History: A Defence* (Oxford, 1978).

Cole, M., et. al., *The Cultural Context of Learning and Thinking* (New York, 1969).

Collinson, P., *The Birthpangs of Protestant England: Religious and Cultural Change in the Sixteenth and Seventeenth Centuries* (Basingstoke, 1988).

Conrad, J., *The German Universities for the Last Fifty Years* (Glasgow, 1885).

Cooper, D. E., *Metaphor* (Oxford, 1986).

Cottignoli, A., 'I "Promessi Sposi" nella storia del realismo desanctisiano', in G. Cuomo (ed.), *De Sanctis e il realismo* (2 vols: Naples, 1978), 1.455– 70.

Courth, F., *Das Wesen des Christentums in der liberalen Theologie* (Frankfurt, 1977).

Cragg, G. R., *The Church and the Age of Reason* (London, 1976).

Cullmann, O., *Die ersten christliche Glaubensbekenntnisse* (Zurich, 2nd edn, 1949).

——, 'Scripture and Tradition', in D. J. Callahan, H. A. Oberman and D. J. O'Hanlon (eds), *Christianity Divided* (London/New York, 1962), 7–33.

Cumming, R. D., *Human Nature and History* (Chicago, 1969).

Cupitt, D., *Taking Leave of God* (London, 1980).

Curtis, J. E., and Petras, J. W., *The Sociology of Knowledge* (London, 1970).

Dahl, N. A., 'Eschatologie und Geschichte im Lichte der Qumrantexte', in E. Dinkler (ed.), *Zeit und Geschichte* (Tübingen, 1964), 3–18.

Danto, A. C., *Analytical Philosophy of History* (Cambridge, 1965).

——, 'The Problem of Other Periods', *JPh* 63 (1966), 566–77.

——, 'Historical Language and Historical Reality', *Review of Metaphysics* 27 (1973), 219–59.

Davidson, D., 'On the very idea of a conceptual scheme', *Proceedings and Addresses of the American Philosophical Association* 47 (1974), 5–20.

Davis, D. B., *The Problem of Slavery in an Age of Revolution 1770–1823* (Ithaca/London, 1967).

Dawkins, R., *The Blind Watchmaker* (London, 1985).

Deneffe, A., 'Dogma: Wort und Begriff', *Scholastik* 6 (1931), 381–400; 505–38.

De Sanctis, F., *Teoria e storia della letteratura* (2 vols: Bari, 1926).

——, *Lezioni zurighesi sul Petrarca* (Padua, 1955).

——, *Lezioni e saggi sul Dante* (Turin, 1955).

Dewart, L., *The Future of Belief: Theism in a World Come of Age* (New York, 1966).

Dickens, A. G., and Tonkin, J. M., *The Reformation in Historical Thought* (Cambridge, Mass., 1985).

Dieterici, W., *Geschichtliche und statistische Nachrichten über die Universitäten im preussischen Staat* (Berlin, 1836).

Dillenberger, J., *God Hidden and Revealed: The Interpretation of Luther's Deus Absconditus* (Philadelphia, 1953).

Dillon, J. M., 'Self-Definition in Later Platonism', in E. P. Sanders (ed.), *Jewish and Christian Self-Definition* (3 vols: London, 1980–2), 3.60–75.

Dodd, C. H., *The Interpretation of the Fourth Gospel* (Cambridge, 1953).

Dörrie, H., 'Was ist "spätantiker Platonismus"? Überlegungen zur Grenzziehung zwischen Platonismus and Christentum', *Theologische Rundschau* 36 (1971), 285–302.

Douglas, M., *Implicit Meaning: Essays in Anthropology* (London, 1975).

Dowey, E. A., *The Knowledge of God in Calvin's Theology* (New York, 1952).

Downing, F. G., *Has Christianity a Revelation?* (Philadelphia, 1964).

Draper, J., 'The Jesus Tradition in the Didache', in D. Wenham (ed.), *The Jesus Tradition outside the Gospels* (Sheffield, 1984), 269–87.

Dray, W. H., 'The Historical Explanation of Actions Reconsidered', in S. Hook (ed.), *Philosophy and History* (New York, 1963), 105–35.

Driver, T. F., *Patterns of Grace: Human Experience as Word of God* (San Francisco, 1977).

Dülman, R. van, *Reformation als Revolution: Soziale Bewegung und apokalyptische Visionen im Zeitalter der Reformation* (Göttigen, 1979).

Dulles, A., 'The Hermeneutics of Dogmatic Statements', in *The Survival of Dogma* (New York, 1973), 176–91.

———, *Models of Revelation* (Dublin, 1983).

Dummett, M., *Truth and Other Enigmas* (London, 1978).

Dunn, J. D. G., *Unity and Diversity in the New Testament* (Philadelphia, 1977).

Dupré, L., 'Experience and Interpretation: A Philosophical Reflection on Schillebeeckx' *Jesus* and *Christ*', *Theological Studies* 43 (1982), 30–51.

Duska, R., and Whelan, M., *Moral Development* (Dublin, 1977).

Dyson, A. O., 'Theological Legacies of the Enlightenment: England and Germany', in S. W. Sykes (ed.), *England and Germany: Studies in Theological Diplomacy* (Frankfurt, 1982), 45–62.

Ebeling, G., 'The Significance of the Critical Historical Method for Church and Theology in Protestantism', in *Word and Faith* (London, 1963), 17–61.

———, 'The Significance of Doctrinal Differences for the Division of the Churches', in *Word and Faith*, 162–90.

———, *Das Wort Gottes und Tradition: Studien zu einer Hermeneutik der Konfessionen* (Göttingen, 1964).

———, 'Die Notwendigkeit des christlichen Gottesdienstes', *ZThK* 67 (1970), 232–49.

———, 'Die Anfänge von Luthers Hermeneutik', in *Lutherstudien I* (Tübingen, 1971), 1–68

———, 'Die Klage über das Erfahrungsdefizit in der Theologie als Frage nach ihrer Sache', in *Wort und Glaube III* (Tübingen, 1975), 3–28.

Edwards, R. B., 'The Pagan Doctrine of the Absolute Unchangeableness of God', *Religious Studies* 14 (1978), 305–13.

Elert, W., *Der Ausgang der altkirchlichen Christologie* (Berlin, 1957).

Elliott, J. H., *A Home for the Homeless: A Sociological Exegesis of I Peter, its Situation and Strategy* (Philadelphia, 1981).

Elster, J., 'Belief, Bias and Ideology', in M. Hollis and S. Lukes, (eds), *Rationality and Relativism* (Oxford, 1985), 123–48.

Elze, M., 'Der Begriff des Dogmas in der Alten Kirche', *ZThK* 61 (1964), 421–38.

Emerson, R. W., 'Phi Beta Kappa Address', in B. Atkinson (ed.), *The Complete Essays and Other Writings of Ralph Waldo Emerson*, (New York, 1940), 45–63.

Epstein, K., *The Genesis of German Conservatism* (Princeton, 1966).

Evans, G. R., *Old Arts and New Theology: The Beginnings of Theology as an Academic Discipline* (Oxford, 1980).

———, *Alan of Lille: The Frontiers of Theology in the Later Twelfth Century* (Cambridge, 1983).

Evans-Pritchard, E. E., *Witchcraft, Oracles and Magic among the Azande* (Oxford, 1937).

———, *Theories of Primitive Religion* (Oxford, 1965).

———, 'Religion and the Anthropologists', *Practical Anthropology* 19 (1972), 193–206.

Faber, K.-G., 'Ausprägungen des Historismus', *Historische Zeitschrift* 228 (1979), 1–22.

Fackenheim, E. L., 'Kant and Radical Evil', *University of Toronto Quarterly* 23 (1953), 339–52.

Farner, A., *Huldrych Zwingli* (4 vols: Zürich, 1943–60).

Farrer, A., *A Rebirth of Images* (London, 1944).

Federer, K., *Liturgie und Glaube: eine theologiegeschichtliche Untersuching* (Freiburg, 1950).

Fenn, R., 'The Sociology of Religion: A Critical Survey', in T. Bottomore et al. (eds), *Sociology: The State of the Art* (London, 1982), 101–27.

Ferré, F., *Language, Logic and God* (London, 1962).

Ferreira, M. J., *Scepticism and Reasonable Doubt* (Oxford, 1986).

Feyerabend, P., *Science in a Free Society* (London, 1978).

Flückiger, F., *Der Ursprung des christlichen Dogmas: Eine Auseinandersetzung mit Albert Schweitzer und Martin Werner* (Zurich, 1955).

———, *Existenz und Glaube: Kritische Beobachtungen zur existentialen Interpretation* (Wuppertal, 1966).

Ford, D. F., 'Barth's Interpretation of the Bible', in S. W. Sykes (ed.), *Karl Barth: Studies of His Theological Method* (Oxford, 1979), 55–87.

Forsyth, P. T., *The Cruciality of the Cross* (London, 1909).

———, *The Person and Place of Jesus Christ* (London, 4th edn, 1930).

Fortes, M., *Oedipus and Job in West African Religion* (Cambridge, 1959).

Foucault, M., *The Order of Things* (London, 1970).

———, *Language, Counter-Memory, Practice* (London, 1977).

———, *Politics, Philosophy and Culture* (London, 1988).

de Fourny, P., 'Histoire et éloquence d'après Ciceron', *Etudes Classiques* 21 (1953), 156–66.

Fowler, J. W., *Stages of Faith* (New York, 1981).

Fraenkel, P., *Testimonia Patrum: The Function of the Patristic Argument in the Theology of Philip Melanchthon* (Geneva, 1961).

Francastel, P., 'Valeurs socio-psychologiques et de l'espace-temps figuratif de la Renaissance', *Année Sociologique* (1965), 3–68.

————, *La figure et le lieu: l'ordre visuel du quattrocento* (Paris, 1967).

François, G., *Le polythéisme et l'emploi au singulier des mots THEOS, DAIMON* (Paris, 1957).

Frankfort, H. et al., *Before Philosophy: The Intellectual Adventure of Ancient Man* (Harmondsworth, 1968).

Fredriksen, P., 'Paul and Augustine: Conversion, Narratives, Orthodox Traditions and the Retrospective Self', *JThS* 37 (1986), 3–34.

Frei, H. W., *The Eclipse of Biblical Narrative* (New Haven/London, 1974).

Frend, W. H. C., 'Heresy and Schism as Social and National Movements', *Studies in Church History* 9 (1972), 37–56.

Friedensburg, W., *Geschichte der Universität Wittenberg* (Halle, 1917).

Frye, N., *The Great Code: The Bible and Literature* (London, 1982).

Fumaroli, M., *L'âge de l'éloquence* (Geneva, 1980).

Furlong, M., *A Study in Memory* (London, 1951).

Gadamer, H.-G., *Truth and Method* (London, 1975).

————, *Philosophical Hermeneutics* (Berkeley/Los Angeles, 1976).

Gager, J. G., *Kingdom and Community: The Social World of Early Christianity* (Engelwood Cliffs, NJ, 1975).

Galot, J., *Dieu souffre-t-il?* (Paris, 1976).

Gaventa, B., 'Galatians 1 and 2: Autobiography as Paradigm', *Novum Testamentum* 28 (1986), 309–26.

Geertz, C., 'Religion as a Cultural System', in D. R. Cutler (ed.), *The Religious Situation* (Boston, 1968), 639–88.

Geiger, T., *Ideologie und Wahrheit* (Stuttgart, 1953).

Geiger, W., *Spekulation und Kritik: Die Geschichtstheologie Ferdinand Christian Baurs* (Munich, 1964).

Geisselmann, J. R., 'Das Konzil von Trient über das Verhältnis der Heiligen Schrift und der nicht geschriebenen Traditionen', in *Die mündliche Überlieferung* (Munich, 1957), 125–206.

Gellner, E., *Words and Things* (London, 1963).

Gerrish, B. A., 'The Nature of Doctrine', *JR* 68 (1988), 87–92.

Gerth, H., *Die sozialgeschichtliche Lage der bürgerlichen Intelligenz um die Wende des 18. Jahrhunderts* (Frankfurt, 1935).

Giddens, A., *New Rules of Sociological Method* (London, 1976).

Gilbert, F., 'Florentine Political Assumptions in the Period of Savonarola and Soderini', *Journal of the Warburg and Courtauld Institutes* 20 (1957), 187– 214.

Gilkey, L., *Message and Existence: An Introduction to Christian Theology* (New York, 1979).

Girardin, B., *Rhétorique et théologique. Calvin: le commentaire de l'épître aux Romains* (Paris, 1979).

Glymour, C., *Theory and Evidence* (Princeton, 1980).

Godin, A., *The Psychological Dynamics of Religious Experience* (Birmingham, Ala., 1985).

Goeters, J. F. G., 'Zwinglis Werdegang als Erasmianer', in M. Greschat and J. F. G. Goeters (eds), *Reformation und Humanismus* (Witten, 1969), 255–71.

Goldstein, J., 'Foucault among the Sociologists: The "Disciplines" and the History of the Professions', *History and Theory* 23 (1982), 170–92.

Goldthwaite, R. A., *The Building of Renaissance Florence* (London, 1980).

Gottwald, N. K., *The Tribes of Yahweh: A Sociology of the Religion of Liberated Israel, 1250–1050 B.C.E.* (Maryknoll, N.Y., 1979).

Gouwens, D. J., 'Kierkegaard's Understanding of Doctrine', *MTh* 5 (1988), 12–22.

Gramsci, A., *The Modern Prince* (London, 1957).

Gray, H. H., 'Renaissance Humanism: The Pursuit of Eloquence', in P. O. Kristeller, and P. P. Wiener, *Renaissance Essays* (New York, 1968), 199– 216.

Green, G., 'The Sociology of Dogmatics: Niklas Luhmann's Challenge to Theology', *JAAR* 50 (1982), 19–33.

Greenacre, R., 'Two Aspects of Reception', in G. R. Evans (ed.), *Christian Authority* (Oxford, 1988), 40–58.

Greene, T., *The Light in Troy: Imitation and Discovery in Renaissance Poetry* (New Haven, 1982).

Greenslade, S. L., 'Heresy and Schism in the Later Roman Empire', in D. Baker (ed.), *Studies in Church History 9* (Oxford, 1972), 1–20.

Greffrath, K. R., *Metaphorischer Materialismus: Untersuchungen zum Geschichtsbegriff Walter Benjamins* (Munich, 1981).

Grillmeier, A., 'Hellenisierung-Judaisierung des Christentums als Deuteprinzipien der Geschichte des kirchlichen Dogmas', *Scholastik* 33 (1958), 321–55; 528–55.

Grossmann, M., *Humanism in Wittenberg 1485–1517* (Nieuwkoop, 1975).

Gruneberg, M., 'Memory Processes Unique to Humans', in A. Mayes (ed.), *Memory in Animals and Humans* (Wokingham, 1983), 253–81.

Gunton, C., '*Christus Victor* Revisited: A Study in Metaphor and the Transformation of Meaning', *JThS* 36 (1985), 129–45.

Gurvitch, G., *The Social Frameworks of Knowledge* (Oxford, 1971).

Habermas, J., *Knowledge and Human Interests* (Boston, 1971).

——, *Legitimation Crisis* (Boston, 1975).

——, 'Exkurs zu Benjamins Geschichtsphilosophischen Thesen', in *Der philosophische Diskurs der Moderne* (Frankfurt, 1985), 16–21.

Hacking, I., *Why does Language matter to Philosophy?* (Cambridge, 1975).

——, *The Emergence of Probability* (Cambridge, 1975).

——, 'Spekulation, Berechnung und die Erschaffung von Phänomen', in P. Duerr (ed.), *Versuchungen: Aufsätze zur Philosophie Paul Feyerabends* (Frankfurt, 1981), 126–58.

Hahn, F., *Christologische Hoheitstitel: Ihre Geschichte im frühen Christentum* (Göttingen, 1963).

Hamlyn, D. W., 'Aristotle's God', in G. J. Hughes (ed.), *The Philosophical Assessment of Theology* (Washington DC, 1987), 15–33.

Hamnett, I., 'Sociology of Religion and Sociology of Error', *Religion* 3 (1973), 1–12.

——, 'A Mistake about Error', *New Blackfriars* 67 (1986), 69–78.

Hanson, F. A., and Martin, R., 'The Problem of Other Cultures', *Philosophy of the Social Sciences* 3 (1973), 191–208.

——, *Meaning in Culture* (London, 1975).

Hanson, R. A., *Patterns of Discovery* (Cambridge, 1958).

——, *The Concept of the Positron: A Theoretical Analysis* (Cambridge, 1963).

——, *Perception and Discovery: An Introduction to Scientific Inquiry* (San Francisco, 1969).

——, *Observation and Explanation: A Guide to the Philosophy of Science* (New York, 1971).

von Harnack, A., *Lehrbuch der Dogmengeschichte* (3 vols: Tübingen, 3rd edn, 1894–7).

——, *Das Wesen des Christentums* (Leipzig, 1906).

Harned, D., *Creed and Personal Identity* (Edinburgh, 1981).

Harris, M. J., 'References to Jesus in Early Classical Authors', in D. Wenham (ed.), *The Jesus Tradition outside the Gospels* (Sheffield, 1984) 343–68.

Hart, R. L., *Unfinished Man and the Imagination: Toward an Ontology and Rhetoric of Revelation* (New York, 1968).

Harvey, A. E., 'Attending to Scripture', in *Believing in the Church: The Corporate Nature of Faith* (London, 1981), 25–44.

——, 'Christian Propositions and Christian Stories', in A. E. Harvey (ed.), *God Incarnate: Story and Belief* (London, 1981), 1–13.

Harvey, J. H., and Weary, C., *Perspectives on Attributional Processes* (Iowa, 1981).

Harvey, V. A., *The Historian and the Believer* (London, 1967).

Hasselhorn, M., *Der altwürttembergische Pfarrstand im 18. Jahrhundert* (Stuttgart, 1958).

Hatfield, H., *Aesthetic Paganism in German Literature* (Cambridge, Mass., 1964).

Hay, D., 'Flavio Biondo and the Middle Ages', *Proceedings of the British Academy* 45 (1958), 97–108.

Hay, D., *Exploring Inner Space: Scientists and Religious Experience* (Harmondsworth, 1982).

Haym, R., *Wilhelm von Humboldt: Lebensbild und Charakteristik* (Berlin, 1856).

Hays, R. B., *The Faith of Jesus Christ: An Investigation of the Narrative Substructure of Galatians 3:1–4:11* (Chico, 1983).

Hazard, P., *La pensée européenne au XVIIIe siècle* (3 vols: Paris, 1946).

Heckel, M., 'Reichsrecht und "Zweite Reformation": Theologisch-juristische Probleme der reformierten Konfessionalisierung', in H. Schilling (ed.), *Die reformierte Konfessionalisierung in Deutschland – Das Problem der 'Zweiten Reformation'* (Gütersloh, 1986), 11–43.

Hegel, G. W. F., *Werke* (18 vols: Berlin, 1832–45).

Heidegger, M., *Platons Lehre von der Wahrheit* (Berne, 1947).

——, *Sein und Zeit* (Tübingen, 8th edn, 1957).

Heiler, F., 'The History of Religion as a Preparation for the Cooperation of Religions', in M. Eliade and J. Kitagawa (eds), *The History of Religions* (Chicago, 1959), 142–53.

Hempel, C. G., 'Empiricist Criteria of Cognitive Significance', in C. G. Hempel, *Aspects of Scientific Explanation* (New York, 1965), 101–33.

Hempelmann, H., '"...keine ewige Wahrheiten, als unaufhörlich zeitliche . . ." Hamanns Kontroverse mit Kant über Sprache und Vernunft', *Theologische Beiträge* 18 (1987), 5–33.

Hengel, M., *Judaism and Hellenism* (London, 1974).

Hermann, R., 'Zu Lessings religionsphilosophischer und theologischer Problematik', *Zeitschrift für systematische Theologie* 22 (1953), 127–48.

Hesse, M., *Revolutions and Reconstructions in the Philosophy of Science* (Brighton, 1980).

Hick, J. (ed.), *The Myth of God Incarnate* (London, 1977).

Hirsch, E., *Geschichte der neuern evangelischen Theologie* (5 vols: Gütersloh, 1949–54).

Hodgson, L., 'The Doctrine of the Church as held and taught in the Church of England', in Flew, R. N. (ed.), *The Nature of the Church* (London, 1952), 121–46.

Hodgson, P. C., *The Formation of Historical Theology: A Study of Ferdinand Christian Baur* (New York, 1966).

Holmer, P. L., 'Kierkegaard and Religious Propositions', *JR* 35 (1955), 135–46.

Horton, R., 'Tradition and Modernity Revisited', in M. Hollis and S. Lukes, (eds), *Rationality and Relativism* (Oxford, 1985), 201–60.

Illingworth, J. R., 'The Incarnation in Relation to Development', in C. Gore (ed.), *Lux Mundi: A Series of Studies in the Religion of the Incarnation* (London, 10th edn, 1890), 179–214.

Jaspers, K., *Philosophical Faith and Revelation* (New York, 1967).

Jennings, T. W., *Beyond Theism: A Grammar of God-Language* (New York/Oxford, 1985).

Jenson, R. W., *The Triune Identity: God According to the Gospel* (Philadelphia, 1982).

Johnson, E. A., 'Marian Devotion in the Western Church', in J. Raitt (ed.), *Christian Spirituality: High Ages and Reformation* (New York, 1987), 392–414.

Jones, L. G., 'Alasdair MacIntyre on Narrative, Community, and the Moral Life', *MTh* 4 (1987), 53–69.

Jüngel, E., *God as the Mystery of the World* (Edinburgh, 1983).

Kain, P. J., 'History, Knowledge and Essence in the Early Marx', *Studies in Soviet Thought* 25 (1983), 261–83.

Kant, I., *Kant's Political Writings*, ed. Hans Reiss (Cambridge, 1970).

Kantzenbach, F. W., *Evangelium und Dogma: Die Bewältigung des theologischen Problems der Dogmengeschichte im Protestantismus* (Stuttgart, 1959).

Kaspar, W., *Dogma unter dem Wort Gottes* (Mainz, 1965).

———, 'Tradition als theologisches Erkenntnisprinzip', in W. Löser, K.

Lehmann and M. Lutz-Bachmann (eds), *Dogmengeschichte und katholische Theologie* (Würzburg, 1985), 376–403.

Kavanagh, A., *On Liturgical Theology* (New York, 1984).

Keck, L. E., 'On the Ethos of Early Christians', *JAAR* 42 (1974), 435–52.

Kee, H. C., *Jesus in History: An Approach to the Study of the Gospels* (New York, 2nd end, 1977).

Kellenberger, J., *Religious Discovery, Faith and Knowledge* (Englewood Cliffs, N.J., 1972).

———, *The Cognitivity of Religion: Three Perspectives* (London, 1985).

Kelley, D. R., *The Foundations of Modern Historical Scholarship* (New York, 1970).

———, *The Beginning of Ideology: Consciousness and Formation in the French Reformation* (Cambridge, 1981).

Kelsen, H., *Aufsätze zur Ideologiekritik* (Neuwied, 1964).

Kennedy, E., *A Philosophe of the Age of Reason: Destutt de Tracy and the Origins of Ideology* (Philadelphia, 1978).

Kenny, A., *The Five Ways* (London, 1969).

Kent, D. V., *The Rise of the Medici: Faction in Florence, 1426–1434* (Oxford, 1978).

Kermode, F., *The Classic: Literary Images of Permanence and Change* (New York, 1975).

Kern, W., 'Atheismus – Christentum – emanzipierte Gesellschaft', *Zeitschrift für katholische Theologie* 91 (1969), 289–321.

Kerr, F., *Theology after Wittgenstein* (Oxford/New York, 1986).

Kierkegaard, S., *Unscientific Postscript* (Princeton, 1941).

Kisch, G., *Humanismus und Jurisprudenz: Der Kampf zwischen mos italicus and mos italicus an der Universität Basel* (Basle, 1955).

Klemm, D. E., 'Toward a Rhetoric of Postmodern Theology: Through Barth and Heidegger', *JAAR* 56 (1988), 443–69.

Koehler, R., 'Der *Deus absconditus* in Philosophie und Theologie', *Zeitschrift für Religions- und Geistesgeschichte* 7 (1955), 46–58.

Koehler, W., *Dogmengeschichte als Geschichte des christliche Selbstbewusstseins* (2 vols: Zurich, 1938–51).

Kolakowski, L., 'Karl Marx and the Classical Definition of Truth', in *Marxism and Beyond* (London, 1969), 59–87.

———, 'Der Anspruch auf die selbstverschuldete Unmündigkeit', in *Vom Sinn der Tradition* (Munich, 1970), 1–15.

———, *Positivist Philosophy: From Hume to the Vienna Circle* (Harmondsworth, 1972).

Kolfhaus, W., *Christusgemeinschaft bei Johannes Calvin* (Neukirchen, 1939).

Krieger, L., *The German Idea of Freedom: History of a Political Tradition* (Boston, 1957).

Krusche, W., *Das Wirken des heiligen Geistes nach Calvin* (Göttingen, 1957).

Küng, H., *The Incarnation of God* (Edinburgh, 1987).

Kuhn, T. S., *The Structure of Scientific Revolutions* (Chicago, 2nd edn, 1970).

———, 'Reflections on my Critics', in I. Lakatos and A. Musgrave (eds), *Criticism and the Growth of Knowledge* (Cambridge, 1979), 231–78.

Laeuchli, S., 'Das "Vierte Jahrhundert" in Karl Barths Prolegomena', in W. Dantine and K. Lüthi (eds), *Theologie zwischen Gestern und Morgen* (Munich, 1968), 217–34.

Lakoff, G., and Johnson, M., *Metaphors we live by* (Chicago, 1980).

Landucci, S., *Cultura e ideologia in Francesco De Sanctis* (Milan, 1964).

Lang, A., 'Der Bedeutungswandel der Begriffe "fides" und "haeresis" von Vienne und Trient', *Münchener theologische Zeitschrift* 4 (1953), 133–46.

Lange, D., *Erfahrung und die Glaubwürdigkeit des Glaubens* (Tübingen, 1984).

Lash, N., *Change in Focus: A Study of Doctrinal Change and Continuity* (London, 1973).

———, *A Matter of Hope: A Theologian's Reflections on the Thought of Karl Marx* (London, 1981).

———, *Easter in Ordinary* (London, 1989).

Laube, A., 'Radicalism as a Research Problem in the History of Early Reformation', in Hillerbrand, H. J. (ed.), *Radical Tendencies is the Reformation* (Kirksville, MO, 1988), 9–24.

Laudan, L., *Progress and Its Problems* (Berkeley, 1977).

Leer, E. F. van, *Tradition and Scripture in the Early Church* (Assen, 1953).

Leff, G., *Heresy in the Later Middle Ages* (2 vols: Manchester, 1967).

Lehmann, H., *Pietismus und weltliche Ordnung in Württemberg vom 17. bis zum 20. Jahrhundert* (Stuttgart, 1969).

Lengsfeld, P., *Überlieferung: Tradition und Schrift in der evangelischen und katholischen Theologie der Gegenwart* (Paderborn, 1960).

Lenhardt, C., 'Anamnetic Solidarity: The Proletariat and its *Manes*', *Telos* 25 (1975), 133–54.

Lessing, G. E., *Gesammelte Werke*, ed. P. Rilla (10 vols: Berlin, 1954–8).

Lewis, C. S., 'The Weight of Glory', in *Screwtape Proposes a Toast* (London, 1974), 94–110.

————, 'The Language of Religion', in *Christian Reflections* (London, 1981), 164–79.

von Leyden, W., 'Antiquity and Authority: A Paradox in the Renaissance Theory of History', *JHI* 19 (1958), 473–92.

Lindbeck, G., *The Nature of Doctrine: Religion and Theology in a Post-Liberal Age* (Philadelphia, 1984).

Locher, G. W., 'Von Bern nach Genf: Die Ursachen der Spannung zwischen zwinglischer und calvinistischer Reformation', in W. Balke, C. Graafland and H. Harkema (eds), *Wegen en Gestalten in het Gereformeerd Protestantisme* (Amsterdam, 1976), 75–87.

Loewenich, W. von, *Luther's Theology of the Cross* (Minneapolis, 1976).

Lohff, W., 'Legitimate Limits of Doctrinal Pluralism according to the Formula of Concord', in *The Formula of Concord: Quadricentennial Essays* (Kirksville, Mo., 1977), 23–38.

Lohse, B., 'Was verstehen wir unter Dogmengeschichte innerhalb der evangelischen Theologie?', *KuD* 8 (1962), 27–45.

————, 'Theorien der Dogmengeschichte im evangelische Raum heute', in W. Löser, K. Lehmann and M. Lutz-Bachmann (eds), *Dogmengeschichte und katholische Theologie* (Würzburg, 1985), 97–109.

Lonergan, B. J. F., 'The Dehellenization of Dogma', *Theological Studies* 28 (1967), 336–51.

————, *Philosophy of God and Theology* (London, 1973).

————, *Method in Theology* (London, 2nd edn, 1975).

Loofs, F., *Leitfaden zum Studium der Dogmengeschichte* (Halle, 4th edn, 1906).

Lopez, R. S., 'Quattrocento genovese', *Rivista storica Italiana* 75 (1963), 709–27.

Louth, A., 'The Nature of Theological Understanding: Some Parallels between Newman and Gadamer', in Rowell, D. (ed.), *Tradition Renewed* (London, 1986), 98–109.

Lowenthal, D., *The Past is a Foreign Country* (Cambridge, 1985).

Lucas, J. R., 'True', *Philosophy* 44 (1969), 175–86.

Luhmann, N., *Vertrauen: Ein Mechanismus der Reduktion sozialer Komplexität* (Stuttgart, 1974).

————, *Soziologische Aufklärung* (2 vols: Opladen, 4th edn, 1974).

————, *Funktion der Religion* (Frankfurt, 1977).

Lukács, G., *Geschichte und Klassenbewusstsein* (Berlin, 1923).

Lukes, S., 'Some Problems about Rationality', in B. R. Wilson (ed.), *Rationality* (Oxford, 1970), 194–213.

————, 'Relativism: Cognitive and Moral', *Supplementary Proceedings of the Aristotelian Society* 68 (1974), 165–89.

————, 'Relativism in Its Place', in Hollis, M., and Lukes S., (eds), *Rationality and Relativism* (Oxford, 1985), 261–305.

Lutz-Bachmann, M., 'Das philosophische Problem der Geschichte und Theologie', in W. Löser, K. Lehmann and M. Lutz-Bachmann (eds), *Dogmengeschichte und katholische Theologie* (Würzburg, 1985), 19–36.

McCarthy, T., *The Critical Theory of Jürgen Habermas* (Cambridge, 1984).

McFague, S., *Metaphorical Theology: Models of God in Religious Language* (Philadelphia, 1985).

McGrath, A. E., '"The Righteousness of God" from Augustine to Luther', *Studia Theologica* 36 (1982), 63–78.

———, *Luther's Theology of the Cross* (Oxford/New York, 1985).

———, *The Making of Modern German Christology* (Oxford/New York, 1986).

———, *Iustitia Dei: A History of the Christian Doctrine of Justification* (2 vols: Cambridge, 1986).

———, 'Geschichte, Überlieferung und Erzählung: Überlegungen zur Identität und Aufgabe christlicher Theologie', *KuD* 32 (1986), 234– 53.

———, 'Reformation to Enlightenment', in P. D. L. Avis (ed.), *The Science of Theology* (History of Christian Theology 1: Grand Rapids, 1986), 105–229.

———, 'The Article by which the Church stands or falls', *Evangelical Quarterly* 58 (1986), 207–28.

———, *The Intellectual Origins of the European Reformation* (Oxford/New York, 1987).

———, *The Enigma of the Cross* (London, 1987); American edition published as *The Mystery of the Cross* (Grand Rapids, 1988).

———, *Reformation Thought* (Oxford/New York, 1988).

———, 'Christian Ethics', in R. Morgan (ed.), *The Religion of the Incarnation: Anglican Essays in Commemoration of Lux Mundi* (Bristol, 1989), 189–204.

MacIntyre, A., and Ricoeur, P., *The Religious Significance of Atheism* (New York, 1969).

———, 'Epistemological Crises, Dramatic Narrative and the Philosophy of Science', *The Monist* 61 (1977), 453–72.

———, *After Virtue* (Notre Dame, 2nd edn, 1984).

———, *Whose Justice? Which Rationality* (Notre Dame, 1988).

Macquarrie, J., *God-Talk: An Examination of the Language and Logic of Theology* (London, 1967).

———, *Principles of Christian Theology* (London, 1966).

———, 'The Concept of a Christ-Event', in A. E. Harvey (ed.), *God Incarnate: Story and Belief* (London, 1981), 69–80.

———, 'Tradition, Truth and Christology', in *Theology, Church and Ministry* (London, 1986), 34–47.

MacRae, G. W., 'Why the Church rejected Gnosticism', in E. P. Sanders (ed.), *Jewish and Christian Self-Definition* (3 vols: London, 1980–2), 1.126– 33.

McSorley, H. J., *Luther – Right or Wrong? An Ecumenical-Theological Study of Luther's Major Work, The Bondage of the Will* (Minneapolis, 1969).

Malantschuk, G., *Kierkegaard's Thought* (Princeton, 1971).

Malinowski, B., *The Sexual Life of Savages in North-Western Melanesia* New York, 1932).

Mannheim, K., 'Das konservative Denken. Soziologische Beiträge zum Werden des politisch-historischen Denkens in Deutschland', *Archiv für Sozialwissenschaft und Sozialpolitik* 57 (1927), 470–95.

———, *The Sociology of Culture* (New York, 1956).

Manzoni, A., *I promessi sposi: storia milanese del secolo XVII* (Milan, 1950).

Marías, J., *Reason and Life: The Introduction to Philosophy* (London, 1956).

Markus, R. A., 'The Problem of Self-Definition: From Sect to Church', in E. P.

Sanders (ed.), *Jewish and Christian Self-Definition* (3 vols: London, 1980–2), 1.1–15.

Marshall, I. H., 'Incarnational Christology in the New Testament', in Rowdon, H. H. (ed.), *Christ the Lord* (Leicester, 1982), 1–16.

Marti, M., 'De Sanctis e il realismo dantesco', in G. Cuomo (ed.), *De Sanctis e il realismo* (2 vols: Naples, 1978), 1.293–318.

Martin, R., 'Sociology and Theology', in D. E. H. Whiteley and R. Martin (eds), *Sociology, Theology and Conflict* (Oxford, 1969), 14–37.

Martines, L., *The Social World of the Florentine Humanists* (London, 1963).

——, *Power and Imagination: City-States in Renaissance Italy* (New York, 1979).

Mascall, E. L., *Existence and Analogy* (London, 1949).

Massey, M. C., 'The Literature of Young Germany and D. F. Strauss's *Life of Jesus*', *JR* 59 (1979), 298–323.

Mastermann, M., 'The Nature of a Paradigm', in I. Lakatos and A. Musgrave (eds), *Criticism and the Growth of Knowledge* (Cambridge, 1979), 59–89.

Meeks, W. A., 'The Stranger from Heaven in Johannine Sectarianism', *JBL* 91 (1972), 44–72.

——, *The First Urban Christians: The Social World of the Apostle Paul* (New Haven/London, 1983).

Ménard, J. E., 'Normative Self-Definition in Gnosticism', in E. P. Sanders (ed.), *Jewish and Christian Self-Definition* (3 vols: London, 1980–2), 1.134–50.

Meijering, E. P., *Orthodoxy and Platonism in Athanasius* (Leiden, 1976).

——, *Theologische Urteile über die Dogmengeschichte: Ritschls Einfluß auf von Harnack* (Leiden, 1978).

——, *Melanchthon and Patristic Thought: The Doctrines of Christ and Grace, the Trinity and the Creation* (Leiden, 1983).

——, *Der 'ganze' und der 'wahre' Luther: Hintergrund und Bedeutung der Lutherinterpretation A. von Harnacks* (Amsterdam, 1983).

——, *Die Hellenisierung des Christentums im Urteil Adolf von Harnack* (Amsterdam, 1985).

Meissner, W. W., *Psychoanalysis and Religious Experience* (New Haven/London, 1984).

Michalson, G. E., 'Pannenberg on the Resurrection and Historical Method', *SJTh* 33 (1980), 345–59.

——, 'Faith and History: The Shape of the Problem', *MTh* 1 (1985), 277–90.

——, *Lessing's 'Ugly Ditch': A Study of Theology and History* (University Park/London, 1985).

——, 'The Response to Lindbeck', *MTh* 4 (1988), 107–20.

Michel, D., 'Amät: Untersuchung über Wahrheit im Hebräische', *Archiv für Begriffsgechichte* 12 (1968), 30–57.

Miller, P. D., 'Faith and Ideology in the Old Testament', in F. M. Cross (ed.), *Magnalia Dei: The Mighty Acts of God* (Garden City, N.Y., 1976), 464–70.

Mirri, M., *Francesco De Sanctis politico e storico della civiltà moderna* (Messina/Florence, 1961).

Mitchell, B., 'Doctrinal Disagreements', *The Independent*, 5 November 1988, 13.

Moeller, B., 'Die deutschen Humanisten und die Anfänge der Reformation', *Zeitschrift für Kirchengeschichte* 70 (1959), 46–61.

——, *Reichstadt und Reformation* (Gütersloh, 1962).

Monzel, N., *Die Überlieferung: Phänomenologische und religionssoziologische Untersuchungen über den Traditionalismus der christlicher Lehre* (Bonn, 1950).

Moore, J., 'Herbert Spencer's Henchmen: The Evolution of Protestant Liberals in Late Nineteenth Century America', in J. Durant (ed.), *Darwinism and Divinity* (Oxford/New York, 1985), 76–100.

Morgan, R., with Barton, J., *Biblical Interpretation* (Oxford, 1988).

———, 'Faith', in R. Morgan (ed.), *The Religion of the Incarnation: Anglican Essays in Commemoration of Lux Mundi* (Bristol, 1989), 1–32.

Moule, C. F. D., *The Origin of Christology* (Cambridge, 1977).

Murdoch, I., *The Sovereignty of the Good* (London, 1970).

Nabrings, A., 'Historismus als Paralyse der Geschichte', *AKuG* 65 (1983), 157–212.

Neill, S. C., *Anglicanism* (Harmondsworth, 1958).

Nelson, W., *Fact or Fiction: The Dilemma of the Renaissance Storyteller* (Cambridge, Mass., 1973).

Neufeld, K. H., *Adolf von Harnack: Theologie als Suche nach der Kirche* (Paderborn, 1977).

———, 'Gebundenheit und Freiheit: Liberal Dogmengeschichtserforschung in der evangelischen Theologie', in W. Löser, K. Lehmann and M. Lutz-Bachmann (eds), *Dogmengeschichte und katholische Theologie* (Würzburg, 1985), 78–96.

Neuhaus, G., *Transzendentale Erfahrung als Geschichtsverlust?* (Düsseldorf, 1982).

Neuser, W. H., *Die reformatorische Wende bei Zwingli* (Neukirchen, 1977).

Neusner, J., Green, W. S., and Smith, J. Z. (eds), *Judaisms and their Messiahs at the Turn of the Christian Era* (Cambridge, 1988).

Newald, R., *Nachleben des antiken Geistes im Abendland bis zum Beginn des Humanismus* (Tübingen, 1960).

Newman, A. J., 'Aesthetic Sensitizing and Moral Education', *Journal of Aesthetic Education* 14 (1980), 93–101.

Niebuhr, R. R., *Schleiermacher on Christ and Religion* (London, 1965).

Nielsen, K., 'Wittgensteinian Fideism', *Philosophy* 42 (1967), 191–209.

Nineham, D. E., *The Use and Abuse of the Bible* (London, 1976).

Oberman, H. A., 'Reformation: Epoche oder Episode?', *ARG* 68 (1977), 56–111.

———, *Werden und Wertung der Reformation* (Tübingen, 1977).

O'Cleirigh, P. M., 'The Meaning of Dogma in Origen', in E. P. Sanders (ed.), *Jewish and Christian Self-Definition* (3 vols: London, 1980–2), 1.201–16.

Oexle, O. G., 'Die Geschichtswissenschaft im Zeichen des Historismus: Bemerkungen zum Standort der Geschichtforschung', *Historische Zeitschrift* 238 (1984), 17–55.

Offermann, D., *Schleiermachers Einleitung in die Glaubenslehre* (Berlin, 1969).

Ogden, S., *Christ without Myth* (New York, 1961).

———, *The Reality of God* (New York, 1966).

Olsen, M. E., *The Process of Social Organization* (New York, 1968).

Ommen, T. B., *The Hermeneutic of Dogma* (Missoula, Mont., 1975).

Pannenberg, W., 'The Appropriation of the Philosophical Concept of God as a Dogmatic Problem of Early Christian Theology', in *Basic Questions in Theology II* (London, 1971), 119–83.

———, 'What is Truth?', in *Basic Questions in Theology II*, 1–27.

———, *Jesus – God and Man* (Philadelphia, 1978).

———, 'Religion in der säkularen Gesellschaft: Niklas Luhmanns Religionssoziologie', *Evangelische Kommentare* 11 (1978), 99–103.

——, 'Revelation in Early Christianity', in G. R. Evans (ed.), *Christian Authority* (Oxford, 1988), 76–86.

Parent, J. M., 'La notion de dogme au XIIIe siècle', in *Etude d'histoire litteraire et doctrinaire du XIIIe siècle* (Paris, 1932), 141–63.

Pascal, B., *Pensées* (Paris, 1962).

Peacocke, A., 'Biological Evolution and Christian Theology – Yesterday and Today', in J. Durant (ed.), *Darwinism and Divinity: Essays on Evolution and Religious Belief* (Oxford/New York, 1985), 101–30.

Pelikan, J., *Development of Christian Doctrine: Some Historical Prolegomena* (New Haven/London, 1969).

——, *Historical Theology: Change and Continuity in Christian Doctrine* (New Haven/London, 1971).

——, *Jesus through the Centuries: His Place in the History of Culture* (New Haven/ London, 1985).

Penelhum, T., *God and Scepticism: A Study in Scepticism and Fideism* (Dordrecht, 1983).

Peters, A., *Glaube und Werk: Luthers Rechtfertigungslehre im Lichte der heiligen Schrift* (Berlin/Hamburg, 2nd edn, 1967).

Phillips, D. Z., *Death and Immortality* (London, 1970).

——, 'Lindbeck's Audience', *MTh* 4 (1988), 133–54.

Piaget, J., *The Child's Construction of Reality* (London, 1955).

Pieper, J., *Über den Begriff der Tradition* (Cologne/Opladen, 1958).

——, *Über die platonischen Mythen* (Munich, 1965).

Plaisance, M., 'Culture et politique à Florence de 1542 à 1551', in A. Rochon (ed.), *Les écrivains et le pouvoir en Italie à l'époque de la Renaissance* (Paris, 1974), 149–228.

Plekhanov, G. V., *Fundamental Problems of Marxism* (London, 1969).

Polanyi, M., *Personal Knowledge* (London, 1958).

Pollard, T. E., 'The Impassibility of God', *SJTh* 8 (1955), 353–64.

——, *Johannine Christology and the Early Church* (Cambridge, 1970).

Popkes, W., *Christus Traditus: Eine Untersuchung zum Begriff der Dahingabe im Neuen Testament* (Zurich, 1967).

Porter, R., and Teich, M. (eds), *The Enlightenment in National Context* (Cambridge, 1981).

de la Potterie, I., *La verité dans saint Jean* (2 vols: Rome, 1977).

Powicke, F. M., *The Reformation in England* (London, 1941).

Prickett, S., *Words and The Word: Language, Poetics and Biblical Interpretation* (Cambridge, 1986).

Puntel, L. B., *Wahrheitstheorien in der neueren Philosophie* (Darmstadt, 1978).

Radcliffe, T., 'Relativising the Relativisers: A Theologian's Assessment of the Role of Sociological Explanation of Religious Phenomena and Theology Today', in D. Martin, J. O. Milles and J. S. F. Pickering (eds), *Sociology and Theology: Alliance and Conflict* (Brighton, 1980), 151–62.

Rahner, K., and Lehmann, K., 'Kérygme et dolgme', in *Mysterium Salutis: dogmatique de l'histoire du salut* I/3 (Paris, 1969), 183–280.

——, 'What is a Dogmatic Statement?', *Theological Investigations* 5 (New York, 1975), 42–66.

Ramsden, H., *The 1898 Movement in Spain* (Manchester, 1974).

Ramsey, I. T., *Religious Language: An Empirical Placing of Theological Phrases* (London, 1957).

——, *Models and Mystery* (Oxford, 1964).

——, *Christian Discourse* (Oxford, 1965).

Rawls, J., *A Theory of Justice* (Cambridge, Mass., 1972).

Reiff, R., and Scheerer, M., *Memory and Hypnotic Age Regression* (New York, 1959).

Reilly, R. J., *Romantic Religion: A Study of Barfield, Lewis, Williams and Tolkien* (Athens, Ga., 1971).

Reventloh, H. G., *The Authority of the Bible and the Rise of the Modern World* (London, 1984).

Richards, I. A., *The Philosophy of Rhetoric* (Oxford, 1971).

Richardson, A., *History Sacred and Profane* (London, 1964).

Ricken, F., 'Nikaia als Krisis des altchristlichen Platonismus', *Theologie und Philosophie* 44 (1969), 321–51.

Ricoeur, P., 'Ethics and Culture: Habermas and Gadamer in Dialogue', *Philosophy Today* 17 (1973), 153–65.

——, *Le temps raconté* (Paris, 1985).

Riehl, W. H., *Die bürgerliche Gesellschaft* (Stuttgart, 1851).

Ringer, F. K., *The Decline of the German Mandarins: The German Academic Community, 1890–1933* (Cambridge, Mass., 1969).

Rist, G., 'La modernité de la méthode théologique de Calvin', *Revue de théologie et philosophie* 1 (1968), 19–33.

Ritter, A. M., *Das Konzil von Konstantinopel und sein Symbol* (Göttingen, 1965).

Ritter, J., 'Aristoteles und die Vorsokratiker', in *Metaphysik und Politik: Studien zu Aristoteles und Hegel* (Frankfurt, 1969), 34–56.

Ritter, W. H., 'Theologie und Erfahrung', *Luther* 53 (1982), 23–37.

Robinson, J. A. T., *Honest to God* (London, 1963).

Rogge, J., 'Zur Frage katholischer und evangelischer Dogmenhermeneutik. Ein paraphrasierender Literaturbericht', *Theologische Literaturzeitung* 98 (1973), 641–55.

Root, M., 'The Narrative Structure of Soteriology', *MTh* 2 (1986), 145–58.

Rorty, R., *Philosophy and the Mirror of Nature* (Princeton, 1980).

——, *The Consequences of Pragmatism* (Brighton, 1982).

Rosen, M., *Hegel's Dialectic and Its Criticism* (Cambridge, 1984).

Rosenkranz, K., *Das Zentrum der Spekulation: Eine Komödie* (Königsberg, 1840).

Rotermund, H.-M., *Orthodoxie und Pietismus: Valentin Ernst Löschers 'Timotheus Verinus' in der Auseinandersetzung mit der Schule August Hermann Frankes* (Berlin, 1960).

Rundus, O., 'Analysis of Rehearsal Processes in Free Recall', *Journal of Experimental Psychology* 89 (1971), 63–77.

Russell, B., *The Principles of Mathematics* (London, 1903).

Salutati, C., *Epistolario*, ed. F. Novati (4 vols: Rome, 1891–1911).

——, *De laboribus Herculis*, ed. B. L. Ullman (2 vols: Zurich, 1951).

Samuel, R., *Die poetische Staats- und Geschichtsauffassung Friedrich von Hardenbergs* (Frankfurt, 1925).

Sauter, G., 'Dogma – ein eschatologischer Begriff', in *Erwartung und Erfahrung:*

Predigten, Vorträge und Aufsätze (Munich, 1972), 16–46.

——, 'Das Gebet als Wurzel des Redens von Gott', *Glaube und Lernen* 1 (1986), 21–37.

Schaeffler, R., *Fähigkeit zur Erfahrung* (Freiburg, 1982).

Scheld, S., *Die Christologie Emil Brunners: Beitrag zur Überwindung liberaler Jesulogie und dialektisch-doketischer Christologie im Zuge geschichtlich-dialogischen Denkens* (Wiesbaden, 1981).

Schillebeeckx, E., *Christ – The Experience of Jesus as Lord* (New York, 1980).

Schilling, H., 'Die "Zweite Reformation" als Kategorie der Geschichtswissenschaft', in H. Schilling (ed.), *Die reformierte Konfessionalisierung in Deutschland – Das Problem der 'Zweiten Reformation'* (Gütersloh, 1986), 387–437.

Schleiermacher, F. D. E., *The Christian Faith* (Edinburgh, 1960).

——, *Brief Outline of the Study of Theology* (Richmond, Va., 1966).

Schlier, H., 'Kerygma und Sophia: Zur neutestamentlichen Grundlegung des Dogmas', in *Die Zeit der Kirche* (Freiburg, 1958), 206–32.

——, 'Die Anfänge der christologischen Credo', in B. Welte (ed.), *Zur Frühgeschichte der Christologie* (Freiburg/Vienna/Basle, 1970), 109–34.

Schlingensiepen-Pogge, A., *Das Sozialethos der lutherischen Aufklärungstheologie am Vorabend der industriellen Revolution* (Göttingen, 1967).

Schlink, E., 'Die Struktur der dogmatischen Aussagen als ökumenisches Problem', *KuD* 3 (1957), 251–306.

Schmidlin, S., *Frumm byderb lüt: Ästhetische Form und politische Perspektive im schweizer Schauspiel der Reformationszeit* (Frankfurt/Berne, 1981).

Schmitt, A., 'Zur Wiederbelebung der Antike im Trecento: Petrarcas Rom-Idee in ihrer Wirkung auf die Paduaner Malerei', *Mitteilungen des Kunsthistorischen Instituts in Florenz* 18 (1974), 167–218.

Schmitz, H.-J., *Frühkatholizismus bei Adolf von Harnack, Rudolph Sohm und Ernst Käsemann* (Düsseldorf, 1977).

Scholem, G., 'Walter Benjamin und sein Engel', in S. Unseld (ed.), *Zur Aktualität Walter Benjamins* (Frankfurt, 1972), 87–138.

Schouls, P. A., *The Imposition of Method: A Study of Descartes and Locke* (Oxford, 1980).

Schüssler, H., *Der Primät der Heiligen Schrift als theologisches und kanonistisches Problem im Spätmittelalter* (Wiesbaden, 1977).

Schwarz, R., 'Lessings "Spinozismus"', *ZThK* 65 (1968), 271–90.

——, *Die apokalyptische Theologie Thomas Müntzers und der Taboriten* (Tübingen, 1977).

Schweitzer, A., *The Quest of the Historical Jesus* (London, 3rd edn, 1954).

Scipioni, L. I., *Nestorio e il concilio di Efeso* (Milan, 1974).

Scott Holland, H., 'Faith', in C. Gore (ed.), *Lux Mundi: A Series of Studies in the Religion of the Incarnation* (London, 10th edn, 1890), 3–54.

Scribner, R. W., 'Civic Unity and the Reformation in Erfurt', *Past and Present* 66 (1975), 29–60.

——, and Benecke, G., *The German Peasant War, 1525: New Viewpoints* (London, 1979).

Scroggs, R., 'The Earliest Christian Communities as Sectarian Movements', in J. Neusner (ed.), *Christianity, Judaism and Other Greco-Roman Cults* (2 vols: Leiden, 1975), 1–23.

——, 'The Sociological Interpretation of the New Testament: The Present State of Research', *New Testament Studies* 26 (1980), 164–79.

Seigel, J., '"Civic Humanism" or Ciceronian Rhetoric? The Culture of Petrarch and Bruni', *Past and Present* 34 (1966), 3–48.

Shalit, A., 'A Clash of Ideologies: Palestine under the Seleucids and Romans', in A. Toynbee (ed.), *The Crucible of Christianity* (New York, 1969), 47– 76.

Shapiro, B., *Probability and Certainty in Seventeenth Century England* (Princeton, 1983).

Shaw, W. H., *Marx's Theory of History* (Stanford, 1978).

Shelton, R. C., *The Young Hölderlin* (Berne/Frankfurt, 1973).

Simon, Y., *A General Theory of Authority* (Notre Dame, 1980).

Simone, F., 'Il contributo degli umanisti veneti al prima sviluppo dell'umanesimo francese', in V. Branca (ed.), *Umanesimo europeo e umanesimo veneziano* (Venice, 1963), 295–316.

Skorupski, J., *Symbol and Theory* (Cambridge, 1976).

Smalley, B., 'Gilbertus Universalis, Bishop of London (1128–34) and the Problem of the *Glossa Ordinaria*', *RThAM* 7 (1935), 235–62; 8 (1936), 24–46.

——, 'La *Glossa Ordinaria*, quelques prédécesseurs d'Anselme de Laon', *RThAM* 9 (1937), 365–400.

——, *English Friars and Antiquity in the Early Fourteenth Century* (Oxford, 1960).

——, 'Les commentaires bibliques de l'époque romane: glose ordinaire et gloses périmées', *Cahiers de Civilisation Médiévale* 4 (1961), 23–46.

Soden, H. von, *Was ist Wahrheit? Vom geschichtlichen Begriff der Wahrheit* (Marburg, 1927).

Soskice, J. M., *Metaphor and Religious Language* (Oxford, 1985).

Sperber, D., 'Is Symbolic Thought Prerational?', in M. L. Foster and S. M. Brandes (eds), *Symbol and Sense: New Approaches to the Analysis of Meaning* (New York, 1980), 25–44.

——, 'Apparently Irrational Beliefs', in M. Hollis and S. Lukes (eds), *Rationality and Relativism* (Oxford, 1985), 149–80.

Spiegler, G., *The Eternal Covenant: Schleiermacher's Experiment in Cultural Theology* (New York, 1967).

Spilka, B., Hood, R. W., and Gorsuch, R. L., *The Psychology of Religion: An Empirical Approach* (Englewood Cliffs, N.J., 1985).

Spitz, L. W., *The Renaissance and Reformation Movements* (2 vols: St Louis, rev. edn, 1987).

Staples, P., 'Towards an Explanation of Ecumenism', *MTh* 5 (1988), 23– 44.

Stark, W., *The Sociology of Knowledge* (London, 1958).

Stasiewski, B., 'Ursprung und Entfaltung des Christentums in sowjetischer Sicht', *Saeculum* 11 (1960), 157–79.

Stauffer, R., 'Einfluß und Kritik des Humanismus in Zwinglis "Commentarius de vera et falsa religione"', *Zwingliana* 16 (1983), 97–110.

Stayer, J. M., 'Christianity in One City: Anabaptist Münster, 1534–35', in H. J. Hillerbrand (ed.), *Radical Tendencies is the Reformation* (Kirksville, Mo., 1988), 117–34.

Steck, K. G., 'Dogma und Dogmengeschichte in der Theologie des 19. Jahrhunderts', in W. Schneemelcher (ed.), *Das Erbe des 19. Jahrhunderts* (Berlin, 1960), 21–66.

Steinbart, G. S., *System der reinen Philosophie oder Glückseligkeitslehre* (Züllichau, 1778).

Steiner, G., *After Babel: Aspects of Language and Translation* (Oxford, 1975).

Steinmetz, M., *Deutschland von 1476 bis 1648* (Berlin, 1967).

—— (ed.), *Der deutsche Bauernkrieg und Thomas Müntzer* (Leipzig, 1976).

Stephens, J. N., *The Fall of the Florentine Republic, 1512–30* (Oxford, 1983).

Stockman, N., *Antipositivist Theories of the Sciences: Critical Rationalism, Critical Theory and Scientific Realism* (Dordrecht, 1983).

Stout, J., *The Flight from Authority: Religion, Morality and the Quest for Autonomy* (Notre Dame, Ind., 1981),

Struever, N. L., *The Language of History in the Renaissance* (Princeton, 1970).

Suppe, F., 'The Search for Philosophic Understanding of Scientific Theories', in F. Suppe (ed.), *The Structure of Scientific Theories* (Chicago, 2nd edn, 1977), 3–232.

Surin, K., 'The Impassibility of God and the Problem of Evil', *SJTh* 35 (1982), 97–117.

Swanson, G. E., *The Birth of the Gods* (Ann Arbor, Mich., 1964).

Sykes, S. W., 'Ernst Troeltsch and Christianity's Essence', in J. P. Clayton (ed.), *Ernst Troeltsch and the Future of Theology* (Cambridge, 1976), 139– 71.

——, *The Integrity of Anglicanism* (London, 1979).

——, *The Identity of Christianity* (London, 1984).

——, 'Anglicanism and the Anglican Doctrine of the Church', *Anglican Theological Review* Supplementary Series 10: Essays on the Centenary of the Chicago–Lambeth Quadrilateral (1988), 156–77.

Taft, R. J., 'Liturgy as Theology', *Worship* 56 (1982), 113–17.

Tateo, F., 'Il realismo critico desanctisiano e gli studi rinascimentali', in G. Cuomo (ed.), *De Sanctis e il realismo* (2 vols: Naples, 1978), 1.399– 427.

Taylor, C., 'Interpretation and the Sciences of Man', *Review of Metaphysics* 25 (1971), 3–51.

Temple, W., 'Theology Today', *Theology* 39 (1939), 326–33.

Theissen, G., *Urchristliche Wundergeschichten: Ein Beitrag zur formgeschichtlichen Erforschung der synoptischen Evangelien* (Gütersloh, 1974).

——, *Sociology of Early Palestinian Christianity* (Philadelphia, 1978); published in UK as *The First Followers of Jesus* (London, 1978).

——, *On Having a Critical Faith* (London, 1979).

——, *The Social Setting of Pauline Christianity* (Philadelphia, 1982).

Thielicke, H., *Der evangelische Glaube: Grundzüge der Dogmatik* (3 vols: Tübingen, 1968–78).

Thiselton, A. C., *The Two Horizons: New Testament Hermeneutics and Philosophical Description* (Exeter, 1980).

——, 'Academic Freedom, Religious Tradition, and the Morality of Christian Scholarship', in M. Santer (ed.), *Their Lord and Ours* (London, 1982), 20–45.

Thompson, J. B., *Studies in the Theory of Ideology* (Cambridge, 1984).

Thomson, A., *Tradition and Authority in Science and Theology* (Edinburgh, 1987).

Tillard, J. M. R., 'La réception de Vatican II par les non-catholiques', in G. R. Evans (ed.), *Christian Authority* (Oxford, 1988), 20–39.

Tilley, T. W., 'Incommensurability, Intratextuality, and Fideism', *MTh* 5 (1989), 87–111.

Tilly, C., 'Vecchio e nuovo nella storia sociale', *Passato e Presente* (1982), 31–54.

Timpanaro, S., *The Freudian Slip* (London, 1976).

Toews, J. E., *Hegelianism: The Path towards Dialectical Humanism, 1805–41* (Cambridge, 1985).

Toinet, P., *Le problème de la vérité dogmatique: orthodoxie et hétérodoxie* (Paris, 1975).

Topitsch, E., *Vom Ursprung und Ende der Metaphysik* (Vienna, 1958).

Torrance, T. F., *Theological Science* (New York, 1969).

——, *The Trinitarian Faith* (Edinburgh, 1988).

Toulmin, S. E., *Human Understanding* (Oxford, 1972).

Tracy, D., *Blessed Rage for Order: The New Pluralism in Theology* (New York, 1975).

——, 'Lindbeck's New Program for Theology: A Reflection', *The Thomist* 49 (1985), 460–72.

Trigg, R., *Reason and Commitment* (Cambridge, 1973).

Trinkaus, C., *In Our Image and Likeness: Humanity and Divinity in Italian Humanist Thought* (2 vols: Chicago, 1970).

Trocmé, E., *Jésus de Nazareth vu par les témoins de sa vie* (Neuchâtel, 1971).

Troeltsch, E., 'Geschichte und Metaphysik', *ZThK* 7 (1898), 1–69.

Tulving, E., *Elements of Episodic Memory* (Oxford, 1985).

Valjavec, F., *Die Entstehung der politischen Strömungen in Deutschland, 1770–1815* (Munich, 1951).

Vallée, G., 'Theological and Non-Theological Motives in Irenaeus' Refutation of the Gnostics', in E. P. Sanders (ed.), *Jewish and Christian Self-Definition* (3 vols: London, 1980–2), 1.174–85.

Vass, G., 'On the Historical Structure of Christian Truth', *HeyJ* 9 (1968), 129–42; 274–89.

Vermes, G., *Jesus the Jew* (London, 1973).

Vico, G., *The New Science of Giambattista Vico* (Ithaca, N.Y., 1968).

de Vooght, P., *Les sources de la doctrine chrétienne d'après les théologiens du XIVe siècle et du début du XVe* (Paris, 1954).

Voss, J., *Das Mittelalter im historischen Denken Frankreichs* (Munich, 1972).

Wainwright, G., *Doxology: The Praise of God in Worship, Doctrine and Life* (New York, 1980).

Walgrave, J.-H., *Unfolding Revelation: The Nature of Doctrinal Development* (London, 1972).

Walker, M., *German Home Towns: Community, State and General Estate, 1648– 1871* (Ithaca, N.Y., 1971).

Walsh, W. H., *An Introduction to Philosophy of History* (London, 3rd edn, 1967).

Wand, J. W. C., *Anglicanism in History and Today* (London, 1961).

Warnke, G., *Gadamer: Hermeneutics, Tradition and Reason* (Cambridge, 1987).

Warfield, B. B., *Calvin and Augustine* (Philadelphia, 1956).

Watson, F., *Paul, Judaism and the Gentiles: A Sociological Approach* (Cambridge, 1986).

Watson, J. R., *Wordsworth's Vital Soul: The Sacred and Profane in Wordsworth's Poetry* (London, 1982).

Watts, T., and Williams, M., *The Psychology of Religious Knowing* (Cambridge, 1988).

Waugh, E., *Brideshead Revisited* (London, 1983).

Weisinger, H., 'The English Origins of the Sociological Interpretation of the Renaissance', *JHI* 11 (1950), 321–38.

Weiss, R., *The Renaissance Discovery of Classical Antiquity* (Oxford/New York, 1988).

Werner, M., *The Formation of Christian Dogma* (London, 1957).

White, H., *Metahistory: The Historical Imagination in Nineteenth-Century Europe* (Baltimore, 1975).

———, *Topics of Discourse: Essays in Cultural Criticism* (Baltimore, 1978).

Wilder, A. M., *Early Christian Rhetoric: The Language of the Gospel* (London, 1964).

Wiles, M. F., *The Making of Christian Doctrine* (Cambridge, 1967).

———, *The Remaking of Christian Doctrine* (London, 1974).

———, 'Looking into the Sun', in *Working Papers in Doctrine* (London, 1976), 148–63.

Wilken, R. L., *The Myth of Christian Beginnings* (London, 1971).

Williams, B. A. O., 'The Truth in Relativism', *Proceedings of the Aristotelian Society* 75 (1974–5), 215–28.

Williams, R., 'Base and Superstructure in Marxist Cultural Theory', *New Left Review* 82 (1973), 3–16.

Williams, R., '"Religious Realism": On not quite agreeing with Don Cupitt', *MTh* 1 (1984), 3–24.

———, 'Trinity and Revelation', *MTh* 2 (1986), 197–212.

———, *Arius: Heresy and Tradition* (London, 1987).

———, 'The Incarnation as the Basis of Dogma', in R. Morgan (ed.), *The Religion of the Incarnation: Anglican Essays in Commemoration of Lux Mundi* (Bristol, 1989), 85–98.

Williams, S., 'Lindbeck's Regulative Christology', *MTh* 4 (1988), 173–86.

Willis, G. G., *Saint Augustine and the Donatist Controversy* (London, 1950).

Wilson, B. R., *Sects and Society* (Berkeley, 1961).

———, *Religious Sects: A Sociological Study* (London, 1970).

Winch, P., *The Idea of a Social Science and Its Relation to Philosophy* (London, 1964).

———, 'Understanding a Primitive Society', *American Philosophical Quarterly* 1 (1965), 307–24.

Wiredu, K., *Philosophy and an African Culture* (Cambridge, 1980).

Wisan, W. L., 'Galileo and the Emergence of a New Scientific Style', in J. Hintikka et al. (eds), *Theory Change, Ancient Axiomatics and Galileo's Methodology* (Dordrecht, 1981), 311–39.

Wisdom, J., *Paradox and Discovery* (Oxford, 1965).

Wittgenstein, L., *Philosophical Investigations* (Oxford, 1953).

Wolf, E., 'Die Rechtfertigungslehre als Mitte und Grenze reformatorischer Theologie', in *Peregrinatio II: Studien zur reformatorische Theologie, zum Kirchenrecht und zur Sozialethik* (Munich, 1965), 11–21.

———, '"Kerygma und Dogma"? Prolegomena zum Problem und zur Problematik der Dogmengeschichte', in *Peregrinatio II*, 318–48.

Wolff, H. M., *Weltanschauung der deutschen Aufklärung* (Berne, 1949).

Woolman, J., *The Journal of John Woolman* (New York, 1922).

Woods, G. F., 'Doctrinal Criticism', in F. G. Healey (ed.), *Prospect for Theology* (London, 1966), 73–92.

Wordsworth, P., *William Wordsworth: The Borders of Vision* (Oxford, 1984).

Wright, J. R., 'Anglicanism, *Ecclesia Anglicana*, and Anglican: An Essay on Terminology', in S. Sykes and J. Booty (eds), *The Study of Anglicanism* (London, 1988), 424–9.

Wrzecionko, P., *Die philosophische Wurzeln der Theologie Albrecht Ritschls* (Berlin, 1964).

Yolton, J., Porter, R., Rogers, P., and Stafford, B. (eds), *The Blackwell Companion to the Enlightenment* (Oxford/New York, 1990).

Ziegler, E., 'Zur Reformation als Reformation des Lebens und der Sitten', *Rorschacher Neujahrsblatt* (1984), 53–71.

Ziman, J., *Public Knowledge: The Social Dimension of Science* (Cambridge, 1968).

Zons, R., 'Walter Benjamins "Thesen über den Begriff der Geschichte." Ein Kommentar', *Zeitschrift für philosophische Forschung* 34 (1980), 361–83.

Index

Vass, George 75
Venice, city of 105, 106
verifiability, criterion of, and logical
    positivism 98–9
Verona, city of 107
via moderna 124, 125
Vicenza, city of 107
Vico, Giambattista 19
Vienna, University of 119
Virgil 108, 112, 115
Visconti, Giangaleazzo 107
Voltaire 85, 144

Waldensians 43
Waugh, Evelyn 69

Wiles, Maurice F. 61
Williams, Rowan 30
Winch, Peter 97
Wittenberg, University of 43, 121–4
Wittgenstein, Ludwig 26, 31, 39, 66
Woolman, John 67
Wordsworth, William 68, 69–70
Württemburg, Duchy of 135
Wycliffe, John 120

Ziegler, Ernst 120
Zurich, city of 118
Zwingli, Huldrych 118–22, 123, 127,
    153, 189